ADVANCE PRAISE FOR

The Supreme Court, Crime, & the Ideal of Equal Justice

Smith, DeJong, and Burrow convincingly describe the American criminal justice system as fraught with discriminatory practices and procedures which have not been satisfactorily resolved by the judicial system. This engaging book is a worthy read for anyone interested in criminal justice or judicial politics."
—*Madhavi McCall, San Diego State University*

"The authors analyze the Rehnquist Court's failure to use its authority in interpreting the Equal Protection Clause and other constitutional provisions to advance the American ideal of 'equal justice under law.' This provocative book is a must-read for public officials and informed citizens who are serious about addressing the reality of unequal treatment in the criminal law process."
—*Joyce A. Baugh, Central Michigan University*

The Supreme Court, Crime,
& the Ideal of Equal Justice

STUDIES IN CRIME & PUNISHMENT

David A. Schultz and Christina DeJong
General Editors

Vol. 14

PETER LANG
New York • Washington, D.C./Baltimore • Bern
Frankfurt am Main • Berlin • Brussels • Vienna • Oxford

Christopher E. Smith, Christina DeJong,
& John D. Burrow

The Supreme Court, Crime,
& the Ideal of Equal Justice

PETER LANG
New York • Washington, D.C./Baltimore • Bern
Frankfurt am Main • Berlin • Brussels • Vienna • Oxford

LIBRARY OF CONGRESS CATALOGING-IN-PUBLICATION DATA

Smith, Christopher E.
The Supreme Court, crime, and the ideal of equal justice /
Christopher E. Smith, Christina DeJong, John D. Burrow.
p. cm. —— (Studies in crime and punishment; vol. 14)
Includes bibliographical references and index.
1. Criminal justice, Administration of——United States. 2. Equality before the law——United States.
3. Crime——United States. 4. United States. Supreme Court.
I. DeJong, Christina. II. Burrow, John D. (John David). III. Title. IV. Series.
KF9223 .S574   347.73'26——dc21   2002021408
ISBN 0-8204-6121-0
ISSN 1529-2444

DIE DEUTSCHE BIBLIOTHEK-CIP-EINHEITSAUFNAHME

Smith, Christopher E.:
The Supreme Court, crime, and the ideal of equal justice /
Christopher E. Smith; Christina DeJong; John D. Burrow.
—New York; Washington, D.C./Baltimore; Bern;
Frankfurt am Main; Berlin; Brussels; Vienna; Oxford: Lang.
(Studies in crime and punishment; Vol. 14)
ISBN 0-8204-6121-0

Cover design by Joni Holst

The paper in this book meets the guidelines for permanence and durability
of the Committee on Production Guidelines for Book Longevity
of the Council of Library Resources.

∞

Printed in the United States of America

Table of Contents

Preface

HUMAN INSTITUTIONS ARE inherently imperfect. When human beings are responsible for making decisions within organizations and processes, it is relatively easy to raise questions about biases and errors in their decisions. If an analysis of those decisions is intended merely to find fault, then such an analysis may be regarded as unremarkable and, indeed, merely an exercise in stating the obvious. The analysis in this book, we hope, will not be perceived as merely an exercise in finding fault with the justice system. By choosing to analyze aspects of inequality in criminal law and process, this book seeks to fulfill more important purposes. First, an underlying premise of this book is that governmental institutions, more so than other human institutions, should be evaluated and held accountable for falling short of their intended purposes and principles. In a democratic governing system, it is no mere exercise in criticism to examine whether the institutions of government are serving the people's interests in accordance with the principles of the Constitution. Second, unlike some other human decision-making processes, the criminal justice system has a profound impact on the lives of human beings. Decisions that define the law as well as discretionary decisions within the system determine people's fates, including decisions about which offenders will be selected to die. Thus, flaws and biases in criminal justice decision making have the potential for special impact and importance. Finally, the identification of flaws and biases is the essential prerequisite to considering how human organizations and processes can be improved. If we are reluctant to evaluate critically the institutions and decision makers of the criminal justice system, then we have no realistic hope of suggesting ways to improve the system. Much of the discussion in the book focuses on the ways in which the U.S. Supreme Court has or has not advanced the ideal of equal justice. Although the tone of this discussion is often critical, its underlying intentions flow from the optimistic hope that greater recognition of the facets of persistent inequality will provide a basis for future remedial actions.

Some of the material in Chapter 3 was previously published as Christopher E. Smith and John D. Burrow, "Race-ing Into the Twenty-First Century: The Supreme Court and the (E)Quality of Justice," *University of Toledo Law Review* 28 (1997): 279–300. Similarly, Chapter 4 draws from material that was previously published as Christina DeJong and Christopher E. Smith, "Equal Protection, Gender, and Justice at the Dawn of a New Century," *Wisconsin Women's Law Journal* 14 (1999): 123–154. We are grateful to the *University of Toledo Law Review* and the *Wisconsin Women's Law Journal* for granting permission to incorporate this material.

We would like to express our gratitude to the faculty and doctoral students in the School of Criminal Justice at Michigan State University. Our interactions with these colleagues have significantly enhanced both our curiosity and knowledge about criminal justice. We would also like to thank David A. Schultz for his editorial suggestions and encouragement.

1

The Ideal of Equal Justice

THE STRUCTURES AND processes of government institutions are designed to fulfill specific goals. They do not necessarily succeed in fulfilling these goals, but presumably the people who work within these institutions, if committed to a government's values, will strive to improve their institutions' effectiveness in advancing underlying goals. Among the institutions of government, courts are particularly important. A country's courts enforce its laws and thereby help to ensure that disputes between citizens are resolved peacefully and that individuals who commit crimes are identified and punished appropriately. In criminal cases, courts apply the rules and procedures that determine which individuals will lose their property, liberty, and lives as punishments for violating society's rules. These important, fate-determining decisions made during court proceedings should presumably be reached in accordance with a governing system's goals and values. According to the U.S. Constitution and U.S. Supreme Court decisions defining constitutional law, the fair and equal treatment of people in the criminal law process is a paramount objective of the American legal system. The chapters of this book will examine whether American law and judicial processes actually achieve this goal and, more importantly, whether the justices of the U.S. Supreme Court, who are key decision makers in the system, strive to improve the legal system's effectiveness in advancing the underlying goal of equal justice.

The Goals of Legal Systems

How does one identify the goals of a legal system and evaluate whether those goals are attained in the processing of criminal cases? In essence, any analysis of system goals must begin with an examination of a system's rules and processes. Each country's legal system has its own structures, rules, and procedures for processing criminal cases. Each system also has specific officials empowered to make decisions that help to determine the fates of people drawn into the criminal law process. When comparing legal systems and how they operate, evident differences between systems reflect divergent traditions, values, and objectives. For example, many European countries use an "inquisitorial" process in which judges actively participate in the investigation and processing of cases, especially by asking questions of witnesses during court proceedings (Provine 1996). By contrast, trials in the United States are based on an "adversarial" process in which the judge is relatively passive, the truth is presumed to emerge from the clash between the opposing lawyers who advocate vigorously on behalf of each side, and a jury of citizens makes determinations of guilt or innocence (Abraham 1993). The inquisitorial system seeks to discover the truth about legal cases by utilizing a truth-seeking process that places great reliance on thorough investigations and considered judgments by law-trained professionals employed by the government. Obviously, the American system's goal of discovering the truth is pursued through an alternative process. The American system evolved from English roots and reflects the Anglo-American tradition of involving lay citizens as decision makers in trials. In its use of citizen-jurors, the American system differs from inquisitorial processes by incorporating skepticism about the risks of excessive prosecutorial and judicial power. Moreover, in its use of zealous defense attorneys and an adversarial process, the American system emphasizes the additional goal of protecting the interests of defendants from any abusive exercise of governmental authority. Truth-seeking, citizen decision making, and protection of defendants' rights are not the only goals advanced by the American legal system. These specific goals are highlighted in the use of an adversary system in American courts, but additional goals are reflected in other aspects of the laws and legal procedures employed in the United States.

Legal systems do not develop entirely by accident. As indicated by the foregoing examples, a close examination of rules and procedures can illuminate underlying traditions and values. Systemic goals may be easy to identify and evaluate in a country with a criminal law process that has only a few specific objectives. If, for example, the sole or primary purpose of a legal process is to preserve and maintain the power of a specific leader or regime, then one would expect to see this limited objective reflected in broad law enforcement powers, summary proceedings, draconian punishments, and few legal protections, if any, for individuals. Critics of the government would be arrested upon mere suspicion and then summarily punished in severe ways. If the regime maintained its power and opponents of the regime were either eliminated or terrorized into silent submission, then the legal process could be judged effective in fulfilling its intended function of regime maintenance.

By contrast, it is more difficult to evaluate the criminal law process of the United States because there is a broader array of values and objectives, not all of which can be pursued simultaneously in a harmonious fashion. The American legal process seeks to repress crime and punish criminal offenders, but it also seeks to pursue these objectives while protecting the rights of individuals and limiting the power of government (Cole & Smith 2001). One measure of the success of the criminal law process would be the extent to which criminal offenders are apprehended and punished. However, other measures must necessarily focus on the extent to which law fulfills the expectations of citizens in a constitutional democracy by adhering to espoused principles. For Americans, the suppression of crime is one important objective, but the success of the criminal law process must also be evaluated according to the provision of fair processes and the fulfillment of the rights promised in the U.S. Constitution and state constitutions. In addition, there are other objectives whose attainment is necessary to fulfill Americans' conceptions of justice. These additional objectives include accurate decisions about which defendants are guilty and appropriate, proportional punishments for convicted criminal offenders. The news media, commentators, and the public devote significant attention to instances when a prisoner is released, sometimes after sitting in prison for decades, because new evidence demonstrates his or her innocence (Finucane 2001). Similarly, public debates about the attainment of justice emerge when there are concerns about disproportionate or otherwise inappropriate punishments being imposed on a particular offender (Clary 2001).

Equal Justice in the American System

One especially important objective underlying American legal processes is equal treatment of similarly situated criminal suspects, defendants, and offenders. Equal justice is a central component of the conception of law in the United States. According to Professor Ronald Allen (2000, xviii), "[T]he notion of equality, of treating like cases alike, is both integral to the nature of law and uncontainable once identified." Egalitarianism is a core element of the "American ideology" that shaped the governing institutions and laws of the United States (Ladd 1987). At the founding of the nation, this idea is most famously embodied in Jefferson's statement that "all men are created in equal" in the Declaration of Independence. Obviously, American history's legacy of inequality predicated on race, gender, immigrant status, and other demographic factors indicates that the nation has fallen short of achieving an idealistic conception of egalitarianism. Indeed, some commentators argue that inequality is an established, accepted element of American political culture (R. Smith 1997). Despite the gap between the espoused ideal and reality throughout American history, most of the formal mechanisms for legal discrimination, such as racial exclusion from voting and gender exclusion from jury service, were eliminated by the late twentieth century. In *Taylor v. Louisiana* (1975), for example, the U.S. Supreme Court invalidated a state statute that excluded women from jury service unless they made a special request to be considered for participation. The Supreme Court's decisions in *Taylor* and other cases serve as important statements about the high priority that the American governing system places on treating people equally in their contacts with government institutions and processes. In light of these judicial decisions that purport to advance equal treatment, it is appropriate to evaluate the extent to which the legal system actually achieves the ideal of equal justice, especially because judicial institutions and processes are key purveyors of this ideal through the words of publicly announced decisions.

The justices of the United States Supreme Court work within a building which itself proclaims the message of the judicial system's aspirational goal. Prominently displayed above the Court's high columns and massive bronze door are the words, "Equal Justice Under Law." These words are literally etched in stone. While the Court's interpretation of the U.S. Constitution's provisions inevitably change as justices come and go and as society's values change, "Equal Justice Under Law" will remain as an enduring and unalterable proclamation, visible to all who pass by or enter the nation's highest court. In addition, the Supreme Court and other courts bear responsibility for interpreting, applying, and defending the Constitution's explicit command, contained in the words of the Fourteenth Amendment, to provide "equal protection of the laws" for all people. The courts also interpret and enforce other constitutional provisions designed to achieve "equal justice under law," such as the appointment of defense attorneys for indigent defendants under the Sixth Amendment's guarantee of a "right to counsel."

Evaluating Equal Justice

In light of the courts' central role in the advancement of the ideal of equal justice, how should these institutions be evaluated to assess their commitment to and success in attaining equal treatment for all people? Sometimes authors use "straw man" arguments and analyses to make their points by presenting a hollow or superficial representation of an opposing viewpoint that can be easily demolished by their own preferred arguments. Their own conclusions and analyses appear to be deceivingly persuasive or strong when contrasted only with a weak or unrealistic alternative. In evaluating the achievement (or lack thereof) of equal justice, it would be possible to set the judicial system up as a "straw man" by treating it as if it could be a flawless embodiment of a "textbook" system that fulfills idealistic notions of what a "perfect" criminal law process should be. Then one could criticize existing institutions, rules, and procedures for failing to accomplish an idealized vision of absolutely equal treatment for all people who come into contact with criminal justice officials. In reality, however, the governing system of the United States is specifically designed to ensure that individuals are treated differently in different jurisdictions. The U. S. Constitution is based on a system of federalism in which individual states possess the authority to enact their own laws and to develop their own institutions and procedures. Thus, acts that are legal in some states may bring prosecution and imprisonment in others. For example, prostitution is a legal, regulated business in Nevada but is a crime elsewhere in the country. In addition, states provide different punishments for identical acts. Some people convicted of murder in Texas and other states may be sentenced to death, whereas Michigan, Wisconsin, Minnesota, and a few other states have no death penalty. Because of the federalist model, it may be most appropriate to evaluate the attainment of equal justice within the limited confines of a single jurisdiction governed by a single, common set of laws. Thus, one might argue that equal justice should only be evaluated by examining whether everyone within a specific state is treated the same as everyone else within that specific state. For example, an analyst might ask whether all burglars in Delaware with similar criminal records receive the same punishments as comparable burglars in that state or whether prosecutors in Wyoming pursue the same criminal charges against suspected thieves who commit similar acts of larceny.

Alternatively, one can evaluate equal justice by examining the specific laws that govern the entire country. Federal criminal statutes apply throughout the United States, although they cover only a limited number of offenses, such as drug trafficking, counterfeiting, and fraud, that can be prosecuted and punished through the federal courts. More importantly, most of the constitutional rights contained in the Constitution's first ten amendments, known as the "Bill of Rights" as well as all of the rights in the Fourteenth Amendment are applicable throughout the entire country. The Bill of Rights, including First Amendment rights to freedom of speech and religion, Fourth Amendment rights against unreasonable search and seizure, and Sixth Amendment trial rights, originally provided people only with protections against actions by *federal* law enforcement officials and ensured specific processes in *federal* courts (*Barron v. Baltimore* 1833). Using an interpretive approach known as "incorporation," the U.S. Supreme Court applied most of the rights in the Bill of Rights to state officials and state court proceedings (Hensley, Smith, & Baugh 1997). The Fourteenth Amendment, which was added to the Constitution in 1868 after the conclusion of the Civil War, explicitly gives people legal protections against actions by the states. These protections include the right to "due process of law," the "privileges and immunities of citizenship," and the "equal protection of the laws." In a case-by-case process from 1925 through the end of the 1960s, the Supreme Court interpreted individual provisions of the Bill of Rights as being embodied within or "incorporated into" the Fourteenth Amendment's right to due process and therefore applicable to protect individuals against actions by state officials to the same extent that they provided protections in federal court proceedings (e.g., *Duncan v. Louisiana* 1968). By the end of the 1960s, very few rights in the Bill of Rights had not been incorporated into the Fourteenth Amendment and applied to the states. The handful of unincorporated rights include the Second Amendment's provision on well-regulated militia and the right to bear arms, the Fifth Amendment right to a grand jury, and the Seventh Amendment right to a jury trial in civil cases (e.g., *Hurtado v. California* 1884). Thus, with the exception of the right to a grand jury, all of the important constitutional rights affecting criminal law processes were incorporated and applied against the states. All court proceedings in the country, state and federal, are governed by the Supreme Court's interpretations of rights concerning searches, self-incrimination, double jeopardy, defense counsel, cruel and unusual punishments, and other elements of the Bill of Rights. As a result, one fair means of evaluating the legal system's fulfillment of the ideal of equal justice is to examine the extent to which courts apply the common, universal rights contained in the Bill of Rights for people throughout the country.

Another form of problematic "straw man" arguments about equal justice would be to select a few anecdotes about individuals who received different outcomes in the criminal justice system as the basis for condemning the entire system's failures. Any unequal treatment can provide the basis for examination and criticism, but in a large country with a population in excess of 250 million people, it would be virtually impossible to ensure identical treatment for every individual. Moreover, it can be difficult to compare individual cases because of contextual differences that might affect outcomes and the appearance of equal treatment. For example, one cannot automatically conclude that two individuals are treated differently in sentencing for criminal cases when prison sentences of different lengths are imposed for the same criminal charges. In order to assess accurately the existence of unequal treatment, one would also need to know whether the defendants had the same prior criminal records. Longer sentences for some individuals may stem from more serious criminal records rather than from actual unequal treatment.

Rather than look for anecdotes about individuals as the basis for evaluating the attainment of equal justice, it is more appropriate to consider whether differences in treatment are associated with demographic factors and one's status in society. People who possess power, wealth, and status in a democracy are positioned to influence decision makers and employ mechanisms to protect their interests. These individuals can lobby legislatures and executive officials and hire experienced attorneys, expert witnesses, and jury consultants to advance and protect their interests in judicial processes (Van Horn, Baumer, & Gormley 1992). Moreover, their power and position in society are likely to provide favorable influence over the discretionary decisions of officials in the justice system. Those officials may identify with middle-class and affluent people, leading to empathetic decisions concerning arrests, prosecution, and sentencing. They may also fear repercussions from using discretionary authority against affluent and powerful people. Because many elected officials, including mayors, legislators, sheriffs, and county prosecutors, hold key oversight positions with respect to the criminal justice system, the decision makers whose organizations depend on them for supervision and resources may be wary of making tough decisions concerning people with the resources and power to influence electoral processes (Reiman 2001). Thus, one should expect that individuals who are members of demographic groups that are politically majoritarian and influential will be most likely to have their constitutional rights respected by decision makers in the criminal law process. The benefits for those who are connected to majoritarian political power should (and do) accrue to people who are white, male, middle-class or affluent, middle-aged, and suburban. By contrast, people who are members of political minorities are less likely to receive the benefits of respect and deference when decisions are made in the criminal law process (Smith 1991). Because the American constitutional governing system, purports to promise "equal justice under law" to everyone, one important test of the system's "success" concerns the delivery of that promise for racial and ethnic minorities, women, the poor, youths, and other members of political minorities that are less able to influence policy and practice in legal and governing processes.

This book will examine the extent to which the American criminal law process attains the espoused ideal of "equal justice under law." It will do so by examining the impact of specific aspects of criminal law and process on members of four demographic groups that have historically lacked dominant political influence over policies and practices: racial minorities, especially African Americans; women; the poor; and convicted offenders. The book will not seek to examine all aspects of unequal treatment and disadvantage experienced by these demographic groups in the criminal law process. It would be possible to review and synthesize myriad social science studies of differential treatment and unequal impacts for people from different demographic groups. However, several books and articles by other scholars already document the nature and extent of these issues (e.g., Barak, Flavin, & Leighton 2001; Walker, Spohn, & DeLone 2000; Smith 1991). Instead, this book will pursue a more limited focus.

The chapters that follow will analyze constitutional doctrines and decisions by the U.S. Supreme Court and other courts to evaluate the extent to which unequal justice is fostered, tolerated, or ignored by the judicial guardians empowered to protect constitutional rights. As discussed in the preceding paragraphs, decisions by the Supreme Court and other courts define the rules for criminal law and the judicial process by interpreting, among other provisions of constitutions and statutes, the Equal Protection Clause of the U.S. Constitution. The American legal system falls short of its ideal of equal justice if the Supreme Court and other courts define national legal rules and rights in ways that create opportunities for justice system officials to apply unjustifiably differential treatment to similarly situated people because of their race, social class, gender, or status as a convicted offender.

2

Unequal Justice and the U.S. Supreme Court

IN ORDER TO evaluate the effect of the U.S. Supreme Court and constitutional law on the ideal of equal justice, one must first examine the nature and sources of discrimination in the criminal law process. Moreover, one must understand the nature of the Supreme Court's authority and decision making processes in order to assess whether and how the Court can foster equal treatment of people drawn into the criminal justice system. Can constitutional doctrines be applied to prohibit or redress unequal justice in the criminal law process? The answer to that question requires identification of the potential sources or causes of differential outcomes, especially patterns of differential outcomes that are associated with demographic characteristics such as race, gender, and social status.

Sources of Discrimination and Unequal Justice

Obviously, biased attitudes, whether conscious or unconscious, by those who make decisions concerning criminal justice may be the underlying cause of all forms of unequal justice. However, the contextual bases and structural mechanisms that produce unequal treatment are not identical in every situation. In general, there are four primary sources of discrimination and disadvantage that may impact members of particular demographic groups and thereby potentially generate constitutional claims about discriminatory unequal justice. These sources range from overt causes, such as formal government policies that target specific demographic groups, to more subtle, contextual causes that stem from differential impacts produced by seemingly benign and neutral policies.

Mandated Differential Treatment

The most overt source of unequal justice arises when the government enacts crime-related statutes that single out particular demographic groups for treatment different from that applied to members of other groups. For example, the extensive scheme of criminal laws designed to control African Americans and maintain the system of slavery in the antebellum South provide a very clear example of overt, formal governmental actions to enforce unequal justice (Kolchin 1993). For example, unlike whites, slaves could be convicted and punished by whipping for such crimes as running away, insubordination, and even "provoking language or menacing gestures to a white person" (Friedman 1993, 88). Laws mandating racial discrimination continued after the end of slavery. Although the Supreme Court endorsed the use of formal statutes to enforce racial segregation (e.g., *Plessy v. Ferguson* 1896) prior to the landmark anti-segregation decision in *Brown v. Board of Education* (1954), the Court made a few earlier decisions that invalidated discriminatory laws. In 1880, for example, the Court voided as unconstitutional a West Virginia statute barring African Americans from jury service (*Strauder v. West Virginia* 1880).

Because of the overt and official nature of categorical discrimination embodied in formal statutes, these laws are most susceptible for examination and invalidation by courts applying the Equal Protection Clause. However, such statutes continue to exist in the twenty-first century, especially with respect to distinguishing men and women under criminal law. As we will see in Chapter 4, these statutes are either dormant anachronisms that have never been challenged in court, yet remain available for use by prosecutors, or they are reflections of restrictive, moralistic views of women and their behavior that continue to enjoy acceptance by wide segments of American society. States' laws concerning sex-related matters (e.g., indecent exposure, adultery, rape, and so forth) may explicitly treat men and women differently for purposes of criminal prosecutions. Various states' statutory rape laws, for example, may criminalize in strict liability terms the conduct of males who engage in consensual sexual contacts with females who are younger than a statutorily defined age. Under strict liability, the male may be convicted of the offense without any proof of evil intentions, such as when teenagers have consensual sexual contact. Even if the girl consents, encourages, or invites the sexual contact, the male is guilty of a crime if the girl is under the legal age to provide consent. However, these same states may have no similar law aimed at women who have consensual sexual contacts with teenage boys. Alabama's statute illustrates this point by focusing exclusively on the behavior of males:

> A male commits the crime of rape in the second degree if (1) Being 16 years or older, he engages in sexual intercourse with a female less than 16 and more than 12 years old, provided, however, the actor is at least two years older than the female, [or] (2) [h]e engages in sexual intercourse with a female who is incapable of consent by reason of being mentally defective. (Ala. Code section 13A-6-62)

Women can be prosecuted for the crime of "sexual misconduct" for having sexual intercourse with a male without his consent (Ala. Code section 13A-6-65). Unlike the foregoing statute directed at men, however, there is no statutory sex crime directed at women who have consensual sexual contact with younger males under the age of sixteen. According to critics, statutory rape laws unfairly "restrict the sexual activity of young women and reinforce the double standard of sexual morality" (Olsen 1991, 306), yet the U.S. Supreme Court has approved such laws that treat men and women differently for the purposes of protecting young females from sexual exploitation. The Court declared that such laws do not violate the Equal Protection Clause of the Fourteenth Amendment (*Michael M. v. Superior Court of Sonoma County* 1981).

Discretion and Discrimination

A second source of unequal justice stems from discretionary decision making by authoritative actors in the criminal justice system. The application of discretion can readily produce discrimination as police officers, prosecutors, judges, and other officials make situational decisions about whether and how to draw people into the criminal justice system for processing, prosecution, and punishment. Discretionary authority is pervasive in the criminal justice process and is not easily curbed (Walker 1993). Indeed, discretion is often regarded as an essential element for criminal justice actors because the system lacks sufficient resources to enforce all laws equally and because discretion permits contextual individualization of treatment in order to achieve (what is perceived to be) more appropriate justice (Cole & Smith 2001, 20).

Discretion is applied by actors throughout the justice process. Police officers use discretion in determining whom to stop and arrest. Prosecutors use discretion in determining criminal charges and endorsing plea agreements. Juries use discretion in determining whom to convict and what charges have been proven. Judges use discretion in ruling on motions and, within the constraints imposed by sentencing guidelines, imposing punishment on convicted offenders. At the dawn of the twenty-first century, the connections between discretion and discrimination in criminal justice continue to receive highly publicized attention with respect to traffic stops. The use of racial profiling by police officers in determining whom they will stop and which vehicles they will search has become a major source of controversy. The American Civil Liberties Union issued a report documenting how African American and Hispanic drivers in Illinois, Maryland, Pennsylvania, and elsewhere were much more likely than their white counterparts to be stopped and to have their vehicles searched (Harris 1999). Many prominent African Americans, including Detroit's mayor and former Michigan Supreme Court justice, Dennis Archer, and Harvard professor Cornel West, have suffered harassment and indignity from being stopped for no apparent reason other than their skin color (Eversley 1999; West 1993). Apparently, many police officers use race as a "cue" that triggers their suspicions about possible criminal conduct. Their stereotyped beliefs lead them to intrude improperly on the liberty and privacy of many innocent people. In a study of Maryland's State Police, for example, three-quarters of the motorists who committed traffic violations on interstate highway I-95 were white. However, three-quarters of the motorists detained and searched by the state police were African Americans, despite the fact that African Americans made up less than eighteen percent of the motorists committing traffic violations. African Americans were stopped and searched with much greater frequency, even though the results of such searches indicated that they were no more likely than whites to be found with drugs or other contraband. Only 28 percent of African Americans searched were found to be carrying drugs; the same percentage as among whites who were searched ("ACLU Moves" 1996). The application of police discretion, apparently guided by stereotypes and bias, led to unequal treatment of motorists because of their race. The problem has given rise to legislative proposals to require law enforcement agencies to keep statistics about the traffic stops made by their officers. Obviously, the application of discretion to subject members of a particular demographic group to more frequent stops, searches, and arrests will contribute to unequal outcomes in the criminal justice process. Moreover, the intrusiveness of a stop and search, especially when not justified by legally appropriate neutral factors such as clear evidence of criminality, by itself constitutes a form of unequal, unjust treatment of citizens by justice system officials (Cole 1999).

There are other examples of discretionary decisions producing unequal results associated with race. Historically, rape was punishable by death in many states until the Supreme Court in 1977 (*Coker v. Georgia*) forbade states from applying the ultimate penalty for this particular offense. Despite the possibility of capital punishment for rape throughout most of American history, the death penalty was applied disproportionately, and in some jurisdictions, nearly exclusively to African American men accused of raping white women from the slavery era until the 1970s (Friedman 1993). The disproportionate and discriminatory application of the death penalty for rape resulted from discretionary decisions by prosecutors, juries, and judges. Contemporary sentencing studies have also shown examples of unequal treatment by race. For example, one study of sexual assault cases found that African Americans convicted of victimizing whites received sentences that were, on average, four years longer than those for whites who assaulted other whites and three years longer than those for African Americans who victimized other African Americans (Spohn & Spears 1996).

In Connecticut, a study of the bail process found that judges set the average bail for African American and Hispanic defendants in felony drug cases four times higher than the average bail set for whites facing the same charges (Cole & Smith 2001, 329). This unequal treatment not only increased the likelihood that members of minority groups would be deprived of their liberty and jailed while awaiting processing of their cases, it also made it more difficult for these defendants to assist in the preparation of their cases (e.g., assisting the defense attorney in locating defense witnesses, and so forth). Thus, this application of discretion can also increase the likelihood of conviction.

Discretionary decisions producing unequal justice are not limited to the demographic characteristic of race. Officials' discretionary decisions can also adversely affect women, the poor, and members of other demographic groups, especially when stereotypes and biases color the views of police, prosecutors, judges, and other decision makers. Social class, like race, is also used as a "cue" by many police officers to spur stops and searches without any evidence that would satisfy the standards of "reasonable suspicion" and "probable cause" that are purportedly required by Fourth Amendment jurisprudence for various types of searches. Criminologist John Irwin has described his observations of the differences in police reactions to seeing well-dressed, wealthy opera patrons violating laws against drinking alcohol in public from open containers as the tuxedo-clad elites blocked the sidewalk and street outside of a theater while sipping champagne during intermission at an opera performance. Police officers walked respectfully around these influential, high status people, despite the obvious crime being committed. By contrast, officers employed their discretion to aggressively arrest poor people sipping wine out of a bottle in a vacant alley. Irwin describes the use of police discretion to arrest and jail poor people considered unsightly and threatening by middle-class society as an effort to control the "rabble" and remove uncomfortable social problems, such as homelessness, from public view (Irwin 1992). The effect of such applications of police discretion is to foster unequal justice as, in Irwin's example, people equally guilty of the same crime experience very different treatment at the hands of criminal justice officials.

The creation of unequal treatment for the poor through the application of discretion is evident in other aspects of the criminal law process. For example, police and prosecutors focus their resources on "street crimes" committed primarily by less affluent people (e.g., robberies, burglaries, and so forth). Meanwhile, there is less attention and fewer severe sanctions for offenses by white-collar criminals and corporations that impose significant financial costs on American society and can threaten the health and safety of many people when companies knowingly or negligently violate criminal laws by polluting the environment, selling unsafe products, and other harmful activities (Barak, Flavin, & Leighton 2001).

In an example involving gender discrimination, advocates for women long believed that police officers' reluctance to use their discretionary arrest authority in domestic violence situations ignored the victimization of women, and thus efforts were made to require police officers to make arrests in all domestic violence cases (Karmen 1990). Some police officers refrained from intervening because they labeled domestic violence as a "family problem" or "personal dispute" rather than as a crime involving assault. In effect, this viewpoint reflected a stereotyped assumption that husbands have authority over their wives and that interspousal violence was socially acceptable and "normal." In another example, because of the power position and gender composition of correctional institutions' staff, the exercise of discretion by personnel in their interactions with prisoners can adversely affect female inmates by subjecting them to sexual harassment and exploitation. According to one scholar who studied women in the criminal justice system, "Women [prisoners] also reported being approached by men employed at these [correctional] institutions with proposals for sexual services in exchange for certain privileges" (Miller 1986, 132). The worldwide human rights organization, Amnesty International, reported that there were more than 1,000 cases of women being victimized by sexual abuse in American prisons during the final three years of the twentieth century (Smith 2001).

Disparate Impact

A third source of unequal justice is laws that are facially neutral but have a disparate impact because of their operation in the particular social conditions of American society. The words "facially neutral law" make it appear that the law applies equally to everyone in society without being aimed at any particular demographic group. However, because of the reality of where people live and what they do in their daily lives, certain laws will actually affect specific people in a much more significant way. For example, federal drug laws mandate significantly more severe punishments for crack cocaine than for equivalent amounts of powder cocaine. Thus, despite the fact that both forms of cocaine are chemically identical and similarly harmful to users, inner-city residents, who are likely to have greater access to the crack form of cocaine, are often imprisoned for longer periods of time than their suburban counterparts who are more likely to use powder cocaine. Because of the racial composition of cities and suburbs in much of the United States, the facially neutral law produces a disparate impact along racial lines as well as along social class lines (Tonry 1995).

In Connecticut, ninety percent of people incarcerated for drug offenses are African American or Hispanic, even though half of the people arrested for drug offenses are white. This unequal result was produced, in part, by a state law imposing mandatory sentences for possessing drugs within two-thirds of a mile of schools, day care centers, or public housing projects. In Connecticut's largest cities, where poor and minority people are generally arrested for drug offenses, virtually every spot within the cities' boundaries fall under the mandatory sentencing requirement. By contrast, whites, many of whom are arrested in small towns and rural areas, often do not receive the serious consequences of the facially neutral sentencing law. Many locations where arrests occur in small towns and rural areas are not sufficiently close to schools and housing projects. Thus, there is a disparate impact (Butterfield 2001).

In another kind of example, Cincinnati's ordinance defining the misdemeanor offense of "Interference with or Improper Solicitation of Pedestrian or Vehicular Traffic" makes it a crime to (among other things) "make a solicitation, request, or demand for money or other thing of value, in a manner which would alarm, intimidate, threaten, menace, harass, or coerce a reasonable person" (Cincinnati Municipal Code section 910–13). Although the ordinance applies to all people, it is the poor who most frequently find themselves in the position of begging for money on public streets and thereby come under the coverage of the law. In addition, the application of police discretion in enforcing the law can compound its unequal impact on the poor. Some "reasonable people" could very well feel "harassed" by "requests" for money on public sidewalks outside of businesses from Girl Scouts selling cookies and donation solicitors for the United Way, cancer society, or heart association. However, there is little likelihood that police would enforce the ordinance against them because the unstated purpose underlying the law is to give police the authority to fulfill downtown business owners' desire to clear the sidewalks of homeless panhandlers whose dress, manner, and smell may offend and repel potential middle-class shoppers.

Unequal Resources

A fourth source of unequal treatment may stem from resource inequalities associated with demographic group membership. For example, if members of a racial group are disproportionately represented among less affluent people who cannot afford high quality legal representation, expert witnesses, and other trial resources, then members of that group may receive different, less desirable outcomes in the processing of criminal cases. In capital punishment cases, for example, many scholars have highlighted the detrimental impact on indigent defendants from their representation by inexperienced or incompetent appointed counsel (Bright 1994). A study of capital cases in Illinois from 1977 to 1999 found that thirty-three death row inmates had been represented by attorneys who had been disbarred or suspended and that approximately half of death penalty cases are reversed for error (Claiborne 2000). The results of this study, in conjunction with the significant publicity surrounding the release of a total of thirteen Illinois inmates from death row after they were later discovered to be innocent led the governor of Illinois to impose a moratorium on capital punishment in 2000 (Claiborne 2000.). A similar study focusing on the tenure of then-Governor George W. Bush in Texas found that attorneys for 40 of the 131 inmates executed during the Bush Administration presented either just one witness or no evidence at all in their clients' sentencing hearings. In addition, many failed to present the judge and jury with any evidence of their clients' brain damage, low IQ, childhood abuse experiences, and other factors that could influence the decision about whether to impose the death penalty. Moreover, about one-third of the Texas capital defendants were represented by attorneys who were later disbarred, suspended, or otherwise sanctioned (Sharp 2000). Unlike the governor of Illinois, Governor Bush defended the adequacy of the Texas criminal capital punishment system that he had helped to accelerate by approving legislation to speed up the processing of cases (Sharp 2000).

In the worst-case scenario for detrimental actions, an attorney appointed to represent an indigent capital defendant in North Carolina subsequently admitted he intentionally missed an important filing deadline for an appeal because, in his words, "I decided that Mr. Tucker deserved to die, and I would not do anything to prevent his execution" (Nowell 2000). The low pay provided for appointed counsel in many states discourages many attorneys other than those who are inexperienced or desperate for business from accepting court appointments. In addition, there are concerns that judges do not seek to appoint the best possible attorneys for indigent defendants. Indeed, one survey of judges in Florida found that some judges may even intentionally appoint inept attorneys because they do not want to preside over trials that lead to acquittals, especially in capital cases (Bowers 1983). Defendants who are sufficiently affluent to choose and compensate their own defense attorneys are not likely to experience unequal justice to the same extent as indigent defendants whose fates are placed in the hands of counsel appointed under these circumstances.

Constitutional Doctrines and Unequal Justice
Imagine if someone appealed a case by bluntly saying the following,

My five-year sentence for burglary is longer than Joe's two-year sentence, and he's the guy that committed the burglary with me. It isn't fair to give two people different sentences for the same crime. That is clearly a violation of the promise of "equal justice under law" that the judiciary and the criminal law process proclaim to be their most fundamental and important principle. We both must receive the same punishment since we committed the same crime, or else the criminal law process is unequal and unfair.

This is not a far-fetched example because it is quite common for two offenders who committed the same offense together to receive different punishments. Moreover, this is precisely the kind of outcome regularly produced by the criminal law process that leads offenders to feel that the system is unfair and leads observers to question whether the criminal law process truly strives to achieve the ideal of equal justice.

It is widely acknowledged that the sentences of two co-defendants will sometimes differ because one of them was convicted of other crimes in addition to the burglary. In this case, however, let us assume that both Joe and his co-defendant (the complaining appellant) were convicted of one count of burglary based on their joint and equal participation in the same crime of breaking into a house at night in an attempt to steal a family's jewelry and other valuables. There are many possible reasons for co-defendants to receive different punishments when they are apparently equally culpable for an identical offense. Perhaps Joe is a juvenile and the appellant is an adult. Judges may treat juveniles more leniently than adults or state laws may provide for different punishments for juveniles than those imposed on adults for the same offense. Alternatively, Joe may have cooperated with the police by admitting guilt immediately and providing testimony against the appellant. Thus, Joe's cooperation was rewarded with a lesser sentence. It could also be true that, even if he did not provide information for the police, Joe entered a guilty plea and the appellant claimed to be innocent but was ultimately convicted after a trial. Sometimes defendants who demand the full benefits of the criminal law process, including the time and expense of a jury trial, will pay an extra "penalty" at sentencing. Such actions raise questions about whether people should be penalized for merely asserting their right to a trial, yet differential sentences do occur on that basis. Many people would argue that providing rewards for cooperation is desirable and proper because it increases the effectiveness of law enforcement, encourages contrition and rehabilitation, and conserves scarce system resources. Another explanation might be that the appellant has a prior criminal record while Joe's burglary is his first offense. Prior records are usually considered relevant factors for enhancing criminal sentences in order to incapacitate repeat offenders and give them harsher punishments. The foregoing reasons can produce differential treatment yet they are based on strong policy justifications and reflect goals that the criminal law process seeks to advance. The goals highlighted in these examples include leniency for juveniles, severity for repeat offenders, and encouragement of defendants' cooperation with law enforcement authorities.

Now let us imagine that Joe and the appellant are the same age and neither has a prior criminal record. Moreover, both of them entered guilty pleas. Under these identical circumstances, the complaint about unequal treatment is more obvious and troubling. In spite of the apparent inequality in results, the appellant's statement, as presented above, does not provide a sufficient basis for declaring that the sentencing was improper. In order to provide a proper complaint in an appeal or other post conviction process, the claim must be presented in a legal form that can be received and processed by judges. Rules govern the nature and details of complaints that courts are permitted to consider. They cannot consider general complaints stated in terms familiar to the general public. Instead, complaints must meet legal requirements for acceptance, including the requirement of alleging a violation by officials of an identifiable law. Thus, the appellant must characterize the differential outcome as violating some specific statute or constitutional provision. The most obvious legal basis for the appellant's claim is to assert that the differential sentencing violates the Equal Protection Clause of the Fourteenth Amendment. By its words, the Fourteenth Amendment requires states to provide people with "equal protection of the laws." Unequal treatment of identically situated criminal defendants at sentencing would seem to present a strong basis for the assertion that the sentences violate the right to equal protection.

Although the differential treatment appears to provide the appellant with less than equal protection of the law, this unequal treatment does not actually violate the Constitution unless the Supreme Court (and other courts) interpret the Equal Protection Clause to cover such situations. The Constitution contains words and phrases that are vague as well as those that seem straightforward and clear. The Eighth Amendment prohibition on "cruel and unusual punishments," for example, obviously requires interpretation and definition by judges because it is not self-evident from the phrase exactly which punishments will violate the Amendment. Similarly, the Fourth Amendment's prohibition on "unreasonable searches and seizures" requires interpretation to define which searches and seizures are considered "unreasonable." In addition, seemingly unambiguous phrases of the Constitution have also been interpreted and defined by judges.

The First Amendment says "Congress shall make no law...abridging the freedom of speech." Despite the clarity of this phrase, the Supreme Court has interpreted the First Amendment to permit legislation that limits freedom of speech through reasonable time, place, and manner regulations and other restrictions on speech (e.g., *Madsen v. Women's Health Center* 1994). The words of the Fourteenth Amendment's Equal Protection Clause also seem relatively clear, yet the Supreme Court and other courts have interpreted the words to limit the definition of the constitutional right to equal treatment. Thus, unequal sentences of identically situated defendants would not necessarily violate this constitutional right.

The Fourteenth Amendment was added to the Constitution following the Civil War. A primary impetus for the Equal Protection Clause was the concern about the treatment of African Americans who had recently been released from slavery. Members of Congress who played a primary role in writing and initiating the Equal Protection Clause were justifiably concerned that the former Confederates who had fought for the preservation of states' rights and slavery would enact state laws to discriminate against and disadvantage African Americans living within southern states. As a result of its historical origins, there is general agreement that the Equal Protection Clause was intended to and does protect individuals against unequal treatment by government because of their race (Cox 1987). Except for an occasional decision, such as *Strauder v. West Virginia* (1880) barring formal laws to prohibit African Americans from serving on juries, the Clause was not interpreted and applied with any vigor in opposition to racial discrimination until after the Supreme Court's school desegregation decision in *Brown v. Board of Education* (1954).

One consequence of the race-motivated origins of the Equal Protection Clause is that the Supreme Court has generally evaluated equal protection claims in categorical terms rather than treating the Clause as a general prohibition on unequal treatment. Thus, the Court has tended to analyze claims of unequal treatment by asking, "Is this a claim of racial discrimination? If not, is it a claim based on some other category of discrimination that is covered by the Equal Protection Clause?" The Court's incremental interpretive approach has led it to conclude that the Equal Protection Clause prohibits some categories of discrimination but that other forms of unequal treatment are not covered. An alternative approach to interpretation might have led the Court to ask, "Is this individual claimant being treated in an unequal, disadvantageous manner by state laws or other governmental actions?" Such an approach would have employed the clause to push vigorously for equal treatment of individuals by government in all circumstances. Indeed, an interpretation of the clause that treated it as a general command of equal treatment would provide a strong basis for our hypothetical appellant to present a persuasive claim of a rights violation in light of the favorable sentencing treatment of the co-defendant, Joe. However, because of the Supreme Court's categorical approach to interpreting and applying the Clause, mere unequal treatment does not provide a basis for successfully presenting a claim. The appellant needs to make a further demonstration that the unequal treatment was based on race or some other prohibited category of discrimination.

When the Court is presented with a substantiated claim of racially discriminatory governmental action, it applies "strict scrutiny" under which the government must justify its statute or practice by demonstrating that there is a "compelling" reason for using a racial classification and that the classification is necessarily related to the compelling governmental interest.

This is a difficult burden for the government to carry. The government is required to justify its differential treatment of people from different racial groups by a reason that is so persuasive and powerful that it overcomes the strong legal value against racial discrimination. The government is required, in effect, to convince the Court why it has no alternative other than to engage in racial discrimination in order to accomplish some exceptionally compelling objective. Except for instances in which judges order the use of affirmative action to remedy proven racial discrimination (e.g., *United States v. Paradise* 1987), the only case in which a government has successfully demonstrated a "compelling" reason for a racial classification was the affirmative action case of *Regents of the University of California v. Bakke* (1978). In *Bakke,* a slim majority of justices accepted the need for diversity within a medical school student body as a "compelling" reason to use race as one consideration in admissions decisions.

Race is not the only category of discrimination for which the Supreme Court has applied this "strict scrutiny" analysis. In individual cases, the Court has also demanded a compelling justification for governmental discrimination based on a complainant's status as a non-U.S. citizen (an "alien"). The application of strict scrutiny for equal protection claims based on alienage is situational. The Court applied strict scrutiny in striking down a state statute barring otherwise qualified non-citizens from practicing law (*In re Griffiths* 1973), but the Court declined to apply the same analysis to a law that prevented non-citizens from becoming police officers (*Foley v. Connelie* 1978). In the latter case, the state was permitted to treat people differently without a compelling reason. If a state treated U.S. citizens differently because of their national origin, such as discriminating against Polish-Americans, it is generally believed that the Court would apply strict scrutiny analysis because of the strong parallels between race and national origin as categories of irrelevant immutable characteristics that are often not easily distinguishable.

No more than four justices ever supported applying strict scrutiny to gender discrimination cases in the same manner that the test is applied to racial discrimination cases. Despite never gaining the needed fifth vote to establish the precedent they desired, the justices who supported applying the Equal Protection Clause to gender discrimination succeeded in gaining much of what they wanted. They created a new mid-level or "heightened" scrutiny test for application in gender discrimination cases (*Craig v. Boren* 1976) Under "heightened scrutiny," the government must show that its use of a gender classification is substantially related to an "important" government interest. This test can pose a difficult challenge to a governmental entity seeking to justify differential treatment of men and women. Although some governmental practices will survive heightened scrutiny that may not have avoided invalidation under strict scrutiny, such as treating men and women differently for purposes of Selective Service registration for a possible military draft (*Rostker v. Goldberg* 1981), the heightened scrutiny test provides a significant potential mechanism for judicial examination and elimination of many forms of gender discrimination.

Even under such a limited categorical approach to interpreting and applying the Equal Protection Clause, one might expect that other obvious categories upon which discrimination in American society often rests, such as age or religion or sexual orientation, would also be covered. However, these categories of discrimination do not receive the same kind of legal protection. For some purposes, such as discrimination in employment or federally financed programs, some of these other categories are covered by state or federal *statutes* enacted by legislatures. This protection, though, is narrower, situational, and less encompassing than the *constitutional* protection against discrimination based on race, gender, national origin, and alienage that the courts provide under interpretations of the Equal Protection Clause of the Fourteenth Amendment.

When unequal treatment by government cannot be proven to be based on race, national origin, gender, or illegitimacy, then the Court applies the rational basis test to claims of unequal treatment. Under the rational basis test, discrimination is permissible if it is rationally related to a legitimate governmental purpose. Thus, if unequal treatment occurred because a complainant had long hair, unusual clothes, or a "bad attitude," the government could justify the discrimination by merely showing that it was the rational result of advancing a legitimate governmental objective. For example, the Supreme Court has upheld a regulation requiring police officers to get haircuts (i.e., discriminating against those who wish to determine their own hair length) based on the very un-compelling reason of advancing the government's purported interest in uniformity in police appearance (*Kelley v. Johnson* 1976). The justification is not compelling because officers with long hair can carry out the required tasks for fulfilling their crime control, order maintenance, and service functions. The government's own use of longhaired and unusually attired "undercover" officers for specific investigations and sting operations provides evidence that the government's desire for uniformity in police appearance is merely rational and not compelling.

If we return to our hypothetical example of unequal treatment in sentencing, the appellant must show not merely differential treatment, but also that the treatment was based on race, national origin, gender, or possibly alienage. If the unequal treatment were proven to stem from one of these categories, it would be very difficult to present a compelling justification for the different sentences for identically situated defendants. But how would the appellant prove that the unequal treatment was attributable to one of these categories? Unless the judge or prosecutor made an explicit, negative statement referring to the defendant's race or gender as part of the sentencing process, it would be difficult to prove that the differential treatment was based on these categories—even if it *was* actually based on these categories because of the judge's racist or sexist attitudes. In contemporary times, it is relatively unusual for educated professionals to make overt, discriminatory statements because of the social stigma attached to being labeled as "prejudiced." Even if the defendant treated more harshly by the judge was African American and the other defendant was white, if the prosecutor and judge asserted that the differential sentence was due to the defendant's "bad attitude," then a reviewing court might apply only the rational basis test instead of strict scrutiny. The rational basis test would very likely be seen to justify differences because of the government's objective of saving money by speeding the release of offenders who are amenable to rehabilitation (i.e., those possessing "good attitudes") while giving those whose motives and values remain dangerous to society (i.e., "bad attitude") a longer incapacitative period in which to change their ways. The rational basis test is nearly always applied in a manner that is deferential to the government. Thus, it is exceedingly difficult for complainants to prevail with equal protection claims if they cannot prove that their unequal treatment was based on race, gender, national origin, or alienage. Moreover, the Supreme Court is especially deferential to prosecutors and judges, even in the face of powerful statistical evidence indicating the existence of consistent and systemic differential treatment that can only be explained by racial discrimination (Baldus, Woodworth, & Pulaski 1990). According to the Court, unless evidence is presented of patently discriminatory decisions by specific individuals, there must be deference to criminal justice officials because "[i]mplementation of [criminal justice] laws necessarily requires discretionary judgments. Because discretion is essential to the criminal justice process, we would demand exceptionally clear proof before we would infer that the discretion has been abused" (*McCleskey v. Kemp* 1987, 281).

In considering the extent to which the ideal of "equal justice under law" is attained, the Equal Protection Clause is not the only relevant provision of the Constitution that the Supreme Court and other courts may apply, especially with respect to equal treatment of people who are less affluent or incarcerated. For example, the Sixth Amendment right to counsel provides a potential equalizing resource for less affluent people. If affluent people are able to hire professional representatives to handle their case preparation and arguments, then poor people are significantly disadvantaged in the criminal law process if they do not receive professional representation of equal quality. Thus, the aspiration for equal justice rests on the provision of timely and effective legal resources for the poor. The interpretation and application of the rights to counsel, due process, and jury trials can either enhance or diminish the attainment of equal justice, especially if the effectuation of those rights depends on access to resources.

Individuals who are incarcerated, either as sentenced offenders or as pretrial detainees, cannot readily enjoy the full panoply of rights and liberties possessed by free citizens. The need to maintain order and security in prisons and jails necessarily entails the imposition of limitations on inmates' freedom. However, as we will see in Chapter 6, the Constitution's words do not mandate a forfeiture of all rights for incarcerated persons. Indeed, the Constitution clearly places limitations on the power of government to do whatever it wants to do to detainees and convicted offenders. The Eighth Amendment prohibition on "cruel and unusual punishments" imposes a limitation (albeit an ambiguous one) on governmental power. In addition, the Constitution does not make an exception for incarcerated individuals with respect to other constitutional rights, such as those concerning freedom of religion and due process. Thus, one measure of equal justice is the extent to which detainees and prisoners retain the rights provided by the Constitution. This is especially true of pretrial detainees who are presumptively innocent and, sometimes, actually innocent of any crime. Do judges strike an appropriate balance between the preservation of rights and the maintenance of institutional security in order to fulfill the promise of constitutional rights? Alternatively, do judges permit governmental authorities to assert discretionary powers in ways that needlessly diminish the enjoyment of rights and thereby create inappropriately large differences between the rights of incarcerated persons and those of other citizens?

While some people might argue that it is illegitimate to evaluate the American criminal law process by examining "equal justice" for incarcerated persons, a central feature of descriptions of (as well as criticisms directed at) foreign regimes by Americans and their government has been the mistreatment and denial of rights to prisoners ("From Mao Apologist to Prisoner" 2001; DeYoung & Pianin 2000; Carpenter 1997). This has been especially true with respect to American criticisms of communist regimes such as Cuba, the People's Republic of China, and the old Soviet Union. Implicit in these criticisms is the assertion that the United States is different and, indeed, superior because of the provision of legal rights and humane prison conditions under the American constitutional democracy. The extent to which these rights actually exist or, by contrast, are needlessly diminished provides one measure of the attainment of equal justice in the American system.

Constitutional Interpretation and the Definition of Rights

As indicated by the foregoing discussion, the key actors in determining whether constitutional principles will match the espoused objective of "equal justice under law" are the judges who interpret the Constitution and especially the justices of the U.S. Supreme Court. A five-member majority from among the high court's nine justices can define the meaning of the Constitution's words and phrases, even if their definitions seem too difficult to justify or understand. For example, the Fifth Amendment provides a privilege against compelled self-incrimination, and the Sixth Amendment provides a right to counsel. In 1966, the Supreme Court drew from these provisions of the Bill of Rights to declare that police officers must inform suspects of their right to remain silent and their right to an attorney before undertaking any custodial questioning (*Miranda v. Arizona* 1966). The words of the Constitution do not say anything about informing suspects of their rights, but a majority of Supreme Court justices believed that the policy of providing "Miranda rights" was necessary to make the Fifth and Sixth Amendment rights effective. The justices who dissented against the decision strongly disagreed. Chief Justice William Rehnquist (1987, 291) has written that "[t]he law is at best an inexact science...[so] [t]here is simply no demonstrably 'right' answer to the question involved in many of [the Supreme Court's] difficult cases." Thus, constitutional law, including the definition of rights, is developed as a result of the arguments and reasoning that persuade a majority of justices on the Supreme Court (Epstein & Kobylka 1992).

The justices are not neutral, open-minded decision makers waiting to be persuaded by one side's attorney in a case. The justices have attitudes, values, policy preferences, and role orientations that guide their decision making (Baum 1997). The justices possess judicial philosophies about how the Constitution ought to be interpreted. For example, Justices Antonin Scalia and Clarence Thomas believe that the Constitution should be interpreted according to the original intentions of the authors of each constitutional provision. Thus, they believe the phrase "cruel and unusual punishments" in the Eighth Amendment should have the same meaning as that intended by the men who wrote the Amendment in the eighteenth century (Smith 1993b). Interpretation by original intent is fraught with problems, particularly a lack of historical knowledge about whether any specific meaning was intended for each constitutional provision (Macedo 1987; Baer 1989). The words of the Constitution and Bill of Rights were drafted by legislative bodies and ratified by bodies of decision makers within each state. How can a single intended meaning be attributed to all of these decision makers, especially when they chose to use ambiguous words and phrases? In addition, justices, including Scalia and Thomas, are never completely consistent in their purported adherence to a specific interpretive approach (Smith & Baugh 2000). In spite of these problems, a justice's judicial philosophy and preferred interpretive approach provide an orientation that will determine the justice's receptivity (or lack thereof) to particular arguments presented by lawyers about what the Constitution ought to mean.

Other justices employ different interpretive approaches based on their values and policy preferences. In defining the meaning of constitutional provisions, including rights contained in various amendments, some justices emphasize the maximization of legal protections for individuals. For example, Justice William Brennan believed that, in his own words, "the Constitution embodies the aspirations to social justice, brotherhood, and human dignity that brought this nation into being," and he sought to interpret the document in a manner that advanced those broad goals (Brennan 1997, 200). Other justices, such as Warren Court era Justice John Harlan, place a priority on giving states the broadest possible authority to handle their own affairs (*Duncan v. Louisiana* 1968). Other justices appear to decide issues in an *ad hoc* manner depending on how each case fits with their values and without always manifesting a guiding philosophy. Justice Anthony Kennedy, for example, periodically deviates from his frequent support for conservative outcomes in order to provide the decisive fifth vote for a liberal majority protecting constitutional rights in specific cases (Smith 1992).

In addition to the influence of their own values and arguments formulated by attorneys, the justices' decisions are also shaped by their interactions with each other, especially when they attempt to persuade other justices through the draft opinions that they circulate during the gradual process of developing the Court's final majority opinion (Schwartz 1996). Some justices are also influenced by their concern that law should develop and change in an incremental fashion so that it does not appear that the justices are simply making up rules out of thin air as they issue each decision interpreting the Constitution. In anticipating what kinds of interpretations the public will view as legitimate, these justices may restrain the expression of their own true values and preferences by making more modest decisions or by retaining interpretations that they really believe should be changed. This factor was most apparent when three justices, Sandra O'Connor, Anthony Kennedy, and David Souter, declined to alter the Court's interpretations concerning the right of choice with respect to abortion because they feared that the Court's legitimacy would suffer in the eyes of the public if a twenty-year-old precedent were suddenly changed (*Planned Parenthood v. Casey* 1992). This factor does not affect all justices equally. Some justices appear always inclined to interpret the Constitution according to their preferences even if it means eliminating long-accepted interpretations. Moreover, the reluctance of some justices to alter the definition of rights for a closely scrutinized, controversial issue such as abortion does not mean that they would not overturn established precedents concerning other issues, such as the use of victim impact testimony in death penalty cases (*Payne v. Tennessee* 1991).

A scholar who reviewed research on judicial decision making summed up the basis for judges' actions in the following statement: "Judges' decisions are a function of what they prefer to do, tempered by what they think they ought to do, but constrained by what they perceive is feasible to do" (Gibson 1983, 9). This conclusion has important implications. First, the interpretation of the Constitution and the definition of constitutional rights can change. The Constitution's meaning is not defined by clear, fixed, universally agreed upon principles. Moreover, change can occur incrementally or it can be sudden and dramatic. All it takes is the agreement of five justices, and the meaning of the Constitution can change overnight. A legal protection can be instantly created or it can instantly disappear depending on how the Supreme Court's justices interpret the Constitution in deciding a case.

Second, the interpretation of the Constitution and the definition of rights are defined by the values, beliefs, thought processes, and interactions of a shifting mix of human beings who comprise the nine justices on the U.S. Supreme Court as well as the judges in other courts. These human beings are not delivered to the courts by divine intervention. They are selected through political processes and generally come to the judiciary with substantial political experience and connections. Nearly all of them were active in electoral politics and were closely associated with either the Democratic or Republican party. They are not "neutral" is the sense of being objective and open-minded. They generally aspire to fulfill their professional responsibility to avoid favoring either side as they listen to arguments and evidence. However, they bring values, policy preferences, and experiences to their judicial careers that significantly shape their decision-making orientations. Thus, a key factor influencing the interpretation of the Constitution is the political composition of the Supreme Court and other courts at any given moment in history. That composition is determined to a significant extent by the quirks of fate that determine which judicial officers retire, die, or resign while a specific president is in office or a particular political party controls the U.S. Senate. Although many states elect their judges, a process that infuses judicial selection with a particular kind of relationship to party politics, federal judicial officers on the U.S. Supreme Court and lower federal courts are appointed by the president and confirmed by the U.S. Senate. Thus, for example, when no Supreme Court justices left the high court during Democratic President Jimmy Carter's term (1977–1981), it meant that Republican presidents appointed all ten justices named to the high court from 1969 to 1991. In addition, the timing of fateful departures gives some presidents especially significant opportunities to shape the Court's composition. For example, President Richard Nixon appointed four justices during his six years in office and President Ronald Reagan appointed three justices during his eight years in office. Presidents select nominees to the Supreme Court for political reasons, especially their desire to see their own values and policy preferences represented in the Court's interpretations of the Constitution (Yalof 1999; Maltese 1995). As a result, they nearly always seek to nominate justices whom they believe to share their political orientation.

Political developments that produced changes in the Supreme Court's composition played a primary role in determining the interpretations of the Constitution that defined rights relevant to the attainment of "equal justice under law." Justices appointed by Democratic President Franklin Roosevelt in the 1930s and 1940s accelerated the process of incorporating most of the rights in the Bill of Rights into the Due Process Clause of the Fourteenth Amendment for application to the states. These Roosevelt appointees, especially Hugo Black and William O. Douglas, who each served on the Court for more than thirty years, expanded the definition of rights for individuals and the concept of equal protection. They decided *Brown v. Board of Education* (1954) concerning racial discrimination as well as a variety of cases expanding rights for individuals in the criminal law process. Among President Dwight Eisenhower's appointments to the Supreme Court were two justices whose inclination to interpret the Constitution in ways that expanded individual rights went beyond what Eisenhower desired. These two, Chief Justice Earl Warren and Justice William Brennan, led the Court in making a variety of decisions, including *Miranda v. Arizona* (1966), that outraged political conservatives by providing legal protections for criminal suspects and defendants. During the Warren Court era (1953–1969), the Court incorporated and expanded most of the provisions in the Bill of Rights relevant to the criminal law process.

With respect to the criminal law process, the Supreme Court's history since the 1960s has been largely a reaction to the many precedents established by the Warren Court. Republican Presidents Richard Nixon, Gerald Ford, Ronald Reagan, and George Bush (I) made all of the appointments to the Court from Nixon's election in 1969 until Democratic President Bill Clinton's appointment of Justice Ruth Bader Ginsburg in 1993. With the exception of Ford, all of the Republican presidents were intent on appointing justices who would reinterpret the Constitution in ways that would diminish or eliminate the Warren Court precedents that had expanded rights for criminal defendants. Thus, during the Burger Court era (1969–1986) and the Rehnquist Court era (1986–current), under the leadership of Republican appointees Chief Justice Warren Burger and Chief Justice William Rehnquist, the increasingly conservative Supreme Court issued many decisions that diminished the scope of rights for suspects, defendants, and convicted offenders (Hensley, Smith, & Baugh 1997). Although many Warren-era precedents remained in place, such as *Mapp v. Ohio* (1961) concerning searches and *Miranda v. Arizona* (1966) concerning custodial questioning of suspects, most of them were weakened by the creation of exceptions that permitted law enforcement officials to deviate from the underlying rules in specific situations. Thus, for example, evidence obtained by questioning an arrestee who was not informed of his *Miranda* rights could be used in court against the defendant if the police and the court defined the context of the questioning as a situation in which "public safety" was threatened (*New York v. Quarles* 1984).

If constitutional law were determined by clearly defined and universally accepted immutable principles, then there would be little point in evaluating the criminal law process and its purported objective of "equal justice under law." One could note those instances in which the objective of equal treatment was not achieved in order to highlight the extent to which the goal was merely illusory. By contrast, there are strong reasons to evaluate the ideal of equal justice in light of the human processes that shape constitutional interpretation and the fact that the definitions of rights change in accordance with political developments that determine the composition of the judiciary. The assessment of "equal justice" takes on special importance because doctrinal deficiencies that impede advancement of the goal are not necessarily inevitable and permanent. Deficiencies are the product of human decisions by decision makers who possess the authority to advance rather than diminish the legal system's purported equality goals. This is not to say that a perfect, idealized version of "equal justice under law" is attainable in a complex legal system operated by inherently inconsistent and flawed human processes. Instead, it underscores the point that the justices of the U.S. Supreme Court and judges on other courts could interpret the Constitution and define rights in ways that advance the purported goal of equal justice. Because legal doctrines are not fixed and static, the interpretive powers granted to judges permit those officials to interpret the Equal Protection Clause and other constitutional provisions in ways that seek to ensure that people drawn into the criminal justice system do not receive less than equal treatment because of their race, gender, social status, or other demographic characteristics.

Obviously, any criticisms of the criminal law process and its underlying legal doctrines that focus on inadequate advancement of equal treatment are based on value choices that emphasize the primacy of "equal justice" as a key priority for the American legal system. It is clear that some judicial decision makers give priority to alternative value choices and objectives, such as limiting the role of the judiciary in defining certain public policies or deferring to federalism's objectives by permitting states to define their own laws and policies. Despite these disagreements about prioritization of constitutional values, there is strong reason to emphasize the importance of "equal justice" as a systemic objective and measure of success. The purported goal of "equal justice under law" is an openly touted attribute of the judicial system that provides the system with public support and legitimacy. Unlike such alternative priorities as judicial restraint and federalism, "equal justice" provides a slogan and a belief that Americans use to define their image of themselves and pridefully distinguish their country's system from "undesirable" and "inferior" governing systems elsewhere in the world. Moreover, the concept of equal treatment rests at the heart of American conceptions of justice and directly affects the fates of individuals drawn into the criminal law process.

The chapters of this book will examine the extent to which constitutional doctrines and judicial decisions advance or impede the purported goal of "equal justice under law." Because of the pervasiveness of discretionary decisions in the criminal justice system and the influence of partisan politics over the selection of judicial decision makers, there is no claim, implicit or otherwise, that equal treatment can be guaranteed through constitutional interpretation and the definition of individuals' rights. Judicial decisions defining constitutional rights are often undercut or ignored by police officers, prosecutors, judges, and corrections officers because legal doctrines are not self-effectuating. For example, there were differences in the ways in which police departments implemented, or failed to implement, their new obligation to inform suspects of their rights after the Supreme Court's 1966 decision in *Miranda v. Arizona* (Milner 1971). Mechanisms for the supervision of criminal justice personnel and the implementation of constitutional doctrines are often weak and uncertain (Smith & Hurst 1997). Thus, the fundamental concern of the book is an assessment of the actions of the U.S. Supreme Court and other courts in the advancement of equal justice rather than the actual attainment of an ideal. The Supreme Court cannot ensure that "equal justice under law" is achieved, but it can set the tone and provide the basis for aspiring to improve the efforts of criminal processes and institutions to advance the goal. Judicial decisions interpreting the Constitution and defining rights establish rules and tools for seeking equal treatment while they also send a message to decision makers in the criminal law process about the prioritization of objectives. When the nation's courts do not use their institutional authority and legitimacy to advance the goal of "equal justice under law," there is little reason for other actors in the criminal law process to devote themselves to the goal of equal treatment rather than give primary or exclusive emphasis to crime control, efficiency, political self-interest, and other objectives.

3

Race and Equal Justice

W.E.B. DUBOIS SAID that the color line was the problem of the twentieth century (Jones 1972, 1). In the first decade of the twenty-first century, it is appropriate to ask whether DuBois' observation remains valid, especially for the criminal law process that espouses a commitment to the ideal of "Equal Justice Under Law." To what extent does race affect the quality of justice that people receive when they are drawn into contact with criminal justice officials? One century ago, it was obvious, expected, and accepted by many in society that whites and African Americans would not receive the same treatment. The U.S. Supreme Court's ignominious decision in *Plessy v. Ferguson* (1896) provided the highest court's imprimatur of legitimacy for official racial segregation in governmental services and institutions. Segregation and discrimination continued in the decades following the *Plessy* decision. Nearly fifty years later, the publication of Gunnar Myrdal's monumental work, *An American Dilemma: The Negro Problem and Modern Democracy* (1944), documented the existence and consequences of racial discrimination throughout American society, including the judicial system. In the later decades of the twentieth century, American society made important strides toward reducing the prevalence of racial discrimination through federal and state equal opportunity laws, court decisions mandating equal protection, and changes in societal attitudes about race. Looking back across the decades at how things used to be, it is no surprise to find contemporary commentators noting that the problems which remain are not as universally deep and damaging as the racial problems of the past (Steele 1990). However, from the vantage point of the first years of the twenty-first century, one need only look to the preceding decade's major controversies to recognize that racial divisions and debates about equal justice continue to plague American society.

Continuing Issues of Race and Justice

The acquittal of Hall-of-Fame football player O.J. Simpson on charges of murdering his wife and a man on the sidewalk of his wife's home divided many African Americans and whites in their assessments of the fairness and effectiveness of the criminal law process (Morrow 1995). African Americans focused on the Los Angeles police detective whose racist statements were documented by witnesses and who claimed that he found a bloody glove in Simpson's backyard that was linked to the murders. The nature of the detective's statements and his role in finding key evidence raised concerns that Simpson was being framed for murder. By contrast, many whites believed that the evidence demonstrated Simpson's guilt, and they expressed dissatisfaction with jury processes that could lead to acquittal in the face of Simpson's apparent motive, prior violent behavior toward his wife, and suspicious actions after the murder. In another example, dozens of people were killed in Los Angeles in 1992 as a result of civil disturbances produced when a state court jury acquitted several police officers of beating Rodney King, an African American motorist, despite the fact that a bystander had videotaped the beating (Mydans 1992). Although two of the officers were later convicted in federal court for violating King's civil rights, many African Americans viewed the episode as evidence that racially-motivated abusive behavior by police officers was seldom punished. In 1999, four white police officers in New York City fired forty-one bullets at an unarmed, innocent African immigrant whom they mistakenly thought was a murder suspect. The man was killed in the fusillade. Amid large-scale public protests about racially motivated police brutality, the officers were acquitted of murder charges (Cole & Smith 2001, 222). In 2001, civil disturbances erupted in Cincinnati after a white police officer shot and killed an unarmed African American man. The city responded by imposing a curfew. Nearly ninety percent of those arrested for curfew violations following the disturbances were African Americans (Vela 2001). These examples, as well as others, regularly remind Americans to recognize that racial conflicts persist and that the legal system is intimately tied to those problems.

In some cases, such as O.J. Simpson's, judicial processes are arguably mere focal points for societal reactions that reflect existing racial divisions rather than concrete deficiencies in court processes and outcomes. Both sides in the case possessed the resources to put forward complete presentations about the evidence and then the jury weighed the evidence before making a decision. Other jurors might have made a different decision, but there is little indication that the jurors focused on underlying racial debates as the focal point for their verdict. The fact that disagreements and debates about the role of race in criminal justice lurk beneath many cases does not automatically mean that race is, in fact, a primary influence for the treatment and outcomes experienced by most defendants. Indeed, there are significant debates among contemporary scholars about the extent to which legal institutions and processes employ racist influences and produce discriminatory results. For example, William Wilbanks asserts that the influence of racism in the criminal justice system is a "myth." According to Wilbanks, "It would appear, however, that the size of the race effect *against* blacks is largely balanced by a comparable race effect *for* blacks. The presence of the canceling-out effect is important because there would appear to be no room in the [Discrimination Thesis] for such a result" (Wilbanks 1987, 143). By contrast, other scholars carefully reviewed studies of various aspects of the criminal justice system before concluding that "the criminal justice system is characterized by *contextual* discrimination. Racial minorities are treated more harshly than whites at some stages of the criminal justice process" (Walker, Spohn, & DeLone 1996, 230).

Debates about the nature and existence of inequalities in the criminal law process typically focus on police and trial court processes as sources of racial discrimination. By contrast, the U.S. Supreme Court has enjoyed significant acclaim during the second half of the twentieth century as a legal institution that played an important role in pushing American society away from unthinking acceptance of racism and discrimination. In particular, the Supreme Court's decision in *Brown v. Board of Education* (1954) is praised because of "the groundwork it laid for a massive attack upon Jim Crow itself. *Brown* was the catalyst that shook up Congress and culminated in the two major Civil Rights acts of the century" (Wilkinson 1979, 48–49) As characterized by Roy Brooks (1990, 28–29), "[T]he Supreme Court in *Brown* took a decisive turn for the better in the government's approach to race relations. *Brown* was the first act of government to make the ideal of racial equality—the push for racial inclusiveness—a constitutional imperative and, hence, unequivocally the official civil rights policy of the United States." In looking at the Supreme Court's post-*Brown* decisions, Bernard Schwartz (1993, 309) claimed that "[b]y the end of [Chief Justice Earl] Warren's tenure [1953–1969] ... the [Supreme] Court had virtually rooted out racial discrimination from American law." Although there are lingering questions about the extent of social change actually attributable to the Supreme Court's decisions (Rosenberg 1991), the high court and other federal courts receive credit for leading the movement against racial discrimination (Peltason 1961). According to Archibald Cox (1987, 257), the Court led a "revolution in constitutional law [that] quickly extended the *Brown* principle to other racial segregation laws."

The Supreme Court and Sources of Discrimination

What is the relationship between the Supreme Court's reputation and legacy for combating racial discrimination and the debates about discrimination in criminal justice processes? As discussed in Chapter 2, discrimination in criminal law processes can stem from several sources. One source is formal rules and practices that impose discriminatory treatment on people. For example, a state statute that excluded African Americans from jury service would embody such formal discrimination. The Supreme Court invalidated just such a law in 1880 (*Strauder v. West Virginia*), and there is virtually no likelihood that such a formal law could survive scrutiny by any judge under equal protection analysis. The Supreme Court has consistently issued decisions to eliminate this first source of discrimination. For example, the Court has ruled against corrections policies and practices that routinely segregated prisoners by race (*Lee v. Washington* 1968).

The Problem of Discretion

A second source of discrimination is discretionary decision making by actors in the legal system, which produces differential treatment. When trial judges possess discretionary authority to impose criminal sentences, for example, they may apply that discretion to favor or disadvantage particular defendants because of racial biases. Similarly, selective searches by police and charging decisions by prosecutors may reflect racial discrimination. The Supreme Court possesses the authority to combat, but not cure, this source of discrimination. Through its decisions concerning constitutional rights, the high court can define limitations on the ability of police officers, prosecutors, judges, and corrections officials to discriminate through the application of discretionary decisions. However, this second source of discrimination presents a more significant challenge for the Supreme Court and society because of the difficulties involved in detecting and understanding the discriminatory consequences of discretionary decision making and because of the Rehnquist Court's disinclination to limit the discretion of criminal justice officials.

As described in Chapter 2, the use of racial profiling by law enforcement officers in determining whom they will stop and which vehicles they will search has become a major source of controversy about discriminatory applications of officials' discretionary authority. Studies indicate that African American and Hispanic drivers in Illinois, Maryland, Pennsylvania, and elsewhere were much more likely than their white counterparts to be stopped and to have their vehicles searched. This pattern existed despite the fact that white drivers comprise the largest percentage of motorists and commit a majority of traffic violations (Harris 1999). The federal government's General Accounting Office studied the U.S. Customs Service and found that African American women were nine times more likely than whites to be singled out for searches at airports despite a lower probability that they were engaged in illegal conduct (General Accounting Office 2000). In the aftermath of the 2001 suicide attacks of hijacked airliners on the World Trade Center and the Pentagon, there were mounting concerns that people of Middle Eastern ancestry were increasingly targeted for airport searches and other discretionary actions. This form of profiling received heightened publicity after an Arab-American Secret Service agent was removed from an airliner and prevented from flying to his duty assignment as a personal bodyguard for President George W. Bush (Begley & Rosenberg 2002). When police officers use race or ethnicity as a "cue" that triggers their suspicions about possible criminal conduct, they impose discriminatory burdens on the liberty of people selected for stops and searches. Similar discrimination exists when there are racial disparities from discretionary decisions about bail, sentencing, and other aspects of criminal justice. For example, a study in Connecticut found that African American and Hispanic-American males with no prior criminal record were given bail amounts that were double those given to whites. Moreover, in drug cases, the average bail amount imposed on African Americans and Hispanic Americans was four times higher than the amount for whites in the same courthouse (Cole & Smith 2001, 329).

When confronted with cases seeking to limit law enforcement officers' discretionary authority, the Supreme Court has generally supported broad discretion for officials within the criminal justice system. In *Whren v. United States* (1996), the Supreme Court endorsed the authority of undercover police officers in unmarked cars to make stops for routine traffic offenses, even when police departments' policies indicate that uniformed officers in regular patrol cars should make such stops. The decision keeps available the tactic of pretextual traffic stops as a means to examine vehicles and question motorists for drug possession and other illegal activities. Unethical officers can falsely claim that a motorist failed to use a turn signal when changing lanes or exceeded the speed limit, and there is nothing that the motorist can do to prove his or her innocence. Because of the difficulties involved in formulating a rule that would impede officers' ability to make pretextual traffic stops, including those based on racial profiling, one can understand the justices' reluctance to deal with the issue. However, the failure to address the issue continues to facilitate broad opportunities for discriminatory decisions.

Supreme Court decisions concerning other criminal justice issues similarly reinforce law enforcement officers' broad discretionary authority. When the Court established the rules for situations in which officers can "stop and frisk" people on the streets, the Court emphasized that an officer's observations must produce sufficient information to justify a reasonable suspicion that the person to be frisked is armed and poses a danger to the officer and others (*Terry v. Ohio* 1968). By 2000, the Rehnquist Court had expanded the rationale for such stops to permit officers to frisk people whom they see running in a "high-crime neighborhood" or other contexts that arouse suspicion (*Illinois v. Wardlow* 2000). The decision reiterated the Court's reluctance to limit police officers' discretion and, in effect, expanded officers' opportunities to decide when to make stops and to rationalize such stops with vague and possibly pretextual justifications. Similarly, in *Atwater v. City of Lago Vista* (2001), the Court said that officers may arrest and jail people for minor offenses that are punishable only by fines. In the case, a mother was arrested to failing to place seat belts on herself and her children as they drove slowly along the shoulder of a road looking for a child's doll that had fallen out of the window. Because officers can make arrests in such circumstances, they can use those arrests as a justification to conduct complete searches of the arrestees and to conduct complete inventory searches of impounded vehicles. This expanded arrest authority endorsed by the Court gives officers additional discretionary tools that may be applied in a discriminatory fashion, especially if officers engage in racial profiling when enforcing traffic laws.

In one case, the Court was explicitly asked to examine the allegedly discriminatory use of discretion by prosecutors. Defense attorneys in *United States v. Armstrong* (1996) presented information and affidavits from a substance abuse counselor and defense attorney indicating that crack cocaine is used and sold by whites and African Americans. Even so, the U.S. Attorney's Office in Los Angeles only prosecuted African Americans for crack cocaine offenses. The attorneys sought to gain access to prosecutors' records in order to discover whether there was clear evidence of systematic racial discrimination in discretionary prosecutorial decisions. The Supreme Court refused to permit the attorneys to gain access to the prosecutorial records so there was no way for them to pursue the question of whether evidence of provable discrimination existed. Obviously, the Court will be reluctant to permit defense attorneys to explore prosecutorial records based on mere allegations. However, the Court's refusal to look closely at existing indications of discrimination served to reinforce the existence of broad discretion and continuing opportunities for that discretion to produce discrimination.

Disparate Impact and Unequal Resources

Similar problems exist with respect to the Court's lack of attention to the two other sources of unequal treatment. The Court is disinclined to redress the disparate impact of facially neutral laws that create disproportionately adverse impacts on specific groups. Thus, courts have passively permitted legislatures to address, or fail to address, such issues as the differential sentences for crack and powder cocaine offenders that create adverse impacts for African Americans (Tonry 1995). By contrast, the Minnesota Supreme Court demonstrated that a court of last resort could address such issues within its jurisdiction by ruling that the disparate racial impact of Minnesota's cocaine laws violated the right to equal protection under the state constitution (*State of Minnesota v. Russell* 1991). Under the Minnesota law that was invalidated by the state supreme court, offenders convicted of possessing three grams of crack cocaine could receive sentences of up to twenty years in prison while those caught with three grams of powder cocaine could not receive more than five years in prison. The impact of the differential sentences had fallen most heavily on African American defendants. The decision by the Minnesota Supreme Court in interpreting its own constitution provides a demonstration of what the U.S. Supreme Court might have done if it placed a higher priority on advancing equal justice and eliminating racial disparities. The state court invalidated the law without applying the strict scrutiny test for equal protection violations. The strict scrutiny test is applied to challenged statutes that are enacted "'because of [and] not merely in spite of' an anticipated racially discriminatory effect" (*State of Minnesota v. Russell* 1991, 888 n. 2, quoting *McCleskey v. Kemp* 1987, 298). In this case, the disparate impact was a by-product rather than a goal of the statute. Thus, the state court applied the "Minnesota rational basis test" which is more demanding than the U.S. Supreme Court's rational basis test for equal protection because it requires "a reasonable connection between the actual, and not just the theoretical, effect of the challenged classification and statutory goals" (*State of Minnesota v. Russell* 1991, 889).

The State of Minnesota claimed that it created the distinction between crack and powder cocaine in order to target street-level dealers. The State claimed that people with small amounts of crack are dealers rather than mere possessors of cocaine while dealers of powder cocaine carry larger quantities of the drug. The state supreme court rejected this rationale because the State had never studied and documented such differences between crack and powder cocaine dealers. The State's conclusions were based on anecdotal evidence, primarily consisting of a county prosecutor's conversations with police officers and informants. As an additional rationale, the State claimed that crack cocaine is more addictive and therefore more dangerous than powder cocaine. However, the expert testimony by a chemist concerning the two forms of cocaine demonstrated that the method of ingestion rather than composition of each drug determines its impact. In particular, powder cocaine that is dissolved in water and then injected intravenously provides the same potent effects as smoking crack. Thus, the state supreme court rejected the State's second rationale as an invalid justification for providing differentiated punishments. The court also rejected the State's speculative conclusions that trafficking in crack cocaine produces more violence. Again, the State's evidence was limited, anecdotal, and insufficient to justify a policy that produced a racially disparate impact (*State of Minnesota v. Russell* 1991, 890).

With respect to the fourth source of inequality, the Court has historically paid attention to specific aspects of unequal resources, such as the right of indigent defendants to be provided with defense counsel (*Gideon v. Wainwright* 1963). The justices have not focused, however, on the manner in which these resource differences cause unequal racial outcomes because of the strong association between race and income in many American communities. By examining these four sources of unequal treatment, this chapter will examine the Supreme Court's leadership role (or lack thereof) in affecting the continued existence of racial bias within the criminal law process.

Race in the History of the Legal System

The institution of slavery cemented racial ideology into the consciousness, social practices, and formal rules of American society (Kolchin 1993). As observed by Paul Finkelman (1993, 2069–2070), "Obviously slavery was not merely a system of race relations and prejudice; it was also an institution devoted to social control, class stratification, and economic exploitation." Beneath these practices was the core idea that persons of African descent were not equal to whites as human beings. As described by Peter Kolchin (1993, 18), "[M]ost white Americans came to assume that blacks were so different from whites that slavery was their natural state." Such views shaped the definition of law and judicial processes during colonial times and the early years of the nation. For example, criminal law provided less protection to African Americans than to other residents:

> An indication of the regard given to a slave's person is the fact that the maiming of one slave by another was called a "lesser crime" than burglary, robbery, or the burning of houses. It was placed on the level of a "trespass," comparable to the "stealing of fowls [or] provisions." Thus the legislature viewed the "maiming" of one slave by another as a trespass or injury to the slave owner's property, not as a personal injury to the slave. (Higginbotham 1978, 181–182)

As Lawrence Friedman has noted, this differential valuation of African Americans' worth as persons included delegation of punishment powers from the state to the "superior" white citizens: "In a sense, any white man (or woman) ranked higher in society than any black, slave or free, in the states of the slave South; and, at least under certain conditions, the law permitted any white to punish a slave who stepped out of line" (Friedman 1993, 86).

After the demise of slavery, race retained its salience for denying people of color equal protection under the laws. Violent crimes committed against African Americans by whites, especially in the South, received little governmental resistance because "local government was either supine, or helpless, or allied with the Klan" (Friedman 1993, 188). Lynching proliferated as an extra legal means that "suppressed any movement, however small, that disturbed southern white supremacy, or southern 'honor'" (Friedman, 1993, 192). By the mid-twentieth century, racial discrimination remained pervasive in police practices, prosecutorial decision making, jury verdicts, and sentencing in many trial courts (Myrdal 1944, 523–524). Thus, the unequal treatment of Americans according to their racial classification remained deeply entrenched in the legal system after operating in various forms for more than two centuries (Staples 1976).

More than a decade prior to the Supreme Court's monumental condemnation of racial discrimination in *Brown v. Board of Education* (1954), Gunnar Myrdal credited the high court with leading efforts to reduce racial discrimination in the judicial process:

> The Supreme Court is increasingly active in censoring the state courts when they transgress the principles of legal procedure: it is pressing the courts to include Negroes on the jury lists, to curb appeals to race prejudice on the part of public prosecutors and private attorneys, to reject evidence obtained by third degree methods, and so on. (Myrdal 1944, 555)

For example, the Supreme Court recognized a right to counsel for indigent defendants in capital cases after a court in Scottsboro, Alabama quickly convicted several African American men in a controversial rape case in which one of the alleged victims recanted (*Powell v. Alabama* 1932). In another case, the Court found a violation of due process when Mississippi law enforcement officers used beatings and torture as the means to obtain confessions from African American defendants (*Brown v. Mississippi* 1936).

Neither of these cases concerned formal discriminatory rules applied against African Americans. Both cases involved the Court's assessment of the impact of practices employed by criminal justice officials. In addition, neither case involved the right to equal protection. One concerned the right to counsel as a component of due process (*Powell v. Alabama*) and the other concerned a general conception of due process (*Brown v. Mississippi*). Thus, before the Warren Court era (1953–1969), the Supreme Court evinced sensitivity to the reality of unfair treatment of African Americans as a product of the design of the legal process and a consequence of decision making by justice system officials. Such decisions were implicitly informed by empirical observations about the unfairness of certain practices. The words of the Constitution, especially as construed in the 1930s, provided no explicit or precedential basis for concluding either that a fair trial was impossible without defense counsel, or that "due process" precludes the application of what were, at that time, commonplace physical techniques of interrogation. Because the Constitution and the Court's precedents did not explicitly require the presence of defense counsel, there must have been something in the *Powell* case about the reality of the lightning-quick trial, conviction, and sentencing to death of African American defendants in an atmosphere of a howling white lynch mob that spurred the Supreme Court to expand the definition of right to counsel to cover these circumstances. In *Brown v. Mississippi* (1936, 282), the defendants "were laid over chairs and their backs were cut to pieces with a leather strap with buckles on it" until they confessed in the exact words demanded by the police officers. As Lawrence Friedman (1993, 152–153) has noted, in dealing with criminal suspects, "[t]orture and brutality...were common....[Beatings and torture were] only semisecret. The police were, in fact, proud of their physical directness." Moreover, the police officers in the *Brown* case were quite blunt about their racist motivations in abusing the defendants. When testifying at trial, all of the police officers acknowledged that they had beaten the suspects to produce the confessions, and one deputy said, in response to a question about how severely he had whipped the suspects, "Not too much for a negro; not as much as I would have done if it were left to me" (*Brown v. Mississippi* 1936, 284). Their frank admissions in open court provide a clear indication of how common and accepted such abusive police practices were at that moment in history. Even so, by choosing to employ their authority to interpret the malleable concept of "due process" in order to protect the defendants in these cases, the justices of the 1930s Supreme Court demonstrated a capacity to recognize the harsh consequences of racial discrimination in criminal processes.

During the Warren Court era, the justices used a sensitivity to empirical reality in combating racial discrimination, even in the *Brown v. Board of Education* (1954) decision that barred official discriminatory policies. In

Brown v. Board of Education, Chief Justice Warren's majority opinion relied on social science evidence about the adverse impacts of segregation upon African American children. Warren made reference to psychological studies of children that indicated detrimental consequences for African American children's self-esteem as a result of segregation and unequal educational resources (Kluger 1975). Although the use of such considerations has generated controversy about the proper methods of constitutional interpretation, judicial sensitivity to actual discriminatory impacts upon people's lives reflects the modern trend toward legal realism that has been evident since early in the twentieth century (Stumpf 1988).

As indicated by the foregoing discussion, America's racial history produced pervasive, entrenched, and long-standing practices that treated African Americans as less than equal within the legal system. Even before the Warren Court era, the Supreme Court made efforts to combat the pervasiveness of racial discrimination. In making these efforts, the Court's decisions are implicitly informed by sensitivity to the reality of racial discrimination. The high court did not limit its judicial opinions to declarations about the impermissibility of formal and official forms of discrimination. Instead, an awareness of the practical risks of discrimination is evident in the Court's decisions addressing racial injustice within the criminal law process. Given this twentieth-century legacy, how does the contemporary Supreme Court respond to the risks of discrimination in the legal system in the early twenty-first century?

Much has been made of the conservatizing impact of changes in the Supreme Court's composition from 1969 through 1991. Republican presidents from Nixon through the first President Bush appointed new justices who possessed more conservative judicial philosophies than their predecessors while no Democratic presidents had the opportunity to appoint any justices from 1967 until 1993. Despite the enhanced power of the numerically dominant conservative justices after 1986, the Rehnquist Court's new composition produced a less dramatic impact upon the Supreme Court's decisions than many people believe (Hensley & Smith 1995). Although the Court's decisions have generally limited the scope of constitutional rights, the Rehnquist Court has not engaged in wholesale reversals of liberal Warren Court precedents. Thus, such controversial principles as *Miranda* warnings, the exclusionary rule, and a right of choice for abortion continue to exist. It cannot be assumed that the Rehnquist Court's decisions will disfavor individuals' constitutional rights claims at every opportunity. Instead, the actual decisional trends of the contemporary Supreme Court must be examined and analyzed, including trends affecting the risk of racial discrimination in the legal system.

Racial Discrimination in Jury Selection

In *Strauder v. West Virginia* (1880), the Supreme Court made an early decision intended to uphold the Equal Protection Clause by invalidating a state statute that barred African American men from serving on juries. In the decades after that decision, the Court did little to combat discriminatory practices in various states that excluded African Americans from juries without any law that formally barred them from jury service. The Warren Court gave renewed attention to the issue in the mid-twentieth century (*Swain v. Alabama* 1965), but questions lingered about the continued existence of practices that limited the participation of African Americans on juries. At the end of the Burger Court era (1969–1986), the Supreme Court issued a decision that was intended to provide an enforcement mechanism for the previously enunciated prohibition on racial discrimination in jury selection. The Court's decision focused on the use of peremptory challenges. Each side in a legal case is given a specific number of "peremptory challenges" that can be used to exclude individuals from the jury pool without providing any reason. An unlimited number of jurors may be excluded through "challenges for cause" if those potential jurors provide some indication that they may possess a bias that will affect their decision making. The biases at issue in such circumstances are not necessarily related to racial or ethnic prejudice but can be presumptions about the existence of bias based on the potential juror's previous experience as a crime victim or as the relative of a crime victim. The Supreme Court's concern focused on the use of peremptory challenges by prosecutors to exclude African Americans from juries in cases in which African Americans were defendants. In *Batson v. Kentucky* (1986), the Court permitted a defendant to raise an inference of racially discriminatory use of peremptory challenges without showing a long-standing pattern of such behavior by a particular prosecutor. Instead, the appearance of race-based peremptory challenges in the defendant's own case could trigger a burden shift requiring the prosecutor to provide a neutral, non-race-based justification for the suspicious exclusions. Thus, if it appeared that peremptory challenges were being used systematically by the prosecutor to achieve race-related influences on the jury's composition, the prosecutor could be required by the judge to provide a non-race-related reason for the challenges. Previously, attorneys could use peremptory challenges to exclude anyone without providing any explanation, unless the defense could show that a prosecutor repeatedly used such challenges against members of a particular racial group in several different trials (*Swain v. Alabama* 1965).

During the Rehnquist Court era, the Supreme Court expanded the scope of this prohibition on discriminatory peremptory challenges by barring race-based challenges in other contexts. The Court permitted a defendant to challenge the systematic exclusion of jurors from a racial group other than his own (*Powers v. Ohio* 1991). In effect, the Court indicated that the constitutional right at issue was not focused on the defendant's right to have a jury drawn from all segments of the community, but instead involved the equal protection right of individuals to not be denied an opportunity to serve on juries because of their race. Other decisions expanded the anti-discrimination rule beyond prosecutors to also bar civil litigants and criminal defense attorneys from using race-based peremptory challenges (*Edmonson v. Leesville Concrete Co.* 1991; *Georgia v. McCollum* 1992). The prohibition on discriminatory peremptory challenges was later extended to gender-based challenges (*J.E.B. v. Alabama ex rel. T.B.* 1994). This series of decisions created the impression that the conservative Rehnquist Court had taken a strong stand against racial discrimination in jury selection.

Despite the impression conveyed by these decisions, the illusory, symbolic nature of the Court's effort against discrimination became clear in 1995 in its decision in *Purkett v. Elem.* In *Purkett,* a criminal defendant objected to the prosecutor's use of peremptory challenges to strike two

African American men from the jury panel. In offering a purportedly race-neutral explanation for the strikes, the prosecutor said:

> I struck [juror] number twenty-two because of his long hair. He had long curly hair. He had the longest hair of anybody on the panel by far. He appeared to not be a good juror for that fact, the fact that he had long hair hanging down shoulder length, curly, unkempt hair. Also, he had a mustache and a goatee type beard. And juror number twenty-four also has a mustache and goatee type beard. Those are the only two people on the jury... with any facial hair.... And I don't like the way they looked, with the way the hair is cut, both of them. And the mustaches and the beards look suspicious to me. (*Purkett v. Elem* 1995, 766)

The U.S. Court of Appeals for the Eighth Circuit granted the defendant's writ of habeas corpus on *Batson* grounds by finding that the "prosecution's explanation ... was pretextual" (*Elem v. Purkett* 1994, 684). According to the appellate court:

> [W]here the prosecution strikes a prospective juror who is a member of the defendant's racial group, solely on the basis of factors which are facially irrelevant to the question of whether that person is qualified to serve as a juror in the particular case, the prosecution must at least articulate some plausible race-neutral reason for believing that those factors will somehow affect the person's ability to perform his or her duties as a juror. In the present case, the prosecutor's comments, "I don't like the way [he] look[s], with the way the hair is cut.... And the [ ]mustache[ ] and the beard[ ] look suspicious to me," do not constitute such legitimate race-neutral reasons for striking juror 22." (*Elem V. Purkett* 1994, 683)

Without hearing oral arguments, the U.S. Supreme Court reversed the Court of Appeals' decision and issued a *per curiam* opinion that evinced little skepticism about the possibility that pretextual explanations would mask improper motives. In its reasoning, the Court declared that *Batson* "does not demand [a race-neutral] explanation that is persuasive, or even plausible" (*Purkett v. Elem* 1995, 768). Moreover, trial judges are not required to find improper use of peremptory challenges even when the race-neutral reason is "silly or superstitious" or, alternatively, "implausible or fantastic" (*Elem v. Purkett* 1994, 683). By contrast, dissenting Justices John Paul Stevens and Stephen Breyer argued that, "It is not too much to ask that a prosecutor's explanation for his strikes be race neutral, reasonably specific, and trial related. Nothing less will serve to rebut the inference of race-based discrimination that arises when the defendant has made out a prima facie case" (*Elem v. Purkett* 1994, 775). Despite the dissenters' complaints that the Court had, in effect, established new standards without even hearing oral arguments, the majority minimized the importance of *Batson's* statements about the need for "clear and reasonably specific ... legitimate reasons" that are "related to the particular case to be tried" (*Batson v. Kentucky* 1986, 98). Instead, the Court opted for a standard endorsing judicial deference to proffered race-neutral explanations, despite their patent implausibility or disconnectedness from issues related to the trial at hand.

After spending several years developing doctrines ostensibly designed to eliminate discrimination in the use of peremptory challenges, the Supreme Court's *Purkett* opinion subtly revealed that it lacked a substantive commitment to a reduction in discrimination. As one critic has observed, "*Batson* and its progeny have proven less an obstacle to discrimination than a road map to it. Parties now have a good idea of what they can and cannot get away with in eliminating jurors and adjust their means to suit their desired end" (Bray 1992, 554–555). *Purkett* confirms that discriminatory motives are permissible in the use of peremptory challenges as long as attorneys claim to be acting on some other motive, no matter how suspiciously pretextual that claimed motive may be.

As a result of these decisions, defendants in certain cases may not be judged by representatives from a fair cross-section of the community. More importantly, the net effect may be to deny African Americans and others the equal opportunity to serve on juries. Because the jury is the "primary institutional embodiment of democratic decision making within the judicial branch of government" (Smith 1994, 79), the Supreme Court's tolerance for pretextual, race-based exclusion of African American and other jurors serves to prevent some citizens from enjoying participation in governing processes as full and equal citizens.

Racial Discrimination in Capital Punishment

In *McCleskey v. Kemp* (1987), the Rehnquist Court examined a detailed statistical study showing the impact of race upon sentencing in capital cases. Professor David Baldus and his colleagues examined 2,000 murder cases in Georgia during the 1970s. After taking account of as many as 230 variables, Baldus found racial differences in the sentencing of capital defendants. The Baldus study was not unique in its findings (Baldus, Woodworth, & Pulaski 1990). Other studies also found evidence of racial discrimination in capital sentencing in various states (Nakell & Hardy 1987; Bohm 1994; Sorenson & Wallace 1995). In Georgia, these differences encompassed differential treatment of both defendants and victims by race:

> [Professor Baldus] found that the death penalty was assessed in 22% of the cases involving black defendants and white victims; 8% of the cases involving white defendants and white victims; 1% of the cases involving black defendants and black victims; and 3% of the cases involving white defendants and black victims. (*McCleskey v. Kemp* 1987, 286)

The statistics indicated that African Americans, both as defendants and as victims, were not being accorded the full protection and equal application of the law, a conclusion that echoed of the long and lingering history of less than equal treatment by the legal system.

Despite the indications of systemic racial discrimination, a slim five-member majority on the Court rejected the use of such statistics as a means to establish an Equal Protection Clause violation. This decision, like other capital punishment decisions by the Supreme Court, "revealed a radical schism between legal doctrine and the logical implications of related empirical research evidence: capital punishment practices were upheld notwithstanding impressive social science evidence reflecting the very problems of administration that earlier Court decisions seemingly had condemned" (Acker 1993, 67). The Court's official position that the Equal Protection Clause bars racial discrimination was undercut by its acceptance of a suspicious sentencing scheme that treated African American defendants and victims in a discriminatory fashion.

In another decision that poses risks to the equal valuation of African Americans' lives, the Supreme Court in 1991 permitted the use of victim impact statements in capital sentencing hearings (*Payne v. Tennessee*). Thus, friends and relatives of the victim are permitted to testify about the impact of the victim's death upon them and their community. Such testimony risks turning the jury's and judge's attention away from the nature of the offense and the offender in order to focus on the perceived importance of the victim to society. In order to reach this conclusion, the Court overturned two precedents that were only two and four years old, respectively (*South Carolina v. Gathers* 1989; *Booth v. Maryland* 1987). Previously the Court had concluded that the use of victim impact information for sentencing purposes would enable juries to decide punishment based "on the character and reputation of the victim… [F]actors [which] may be wholly unrelated to the blameworthiness of a particular defendant" (*Booth v. Maryland* 1987, 504). Thus, juries are given the opportunity to determine the worth of the victim's life rather than focus exclusively on the culpability of the defendant and the horribleness of the criminal act. As Justice Stevens noted in dissent:

> Evidence offered to prove such differences [between victims] can only be intended to identify some victims as more worthy of protection than others. Such proof risks decisions based on the same invidious motives as a prosecutor's decision to seek the death penalty if a victim is white but to accept a plea bargain if the victim is black. (*Payne v. Tennessee* 1991, 866)

Supreme Court decisions affecting racial discrimination in jury selection and capital punishment have one key element in common: The Supreme Court endorsed the expansion of discretionary decision making within the legal system. In the jury selection context, the Supreme Court maintained and even advanced its visible effort to combat official discriminatory rules and policies by creating a formal rule against race-based peremptory challenges. However, the Court simultaneously facilitated discrimination in the actual practice of jury selection by expanding discretionary opportunities to undertake such actions. In permitting the pretextual, race-based use of peremptory challenges, the Court enables attorneys to use their discretion in excluding jurors by race as long as they do not admit their true motives. The Court allows trial judges to apply discretion in blindly accepting pretextual discriminatory actions. Rather than combat discrimination in jury selection, the Supreme Court's expansion of discretion has created more opportunities for decision makers to discriminate,

Similarly, the decisions affecting capital punishment involve the preservation or expansion of discretion. In *McCleskey*, the majority opinion explicitly noted that the Court valued the preservation of discretionary decision making in death penalty cases more highly than vigilance against systemic racial discrimination. According to Justice Lewis Powell's majority opinion, "Apparent disparities in sentencing are an inevitable part of our criminal justice system…. Where the discretion that is fundamental to our criminal process is involved, we decline to assume that what is unexplained is invidious" (*McCleskey v. Kemp* 1987, 312–313). Note that Powell characterized disparities as "inevitable" and not presumptively invidious while labeling discretion as "fundamental to our criminal process." In the creation of a new precedent concerning the use of victim impact statements (*Payne v. Tennessee* 1991), the Court gave sentencing judges and juries greater discretion to apply their own valuations to the worth of the victim in determining whether or not the defendant deserved execution.

These are not the only Supreme Court decisions expanding the application of discretion in the legal system. In *Tison v. Arizona* (1987), for example, the Rehnquist Court altered an established rule against imposing the death penalty on felony-murder accomplices who do not participate in killing the victim. Instead, the Court permitted such defendants to be executed if the judge and jury find them to exhibit "reckless disregard" for human life. In effect, the clear rule against executing accomplices changed to a rule that permitted sentencers to impose the death penalty through the discretionary decision to label some defendants' actions as demonstrating "reckless disregard." The concept of "reckless disregard" is not clearly defined so its inevitably inconsistent application by juries and judges will undoubtedly lead to discriminatory death sentences with the possibility that race, social class, or gender will be connected to the use of the label and punishment. As with the examples of disparities in capital punishment and victim impact statements at sentencing, this form of expanded discretion creates opportunities for racial discrimination and a continuation of the historic unequal valuation of African Americans' lives.

Impediments to Supreme Court Action

The Supreme Court frequently receives acclaim as the governing institution that helps to push American society away from its tradition of racial discrimination. In one laudatory description, for example, "the Warren Court did not shy away from the problem of race. It met and directly addressed issues that had long been brushed aside and stymied in the political process" (Barker & McCorry 1976, 167). In the words of another author, "*Brown [v. Board of Education]* opened doors that could never be shut, not just for black Americans but for all who saw themselves as the victims of inequality and discrimination" (Wiecek 1988, 158). Although it may be true that Supreme Court decisions altered legal rules and the legitimacy of discrimination, the examples concerning capital punishment and jury selection indicate that the Court's commitment to and impact on the eradication of discrimination have been limited. In light of the Rehnquist Court's decisions affecting the risk of racial discrimination in the legal system, how do we explain the gap between the Supreme Court's image as a legacy of the Warren Court and the contemporary reality of the Rehnquist Court's decisions?

One major impediment to further action is the sensitivity (or lack thereof) to the problems of racial discrimination possessed by the majority of justices on the Rehnquist Court. The Supreme Court during preceding decades had sought the eradication of formal discrimination against racial minorities and approved remedial efforts toward that end. By contrast, much of the recent attention to racial discrimination has concerned dismantling established remedial efforts that either assist minority group members at the perceived expense of whites (e.g., affirmative action; *see Adarand Constructors v. Pena* 1995) or are now considered beyond the scope of federal judges' proper power (e.g., school desegregation; see *Missouri v. Jenkins* 1995). In sum, the traditional focus on eradicating discrimination against members of minority groups has been eclipsed by an emphasis on limiting the government's power to redress the lingering consequences of pervasive discrimination. The Rehnquist Court has been particularly active in seeking to limit the applicability of civil rights statutes that provided opportunities for aggrieved discrimination victims to seek redress (*Alexander v. Sandoval* 2001). This shift in orientation produced stark lamentations from justices who believe that the power of case law and statutes should be directed toward the redress of historic and continuing discrimination against members of racial minorities groups. Justice Harry Blackmun dissented in one civil rights case by exclaiming, "One wonders whether the majority still believes that race discrimination—or, more accurately, race discrimination against non-whites—is a problem in our society, or even remembers that it ever was" (*Wards Cove Packing Co. v. Atonio* 1989, 662).

In the criminal justice context, the contemporary Court's sensitivity— or lack thereof—was sharply illustrated by an exchange between Justices Antonin Scalia and Thurgood Marshall in *Holland v. Illinois* (1990). The case concerned a white defendant's claim that exclusion of African American jurors through use of peremptory challenges violated his Sixth Amendment right to have a fair cross-section of the community represented on the jury. The Court rejected the defendant's claim, but subsequently revisited the issue in a later case and formally barred such systematic exclusion on Equal Protection grounds (*Powers v. Ohio* 1991). In *Holland,* dissenting Justice Thurgood Marshall argued that racially discriminatory applications of peremptory challenges improperly harm constitutionally protected values whether or not the defendant and excluded jurors are from the same racial group. Marshall asserted that discriminatory applications of peremptory challenges embody a form of exclusion that treats members of minority groups as less than equal citizens:

> [T]he goal of ensuring that no distinctive group be excluded from full participation in our criminal justice system is impaired when the prosecutor implies, through the use of racially motivated peremptory challenges, that he does not trust Afro-Americans to be fair enough or intelligent enough to serve on the case he is trying. (*Holland v. Illinois* 1990, 497)

In the majority opinion, Scalia not only categorically rejected Marshall's recognition of a discriminatory racial impact from such uses of peremptory challenges, he also employed sarcasm to attack the notion that the Supreme Court should evince such sensitivity to the risks of discrimination against minority group members. According to Scalia, "Justice Marshall's dissent rolls out the ultimate weapon, the accusation of insensitivity to racial discrimination-which will lose its intimidating effect if it continues to be fired so randomly" (*Holland v. Illinois* 1990, 486).

The effect of Scalia's statement is to delegitimize the Warren Court's legacy of sensitivity to racial discrimination against members of minority groups. Scalia referred to expressions of concern about discriminatory impacts of policies and practices as "the ultimate weapon" with "intimidating effects," thus implying that justices have felt bullied into demonstrating concern about discrimination. Moreover, Scalia's assertion that concerns about discrimination "continue" to be raised "randomly" demonstrates that he is much less inclined than his Warren Court predecessors to recognize racial discrimination against African Americans and other minorities as a pervasive, harmful problem. Most importantly, Scalia's statement cannot be viewed as an isolated or idiosyncratic comment by a single justice because it was made in a law-establishing majority opinion that was supported by four other justices.

Justice Scalia's use of the term "rando[m]" implied that the Supreme Court's past discussions of and concerns about racial discrimination had been both inaccurate and irrational. Clearly, Scalia's assessment of the reality of discrimination in the United States was very different from Justice Marshall's and, by implication, from other justices who had participated in decisions combating discrimination. Scalia does not ignore the existence of discrimination, but focuses his concern on his belief that it is white males who need judicial protection from racial discrimination. In one affirmative action case, Scalia wrote "In fact, the only losers in this process are the [white males] of the country, for whom Title VII has been not merely repealed but actually inverted. The irony is that these individuals— predominantly unknown, unaffluent, unorganized—suffer this injustice at the hands of a Court fond of thinking itself the champion of the politically impotent" (*Johnson v. Transportation Agency* 1987, 677). His recognition of improper discrimination against African Americans and other members of minority groups differs from that of the Warren Court justices who established the high court's reputation as the institutional guardian of equal justice.

The most vivid example of Scalia's differing assessment of racial discrimination occurred in *McCleskey v. Kemp* (1987), yet it is not well known to the legal community. Scalia was a member of the five-member majority that affirmed the Eleventh Circuit's determination that the statistics in the Baldus study were insufficient to demonstrate unconstitutional systemic racial discrimination in Georgia's death penalty cases. Interestingly, however, a memorandum written by Scalia and sent to his colleagues concerning the case was discovered by scholars in the Thurgood Marshall papers at the Library of Congress. In the memorandum, Scalia stated that he disagreed with the criticisms of the Baldus study contained in the draft of Justice Powell's majority opinion: "I disagree with the argument that the inferences that can be drawn from the Baldus study are weakened by the fact that each jury and each trial is unique, or by the large number of variables at issue" (Dorin 1994, 1038). Thus, Scalia apparently accepted the social science evidence demonstrating the existence of systemic racial discrimination in capital sentencing in Georgia. Rather than view this evidence of discrimination as a basis for invalidating McCleskey's death sentence or prohibiting Georgia from operating a racially discriminatory sentencing process, Scalia simply declared that racial discrimination is an inherent, unchangeable aspect of the justice system. According to Scalia, "Since it is my view that the unconscious operation of irrational sympathies and antipathies, including racial, upon jury decisions and (hence) prosecutorial [ones], is real, acknowledged by the [cases] of this court and ineradicable, I cannot honestly say that all I need is more proof" (Dorin 1994, 1038). Thus, Scalia actually agreed with the four dissenters that the Baldus study had proven the existence of racial discrimination against African Americans, yet he provided the decisive fifth vote to continue the capital sentencing system unchanged because of his belief that racial discrimination is inevitable and impossible to prevent. The words and intentions of the Equal Protection Clause clearly indicate that judges should address racial discrimination by government with something more than expressions of acquiescence or helpless indifference. Scalia certainly never silently acquiesced to his perception of the existence of racial discrimination when white males' asserted interests were at issue (*Johnson v. Transportation Agency* 1987).

Scalia's actions in *McCleskey* apparently indicate that his preference for preserving the policy of capital punishment and imposing it upon convicted offenders outweighs any Equal Protection concerns about the proven existence of racial discrimination against African Americans in capital sentencing. Steven Gey's analysis of the Supreme Court's death penalty cases led him to conclude that "Scalia seems to believe that there are virtually no constitutional limits on a state's imposition of the death penalty" (Gey 1992, 102). It is well known to judicial scholars that "justices' policy preferences are the most important of the factors that affect Supreme Court decisions" and that "policy preferences almost certainly provide the best explanation for differences among the justices in decisional behavior" (Baum 1992, 145). In light of the Supreme Court's reputation and legacy as the institutional entity most actively opposed to racial discrimination, however, it may appear surprising that any policy preferences could outweigh the Equal Protection Clause's acknowledged meaning and purpose to eradicate racial discrimination by the government. Even conservative scholar Robert Bork, an outspoken critic of both the Warren Court and the majority opinion in *Brown v. Board of Education*, has noted that "[t]he purpose that brought the [F]ourteenth [A]mendment into being was [racial] equality before the law" (Bork 1990, 82). The episode concerning Scalia's memorandum illustrates how much the Supreme Court has changed and demonstrates the contemporary inclination to either fail to recognize the existence of racial discrimination, as Powell's majority opinion in *McCleskey* did, or disregard the constitutional importance of equal justice, as Scalia did in *McCleskey*. The first instance constitutes a failure to recognize the continuing reality of discrimination while the second embodies a failure to recognize the realistic consequences and constitutional implications of demonstrable discrimination. According to

Dennis Dorin, who discovered the Scalia memorandum in the Library of Congress, Scalia was:

> simply trivializing [racist practices'] importance by saying, in a single-paragraph memo, that [such practices] were merely an unavoidable and legally unassailable part of life for African Americans. Apparently for Scalia, the capital punishment system's valuing a white life significantly above a black one did not implicate any constitutional provisions. (Dorin 1994, 1077)

Although other justices who joined Scalia in the *McCleskey* majority did so for different reasons (i.e., unwillingness to accept statistical evidence of discrimination), the fundamental consequence of a Court majority that either will not recognize or will not act against racial discrimination in specific contexts is to perpetuate the treatment of African Americans as less than equal citizens in the justice system.

An example of contemporary justices' failure to recognize the reality of continuing racial discrimination and its consequences is evident in the views of Justices Scalia and Thomas about the permissibility and desirability of mandatory death sentences. Under current capital punishment jurisprudence, sentencers in death penalty cases are required to weigh aggravating and mitigating factors in each case while making a thoughtful, considered, and individualized sentencing determination (White 1991). By focusing the sentencer's attention on such factors during the penalty phase of a capital trial, the Supreme Court hopes to avoid the arbitrary and capricious imposition of the death penalty. The Court temporarily halted executions during the 1970s because of a concern about its arbitrary and capricious application (*Furman v. Georgia* 1972). The death penalty was reactivated in the late 1970s after states revised their sentencing procedures to focus deliberations on the punishment decision itself through an examination of specific factors concerning the crime and the offender (*Gregg v. Georgia* 1976). In an effort to insure careful, individualized decisions in each capital case, the Court has barred the imposition of mandatory death sentences (*Woodson v. North Carolina* 1976). By contrast, Justice Scalia believes that mandatory sentences are permissible because such sentences "cannot possibly violate the Eighth Amendment, because it will not be 'cruel' (neither absolutely nor for a particular crime) and it will not be 'unusual' (neither in the sense of being a type of penalty that is not traditional nor in the sense of being rarely or freakishly imposed)" (*Walton v. Arizona* 1990, 671). Justice Thomas goes even further by advocating mandatory death sentences as a means to rid the justice system of racial discrimination. According to Thomas, "One would think...that by eliminating explicit jury discretion and treating all defendants equally, a mandatory death penalty scheme was a perfectly reasonable legislative response to the concerns [about arbitrariness and capriciousness] expressed in *Furman [v. Georgia*, 1972]" (*Graham v. Collins* 1993, 906).

While both Scalia and Thomas recognize that discretionary decision making within the justice system can produce discrimination in capital sentencing, their understanding of discretion and its consequences within the justice system is incomplete. Death sentences are the product of cumulative discretionary decisions beginning with the prosecutor's discretionary decision to seek the death penalty through a judge's or jury's imposition of capital punishment, and including indictment decisions by grand juries, intermediate strategic decisions by prosecutors and defense attorneys, and evidentiary and other rulings by trial judges (see, e.g., Nakell & Hardy 1987; White 1991). Throughout these processes, discriminatory decisions and impacts need not be the product of overt prejudice. They may be produced by unconscious prejudices that value one person's worth more than another's because of ethnicity or skin color (Johnson 1985; 1988). A legislatively mandated death penalty for first-degree murder, for example, might eliminate discriminatory decisions by the final stage sentencers, but would simultaneously ignore and effectuate discriminatory decision making that previously occurred in the myriad, cumulative discretionary decisions that began with the prosecutor's charging decision. These contemporary justices' formal view of the justice process, with its inability to recognize the realistic causes and consequences of discrimination, contributes to Supreme Court decisions that perpetuate the undervaluation of minority group members' rights and lives.

The Loss of an Empathic Advocate

With the retirement in 1991 of Justice Thurgood Marshall, the high court's first African American justice, the Supreme Court lost its empathic advocate for equal justice. Marshall spent his life battling for legal equality as an NAACP attorney and federal judge after experiencing firsthand the impact of racial discrimination. He transformed his observations of the employment discrimination and personal indignities that he observed his parents endure in Maryland in the early twentieth century into a lifetime crusade to eradicate racial discrimination. He personally experienced the worst sort of racial discrimination in the justice system when, as a crusading civil rights lawyer, he was nearly lynched by a mob of Tennessee law enforcement officers who, with a noose already prepared and about to be placed around Marshall's neck, stopped short of hanging him from the nearest tree only when several witnesses refused to leave the scene (Rowan 1993, 108). Marshall's replacement, Justice Clarence Thomas, indicated that his boyhood experiences as an African American victimized by racial discrimination in segregated Georgia of the 1950s had given him a deep understanding of and personal sensitivity to issues of discrimination. According to Thomas, "[I]t is clear from the testimony that I have given you here about where I grew up, that I understand the realities of our country. It should be clear from my biography that I understand that racism exists" (*Nomination of Judge Clarence Thomas* 1991, 262). Moreover, he indicated that he had a special understanding of the social forces that can draw people into the criminal justice system. Thomas described his experiences as a federal appellate judge in Washington, D.C., which brought him into close contact with defendants being transported to and from the courthouse:

> I have occasion to look out the window that faces C Street, and there are converted buses that bring in the criminal defendants to our criminal justice system, busload after busload. And you look out, and you say to yourself, and I say to myself almost every day, "But for the grace of God, there go I." So you feel that you have the same fate, or could have, as those individuals. So I can walk in their shoes, and I can bring something, different to the Court... But with respect to the underlying concerns and feelings about people being left out, about our

society not addressing all the problems of people, I have those concerns. I will take those to the grave with me. I am concerned about the kids on those buses I told you about. I am concerned about the kids who didn't have the strong grandfather and strong grandparents to help them out of what I would consider a terrible, terrible fate. (Nomination of Judge Clarence Thomas 1991, 260)

Thomas's statements about his empathic understanding of racial discrimination and the social forces underlying crime and punishment may have assisted him in gaining confirmation to the Supreme Court, but there has been scant evidence that these factors have shaped his judicial decision making.

Thomas's approach to criminal justice issues has been diametrically opposed to the approach taken by his predecessor, Thurgood Marshall. Unlike Marshall, who supported claimants' rights in criminal justice cases more frequently than any other justice in the Rehnquist era (97%), Thomas rejected such claims more frequently than any other justice (89%) (Schultz & Smith 1996). Thomas's consistent support for the prosecution in such cases raises questions about his capacity to identify racial discrimination and other rights violations. Thomas, joined by such colleagues as Rehnquist and Scalia, has sought to limit federal judges' ability to undertake thorough reviews of state criminal convictions through habeas corpus petitions (*Wright v. West* 1992). In contrast to Marshall, who sought to insure that federal judges could aggressively pursue constitutional rights violations, Thomas has joined the justices who are creating new risks that rights violations will go unremedied as the federal courts become less accessible to habeas petitioners and will thereby produce unjust outcomes, including the risk that innocent people may be executed (Yackle 1993). Thomas has also led the push to declare that convicted offenders should no longer receive any constitutional protection against inhumane conditions and practices in prisons (*Helling v. McKinney* 1993). Even when Thomas voted to bar race-based peremptory challenges by criminal defendants' attorneys, he wrote a puzzling concurring opinion which seemed to support, at least in part, the dissenters by lamenting the reduction in attorneys' discretion in excluding jurors. Thomas wrote "I am certain that black criminal defendants will rue the day that this court ventured down this road that inexorably will lead to the elimination of peremptory strikes" (*Georgia v. McCollum* 1992, 60).

Thomas's apparent antipathy to constitutional rights claims by criminal defendants and convicted offenders is compounded, with respect to racial discrimination issues, by his understanding (or lack thereof) of the American legacy of racism and discrimination. For example, he criticized a district judge's court-ordered remedies for school segregation because Thomas viewed the continuing existence of racially imbalanced schools as the product of "voluntary housing choices or other private decisions" (*Missouri v. Jenkins* 1995, 2062). In doing so, he demonstrated little awareness of the long history of discriminatory actions by government, realtors, and homeowners that produced enduring segregated housing patterns in American cities. As Professor Thomas Pettigrew (1975, 38) has observed, "Residential separation does not simply 'happen,' *de facto;* its structural roots have to be carefully planned and implemented." In addition, Thomas appears to view judicial action to counteract discrimination as an objectionable form of paternalism. Thus, he viewed judicial concern about school segregation as involving the "assum[ption] that anything that is predominantly black must be inferior" (*Missouri v. Jenkins* 1995, 2061) without evincing any recognition that segregation virtually always involved the allocation of inferior resources and conditions for African Americans (Tyack 1974).

Most striking of all is Thomas's status as the lone justice in Supreme Court history to criticize the landmark decision in *Brown v. Board of Education.* According to Thomas:

> [T]he [C]ourt has read our cases to support the theory that black students suffer an unspecified psychological harm from segregation that retards their mental and educational development. This approach not only relies upon questionable social science research rather than constitutional principle, but it also rests on an assumption of black inferiority. (*Missouri v. Jenkins* 1995, 2062)

Whether or not one agrees with the methods and conclusions of the psychological studies cited in *Brown,* Thomas's statement is notable both for its confusion of the realities of discrimination with judicial paternalism and for its apparent rejection of social science. What "constitutional principle" would Thomas have applied to decide the *Brown* case, especially in light of his implicit assertion that segregated schools were not necessarily unequal? In the context of the equal justice issues that have faced the Rehnquist Court, Thomas's limited view of the history and continuing legacy of racial discrimination would likely lead him to decide a *McCleskey*-type equal protection case by applying some unknown "constitutional principle" rather than carefully examining social science evidence, which can provide documentation of the reality of discriminatory outcomes. Thomas has stated, "I believe this Court should leave it to elected state legislators, 'representing organized society,' to decide which factors are particularly relevant to the sentencing decision" (*Graham v. Collins* 1993, 914). Thus, his determinative "constitutional principles" are likely to defer to majoritarian interests that may be insensitive to unequal treatment for minorities, including less than equal valuation and treatment of African Americans.

It may be posited that the foregoing analysis is unfair to Justice Thomas in the sense that he should not automatically be expected to serve as a special advocate for the protection of minority group members simply because he is the lone African American justice. The primary point, however, is that Thomas claimed during his confirmation testimony that his background and experiences would give him a special sensitivity to and understanding of racial discrimination and the social forces affecting criminal justice. In reality, his judicial performance has provided scant evidence that his confirmation testimony claims of empathic understanding accurately describe the knowledge and attitudes brought to bear in his judicial decision-making processes (Smith & Baugh 2000).

Conclusion

The U.S. Supreme Court entered the dawn of a new century in a society with significant racial divisions and a continuing legacy of racial discrimination. Although the high court enjoys a reputation as the institutional guardian of equal protection values, the contemporary justices on the Rehnquist Court are less inclined than their predecessors from the preceding forty years to use their authority to seek the eradication of racial discrimination. As illustrated by the foregoing discussions of examples drawn from criminal justice, Rehnquist Court decisions evince a reduction in sensitivity to the existence and harmfulness of racial discrimination.

While the Court would undoubtedly enforce equal protection values to bar formal laws explicitly mandating racial inequality, the contemporary justices readily accept the preservation of discretionary authority throughout the justice system that serves as the vehicle for less than equal valuation and treatment of African Americans and other minority group members. The Court's 1996 decision in *United States v. Armstrong (1996)*, for example, continued this pattern by creating a difficult burden of proof for defendants seeking to show that prosecutors disproportionately pursue African - Americans in prosecuting cocaine trafficking cases, even though studies show equal or greater drug activity among whites (Tonry 1995). The justices' formalistic views about the justice system and reluctance to employ social science evidence diminish the Court's capacity to recognize and address the realities of racial inequality. As noted by Professor Pettigrew (1985, 694), "modern forms of racial discrimination are typically indirect, and ostensibly nonracial." In the current context of American society, in which discretionary rather than formal mechanisms for discrimination present the most pervasive problems, there is an increased need for a Supreme Court with a sophisticated understanding of racial inequality and an unrelenting emphasis on eradicating discrimination in order to uphold the Equal Protection Clause. Unfortunately, such sensitivity and commitment seems lacking at the very moment when the Court lacks a justice with a demonstrable, empathic understanding of racial inequality who can educate the other justices about such issues. Thus, African Americans and other members of minority groups will enter yet another century while continuing to experience, in some contexts, less than equal treatment and valuation in the justice system. Moreover, the Court's failure to use its full authority to redress racial discrimination in such contexts as jury selection and capital sentencing represents a lost opportunity to use its powerful symbolic voice to remind policy makers and the public of continuing social problems that require attention (Tribe 1989).

In the 1990s, Professor Cornel West (1993, 8) wrote, "[A]s we approach the twenty-first century, th[e] challenge will be to help Americans determine whether a genuine multiracial democracy can be created and sustained in an era of global economy and a moment of xenophobic frenzy." The acclaim showered on the Supreme Court for its courageous decision in *Brown v. Board of Education* demonstrated that our nation's highest court possesses the visibility and authority to play a role in tackling intractable social problems that implicate constitutional values. Unfortunately, however, the Rehnquist Court entered the new century with a level of sensitivity and concern about racial discrimination in the justice system that is more likely to reinforce Professor Derrick Bell's conclusion that racism is here to stay than to move toward Professor West's hopes for a successful multiracial democracy (Bell 1992, ix).

4

Gender and Equal Justice

THE STATUS OF American women as full participants in society and possessors of constitutionally protected rights has changed significantly over the course of United States history. Little more than 125 years ago, the U.S. Supreme Court issued its infamous decision in *Bradwell v. Illinois* (1872), which rejected Myra Bradwell's claim that the Illinois law barring women from obtaining law licenses violated the Fourteenth Amendment. Society has moved from the *Bradwell* case, in which the Supreme Court said that "[t]he natural and proper timidity and delicacy which belongs to the female sex evidently unfits it for many of the occupations of civil life" (*Bradwell v. Illinois* 1872, 141) to the early twenty-first century when a woman, Elizabeth Dole, was a serious presidential candidate, two women, Sandra Day O'Connor and Ruth Bader Ginsburg, are justices on the U.S. Supreme Court, and another woman, Eileen Collins, commanded a space flight mission. The clear evidence of progress toward full participation in society cannot, however, be mistaken for proof that equality has been achieved. Conclusions about the attainment of legal equality, or the lack thereof, must rest on broad examinations of reality rather than anecdotal success stories.

Criminal justice provides a straightforward opportunity to evaluate whether the government treats people differently because of immutable physical characteristics and whether the Supreme Court has applied its authority to prohibit manifestations of discrimination and inequality that clash with constitutional principles. Criminal culpability should be based on behavior and intent and not be defined by race, gender, or other characteristics. Because criminal justice provides a context in which Fourteenth Amendment equal protection principles clearly apply, gender-biased policies and practices should be subject to judicial scrutiny and abolishment. Enforcement of criminal laws and processing of criminal cases are governmental functions subject to the Fourteenth Amendment command that "No State shall... deny to any person within its jurisdiction the equal protection of the laws." Therefore, the Supreme Court clearly has a responsibility to ensure that the promise of "Equal Justice Under Law" is a reality for both men and women.

Equal Protection and Gender

The Fourteenth Amendment was ratified in 1868. Although there are debates about the Amendment's intended effect upon the application of specific rights against state and local governments, there is a general consensus that the Amendment was intended to provide legal protections for the African Americans recently freed from slavery who were at risk of adverse actions by southern states. As described by one prominent constitutional historian, the Republicans in Congress who created the Fourteenth Amendment "wanted to extend legal rights to blacks, [but they] still harbored racial prejudice and had no desire to embrace the freedmen as their social equals" (Urofsky 1988, 442). Indeed, it has been argued that the ratification of the Fourteenth Amendment demonstrates Americans' capacity to transcend their racist impulses in order to advance the principle (if not the practice) of equal application of the law (Ackerman 1998, 164). It seems equally clear that the Fourteenth Amendment, including the Equal Protection Clause, was not intended to bar discrimination against women. Despite the fact that nineteenth-century "advocates of women's suffrage were dedicated foes of slavery... [who] put aside the suffrage issue to join the crusade for Union and emancipation," women did not gain the benefits of constitutional protections when their allies in Congress acted on behalf of African Americans (Foner 1988, 255). Indeed, the failure of the Reconstruction Congress to include women in the ideal of equal protection under constitutional law left "feminist leaders with a deep sense of betrayal, it convinced them, as [Elizabeth Cady] Stanton put it, that women 'must not put her trust in man' in seeking her own rights" (Foner 1988, 255). The

Supreme Court placed its imprimatur on a limited definition for the Equal Protection Clause by declaring in 1873 that

> In the light of the history of these [post-Civil War constitutional] amendments, and the pervading purpose of them, [it] is not difficult to give a meaning to this [Equal Protection] [C]lause. The existence of laws in the States where the newly emancipated negroes resided, which discriminated with gross injustice and hardship against them as a class, was the evil to be remedied by this clause, and by it such laws are forbidden…. We doubt very much whether any action of a State not directed by way of discrimination against the negroes as a class, or on account of their race, will ever be held to come within the purview of this provision. It is so clearly a provision for that race and that [post-Civil War] emergency, that a strong case would be necessary for its application to any [other group]. (*The Slaughterhouse Cases* 1872, 81)

The words of the Equal Protection Clause do not limit its coverage to specific kinds or bases of discrimination, but its initial purposes and interpretations focused the Clause narrowly on racial discrimination against African Americans.

Before the 1970s, the Supreme Court declined to expand the coverage of the Equal Protection Clause to include a constitutional right against gender discrimination by government. At the time of *Bradwell v. Illinois* in 1873 and thereafter through the mid-twentieth century, the limited applicability of the Equal Protection Clause was not surprising; after all the Supreme Court also generally failed to apply the Clause to protect its intended beneficiaries, African Americans. Although the Court began to apply equal protection principles to strike down governmental practices that discriminated against African Americans during the twentieth century, it took several decades for the justices to become receptive to arguments about the applicability of such principles to prevent gender discrimination. For example, by the end of the 1940s, the Supreme Court had applied the Equal Protection Clause to prevent Missouri and Oklahoma from barring African Americans from state university law schools (*Missouri ex rel. Gaines v. Canada* 1938; *Sipuel v. Board of Regents of the University of Oklahoma* 1948). By contrast, in 1948 the Supreme Court upheld a paternalistic Michigan statute that forbade women from working as bartenders unless their husbands or fathers owned the bar in which they worked (*Goesaert v. Cleary* 1948). The notion that women should enjoy protection under the Equal Protection Clause did, however, begin to gain support as three justices dissented against the majority's support for the Michigan statute.

Professor (later Justice) Ruth Bader Ginsburg played a major in role in gaining constitutional protections against gender discrimination during the 1970s. As an attorney for the American Civil Liberties Union, Ginsburg argued a series of gender discrimination cases before the Supreme Court (Cole 1984). Although the Court began to strike down discriminatory laws that used gender to favor men as administrators of decedents' estates (*Reed v. Reed* 1971) and recipients of family support benefits while in military service (*Frontiero v. Richardson* 1973), the justices never formally agreed to give gender the same level of protection against governmental discrimination that they gave to race.

When the Court is presented with a substantiated claim of racially discriminatory governmental action, it applies "strict scrutiny" under which the government must justify its statute or practice by demonstrating that there is a "compelling" reason for using a racial classification and that the classification is necessarily related to the compelling governmental interest (Mezey 1992). This is a difficult burden for the government to carry. Except for instances in which judges order the use of affirmative action to remedy proven racial discrimination (*United States v. Paradise* 1987), the only case in which a government has successfully demonstrated a "compelling" reason for a racial classification was the affirmative action case of *Regents of the University of California v. Bakke* (1978). In *Bakke*, a slim majority of justices accepted the need for diversity within a medical school student body as a "compelling" reason to use race as one consideration in admissions decisions. No more than four justices ever supported applying strict scrutiny to gender discrimination cases in the same manner that the test is applied to racial discrimination cases.

Despite never gaining the needed fifth vote to establish the precedent they desired, the justices who supported applying the Equal Protection Clause to gender discrimination succeeded in gaining much of what they wanted. They created a new mid-level or "heightened" scrutiny test for application in gender discrimination cases (*Craig v. Boren* 1976). Under "heightened scrutiny," the government must show that its use of a gender classification is substantially related to an "important" government interest. Interestingly, the Supreme Court's development of limited Equal Protection Clause coverage against gender discrimination was not based on a specific concern about pervasive discrimination against women. In two of the early key cases developing equal protection principles, the Supreme Court invalidated policies that applied gender discrimination against men. In *Craig v. Boren* (1976), the seminal case in the development of constitutional protection against gender discrimination, the Court invalidated an Oklahoma law that created a lower legal drinking age for women than for men. In *Mississippi University for Women v. Hogan* (1982), the Court prohibited a state university for women from barring the enrollment of men in a graduate nursing program. The existence of discrimination against the group (i.e., men) whose membership comprises the majority of justices on the Supreme Court may have struck an empathic nerve with justices who appear to have more difficulty recognizing the discriminatory implications of policies and practices adversely affecting women, racial minorities, the poor, and other political minorities that are underrepresented among the membership on the high court.

If equal protection analysis is applied rigorously, the heightened scrutiny test can pose a difficult challenge to a governmental entity seeking to justify differential treatment of men and women. Although some governmental practices will survive heightened scrutiny that may not have avoided invalidation under strict scrutiny, such as the application of Selective Service registration solely to males during an era in which women have been integrated into the armed forces (*Rostker v. Goldberg* 1981), the heightened scrutiny test provides a significant potential mechanism for judicial examination and elimination of many forms of gender discrimination.

The Supreme Court and Gender Equality in Criminal Justice

Substantive criminal law statutes provide a potentially fertile ground for actions by the Supreme Court and other courts to apply constitutional equal protection principles. As we will see in subsequent sections of this chapter, many states continue to have laws on the books that explicitly treat men and women differently. These laws were often enacted in the first half of the twentieth century or earlier and they reflect paternalistic attitudes by explicitly treating women as helpless victims of adultery, public profanity, and other offenses for which men are presumed to be the sole perpetrators. Other laws, such as those concerning indecent exposure, may place a harsher burden on women by subjecting them to criminal punishment for behavior, such as the public display of their nipples, that would be considered legal behavior for men. These latter examples do not always reflect explicit differentiation of men and women in the language of statutes, but may stem from discriminatory interpretation and treatment of ostensibly neutral statutes aimed at lewd behavior. Again, the enforcement of these laws may reflect paternalistic attitudes by imposing a higher standard of morality on women. Although these examples provide opportunities for courts to apply equal protection analysis, the Supreme Court has done relatively little to root out these vestiges of gender discrimination. Instead, lower state and federal courts are more likely to address these issues haphazardly as individual cases arise. In addressing these issues, however, they do not necessarily wipe away the discriminatory aspects of the law and thus, for example, anachronistic laws remain on the books (albeit usually not vigorously enforced) and differential treatment of men and women in indecent exposure and other crimes remains the norm in most places.

One of the few gender-related issues in criminal justice that has attracted the Supreme Court's attention concerns differential opportunities for participation in legal processes through service as a juror. In examining issues of jury exclusion, most of which concerned exclusion by race, the Court has utilized two different constitutional provisions to analyze whether any rights have been violated. The Court has relied on the Sixth Amendment to determine whether restrictions on jury service violate the defendant's right to a fair trial by excluding or minimizing the participation of one or more segments of the community from the trial's decision-making processes. The Court has also been concerned with the citizen's right to serve on a jury and thus has applied the Equal Protection Clause to determine whether laws and practices deprive people of the opportunity to participate equally in this important aspect of the American constitutional governing system.

Initially, the Court reflected prevailing social views that accepted the exclusion of women from various sectors of public life by explicitly endorsing the statutory exclusion of women from jury service. When the Supreme Court forbade the formal exclusion of African American men from juries in 1880, the justices simultaneously approved the exclusion of women by saying that a state "may confine the selection [of jurors] to males" (*Strauder v. West Virginia* 1880, 310). Although the English common law excluded women from service as jurors because of a presumption that they were "defective" by lacking the necessary capacity to make appropriate, intelligent decisions, exclusionary American laws tended to rely on paternalistic justifications that focused on the need to protect "fragile" women from the harsh and offensive realities of the world that would be presented in court cases (*United States v. DeGross* 1992, 1438). Such paternalistic justifications were evident through the mid-twentieth century. For example, one Arkansas court opinion in 1949 justified the exclusion of female jurors by saying that "Criminal court trials often involve testimony of the foulest kind, and they sometimes require consideration of indecent conduct, the use of filthy and loathsome words, references to intimate sex relationships, and other elements that would prove humiliating, embarrassing and degrading to a lady" (*Bailey v. State* 1949, 61).

The U.S. Supreme Court took its first limited step to redress the exclusion of women from juries when it ruled in 1946 that women could not be excluded from jury pools for federal trials in states in which they were eligible for jury service under state and local laws (*Ballard v. United States* 1946). The decision fell short of granting women an equal right to participate in the important life determining and policy shaping decision making processes of jury trials, but it forced a change in federal criminal justice practices in some states. By 1961, the Court still accepted mechanisms that effectively excluded women from equal participation on juries. The justices approved a Florida statute that exempted women from mandatory jury service and permitted them to serve on juries only when they contacted the court clerk's office to volunteer (*Hoyt v. Florida* 1961). The government justified the statute by saying that women's role in maintaining their homes and families' lives should not be unnecessarily disrupted by mandatory jury service. It was not until 1975 that the Court stuck down such statutes that required the affirmative act of volunteering for jury service in order for a woman to be called to participate (*Taylor v. Louisiana* 1975). The *Taylor* decision was based on a Sixth Amendment concern with the rights of defendants but the Court later focused on the Equal Protection rights of women excluded from juries. According to Leslie Friedman Goldstein (1988, 152), "*Taylor v. Louisiana* marks the first time that a clear majority [of justices] clearly subjected legislative discrimination against women to rigid scrutiny, and the first time that a clear majority stated that the concededly 'reasonable' grounds of administrative convenience was not enough to justify such a sex classification."

In *J.E.B. v. Alabama ex rel. T.B.* (1994), the Supreme Court considered whether the Equal Protection Clause permits attorneys to use peremptory challenges to exclude women systematically from juries. Unlike challenges for cause, which require attorneys to show evidence of a person's prejudice or potential prejudice in order to exclude that person from the jury pool, peremptory challenges traditionally permitted attorneys to exclude potential jurors without providing any reason. Typically, each side in a case is allotted a specific number of peremptory challenges according to the governing state or federal law. Attorneys use hunches about which potential jurors will be favorable to the opposition or less receptive to their own arguments in deciding whom to exclude from the jury pool (White 1995). Traditionally, attorneys are not required to give the judge any reason for excluding a potential juror when a peremptory challenge is employed. Problems arose when prosecutors used peremptory challenges systematically to exclude all African American jurors from participating in trials of African American defendants. Such practices raised concerns that African American defendants might receive unfair consideration of their cases from all-white juries manufactured in this fashion. Moreover, such racially motivated systematic exclusions also deprived African Americans of equal opportunities to participate in judicial processes as jurors. Thus, the Supreme Court barred the use of peremptory challenges to exclude jurors because of their race. This prohibition applied to prosecutors (*Batson v. Kentucky* 1986), defense attorneys (*Georgia v. McCollum* 1992), and civil litigators (*Edmonson v. Leesville Concrete Co.* 1991). These decisions mandated that attorneys provide a race-neutral justification for peremptory challenges whenever their patterns of exclusions raised the inference that race-based systematic exclusions were occurring. In *J.E.B.*, the Court expanded the prohibition to bar peremptory challenge exclusions based on gender.

The *J.E.B.* case concerned a trial involving paternity and child support claims in which the county prosecutor used nine of the ten available peremptory challenges to remove men from the jury pool and the defense attorney used all of his peremptory challenges to remove women from the jury pool. Because many more women than men were in the jury pool, the use of the peremptory challenges resulted in an all-female jury. As in earlier gender discrimination cases (e.g., *Craig v. Boren* 1976), the specific case accepted for consideration by the Supreme Court concerned gender discrimination against men.

Justice Harry Blackmun's majority opinion made a strong statement about the harms to individuals, society, and the judicial process created by gender discrimination in peremptory challenges:

> Discrimination in jury selection, whether based on race or on gender, causes harm to the litigants, the community, and the individual jurors who are wrongfully excluded from participation in the judicial process. The litigants are harmed by the risk that the prejudice which motivated the discriminatory selection of the jury will infect the entire proceedings.... The community is harmed by the State's participation in the perpetuation of invidious group stereotypes and the inevitable loss of confidence in our judicial system that state-sanctioned discrimination in the courtroom engenders. When state actors exercise peremptory challenges in reliance on gender stereotypes, they ratify and reinforce prejudicial views of the relative abilities of men and women. Because these stereotypes have wreaked injustice in so many other spheres of our country's public life, active discrimination by litigants on the basis of gender during jury selection "invites cynicism respecting the jury's neutrality and its obligation to adhere to the law."... The potential for cynicism is particularly acute in cases where gender-related issues are prominent, such as cases involving rape, sexual harassment, or paternity.

Discriminatory use of peremptory challenges may create the impression that the judicial system has acquiesced in suppressing full participation by one gender or that the "deck has been stacked" in favor of one side. (*J.E.B. v. Alabama ex rel. J.B.* 1994, 140)

Although Blackmun's opinion in *J.E.B.* represented a strong statement against gender-based discrimination in jury selection processes, the practical effects of the decision were undercut the following year by the Court's decision in *Purkett v. Elem* (1995). In *Purkett*, the Supreme Court permitted a trial judge to accept implausible rationalizations to disguise the systematic exclusion of jurors by race. A prosecutor had claimed to exclude African American jurors because of their curly hair, and the trial judge accepted this explanation as being "race neutral" and therefore permissible. Despite two dissenting justices' complaints that permitting such lax examinations of attorneys' justifications invited the use of pretextual excuses to disguise race- and gender-based exclusions, the majority of justices placed the enforcement of equal protection principles in jury selection under the discretionary control of local trial judges. As a result, Blackmun's strong statement against gender discrimination in jury selection will only be meaningful in those cases in which trial judges apply appropriate scrutiny and skepticism to attorneys' justifications for the apparent use of gender to exclude potential jurors.

One area of criminal justice in which there has been clearly unequal treatment of women is in corrections (Morash, Haarr & Rucker 1994). Typically, corrections officials provided fewer services and more limited programs at institutions for women than at institutions for men. These disparities were sometimes rationalized as the result of having relatively few women prisoners within state corrections systems. Thus, states often have only one small women's prison that receives relatively little attention when contrasted to the numerous prisons for men that are the central focus of corrections departments' budgets, planning, and programmatic initiatives. In addition, programs at women's prisons often emphasized traditional female roles, such as teaching, cooking, and cleaning rather than vocational skills that would lead to more numerous and higher paying job opportunities upon release from prison. Unequal programs and services for women prisoners serve as the basis for lawsuits alleging violations of the Equal Protection Clause. Although the U.S. Supreme Court has never decided a major case concerning discrimination against women prisoners, lower courts have decided a number of cases that required state corrections officials to provide additional resources and services for women's correctional institutions. Unequal programs and services are not the sole legal issue that has arisen affecting women prisoners. Lawsuits also focus on the sexual abuse of women prisoners by male corrections officials, and the U.S. Justice Department has investigated alleged abuses in several states (Human Rights Watch 1996). Sexual abuse also leads to criminal prosecution of offending corrections officers ("U.S. Marshal's Conviction for Raping Prisoners Affirmed" 2002).

A key illustrative case concerning the unequal treatment of women prisoners was decided in Michigan by a federal district judge. After finding that the state violated the rights of women prisoners, the judge retained supervisory control over the case and actively monitored the compliance of state officials for nearly twenty years ("Court Ends Federal Jurisdiction over Female Prisons" 1999). The judge's active participation was necessary because state officials resisted implementing changes to achieve equal protection for more than a decade after the judge made his initial findings. Judge George Feikens' opinion describes the basis for identifying unconstitutionally unequal treatment:

> FEIKENS, Chief Judge.
> On May 19, 1977, a civil rights suit was filed on behalf of present and future females incarcerated by the State of Michigan.... Plaintiffs sought a declaration by this Court that the State, through its Department of Corrections, had violated their rights under the Constitution. Plaintiffs also asked for injunctive relief to secure these rights. The original complaint focused on alleged inequalities apparent in the treatment and rehabilitation programs available to Plaintiffs at the Detroit House of Corrections when compared to those programs available to male offenders in various prison facilities throughout the State.
> ...Plaintiffs argue that because the State has chosen to emphasize educational opportunities at three male facilities to which male prisoners may be assigned or transferred, the inmates at the single female facility are disadvantaged because they lack access to institutions with a similar emphasis. Evidence was introduced to show that the community college courses made available to them at Huron Valley

are less adequate than those offered to males because the course selection is narrower, and often so limited as to make it difficult to complete successfully a course sequence leading to a major in a given field…

Training in five broad occupational areas is currently available at Huron Valley: office occupations, food service, graphic arts, building maintenance, and general shop…. By way of comparison, male prisoners have access to some twenty different vocational programs, including automobile servicing, heating and air conditioning, machine shop, and drafting. Furthermore, evidence was taken indicating that the "male" versions of those programs…were often more extensive and more useful to the inmates…

…The women inmates have a right to a range and quality of programming substantially equivalent to that offered the men, and the programs currently offered do not meet this standard… (*Glover v. Johnson*, 478 F.Supp. 1075 (E.D.Mich.1978)).

In 2001, the Supreme Court addressed an issue concerning law enforcement practices directed at women, but not men, because of biological differences between males and females. *Ferguson v. City of Charleston* concerned the public hospital operated by the Medical University of South Carolina, which tested maternity patients for drug use and then supplied evidence of drug use to law enforcement officials so that women could be prosecuted for harm to a fetus and child abuse. Several women challenged the use of such medical tests by a public hospital as an unconstitutional search in violation of the Fourth Amendment's prohibition on unreasonable searches and seizures. A majority of justices ruled that the hospital's practices violated the women's rights. According to the majority opinion by Justice John Paul Stevens, "While state hospital employees, like other citizens, may have a duty to provide the police with evidence of criminal conduct that they inadvertently acquire in the course of routine treatment, when they undertake to obtain such evidence from their patients *for the specific purpose of incriminating those patients*, they have a special obligation to make sure that the patients are fully informed about their constitutional rights, as standards of knowing waiver require" [emphasis in original] (*Ferguson v. City of Charleston* 2001, 220–221). The issue in the case arose in a situation that was unique to women and only violated the rights of female hospital patients. However, the principle and reasoning underlying the case apply generally to protect men as well as women from medical tests for law enforcement purposes that are undertaken without either consent or a search warrant.

The U.S. Supreme Court and other courts have addressed a narrow range of issues concerning gender discrimination in the criminal justice system. This fact does not mean, however, that there are not other clear examples of differential treatment of men and women that have continued to produce discriminatory consequences that clash with the ideal of "Equal Justice Under Law." The existence of discretionary authority exercised by police officers, prosecutors, and judges always serves as a potential source of discrimination in decisions concerning stops, searches, arrests, charges, and sentences. Although these discretionary sources of discrimination have generally escaped judicial scrutiny and control, they are not the only issues that invite further judicial attention. Obvious examples of discriminatory treatment remain codified in formal law. Criminal laws on the books still treat men and women differently with respect to some kinds of crimes. These obvious differences in treatment invite remedial judicial action, yet judges have not acted to correct some of these overt expressions of discrimination.

Equal Justice and Formal Law

It is not difficult to find examples of gender discrimination written into formal criminal statutes. Laws remain on the books from earlier eras in which it was taken for granted that men and women should be treated differently. In some instances, the language of the statute singles out women (or men) for special mention, but it is unclear whether the lack of gender-neutral language has any practical implications that would collide with the Equal Protection Clause. Michigan's adultery statute states, for example, that "Any person who shall commit adultery shall be guilty of a felony; and when the crime is committed between a married woman and a man who is unmarried, the man shall be guilty of adultery, and liable to the same punishment" (Mich. Compiled Laws section 750.30). Does the statute mean to imply that an unmarried woman who has an affair with a married man will be treated differently? It is possible that in the 1930s the authors of the statute would have regarded such an unmarried woman as a "victim" of the married man rather than a culpable "criminal" like the unmarried man involved with a married woman. However, because adultery is defined as "the sexual intercourse of two persons, either of whom is married to a third person," the language actually encompasses the actions of the unmarried woman—if authorities choose to enforce the law toward such individuals.

By contrast, there are other criminal statutes in which women are clearly and intentionally treated differently from men. For example, national attention was drawn to Michigan's statute concerning public cursing when a man was convicted of a misdemeanor for yelling obscenities when he fell out of a canoe on a river packed with vacationing families (Flesher 1999). The prosecution was pursued under a Michigan statute that criminalized cursing in front of women and children, but not in front of men. The statute reads "Indecent, etc., language in the presence of women or children—Any person who shall use any indecent, immoral, obscene, vulgar or insulting language in the presence or hearing of any woman or child shall be guilty of a misdemeanor" (Mich. Compiled Law section 750.337). Such a clear differentiation between men and women invites scrutiny under the Equal Protection Clause. The discriminatory language clearly seems to be a product of the gender paternalism prevalent in American society in 1931, the year the statute was enacted. While the authors of the act might have claimed that the statute was necessary to protect women's presumptively delicate sensibilities, such a justification would seem patently unacceptable as a putative "important" state interest that would fulfill the requirements of the contemporary Equal Protection Clause jurisprudence. In discussing the statute, a criminal law manual for police officers advised that "[T]his statute appears to be a bit of an anachronism, and an officer probably would not get far in applying it against one who uses insulting language within earshot of a woman today" (Edmonds & Fink 1998, 80). Indeed, the judge in the canoeist's case used equal protection principles to reject any prosecution for cursing in front of women and proceeded with the trial and eventual conviction solely on the basis of the statutory prohibition on cursing in front of children (Flesher 1999).

In other examples, Michigan has statutes that define the crimes of "Taking a Woman and Compelling Her to Marry" (Mich. Compiled Laws section 750.11) and "Taking a Woman with Intent to Compel Her to Marry" (Mich. Compiled Laws section 750.12). There are no parallel statutes criminalizing the taking of men or compelling men to marry. Presumably the taking of a man would be prohibited by criminal laws if it fit the elements of kidnapping. It is unclear, however, whether men enjoy the same protection explicitly granted to women against being compelled to marry by force or duress. Similarly, Michigan's statute criminalizing "Sexual Intercourse under Pretext of Medical Treatment" explicitly protects female patients from male health care providers, but does not provide protection for male patients (Mich. Compiled Laws section 750.90).

More difficult issues arise when the language of criminal law is ostensibly gender neutral, but the interpretation of the law creates different applications for men and women. This situation is arguably different from gender differences that emerge from discretionary enforcement. Differences in enforcement of neutral statutes produce, for example, differential arrests of men and women for prostitution. Although both the buyers and sellers of prostitution are criminally culpable, law enforcement officials' focus on women in enforcing such criminal laws is evident in the fact that women account for sixty-one percent of the people arrested for prostitution (Maguire & Pastore 1997, 336). By contrast, there are other statutes in which the definitions of terms within the statute carry different meanings for men and women. Arguably, this latter category creates differential treatment based on the meaning of the law rather than merely discretionary enforcement.

An obvious example of different meanings applied to men and women is in criminal laws concerning indecent exposure. Michigan's statute on indecent exposure states "Any person who shall knowingly make any open or indecent exposure of his or her person or the person of another shall be guilty of a misdemeanor" (Mich. Compiled Laws section 750.335a). The meaning of indecent exposure is different for men and women. Men can remove their shirts and expose their bare chests at the beach, at a sports field, and at almost any outdoor public location in which they choose to do so. Women, by contrast, can be arrested and convicted of a crime for undertaking the identical act of removing their shirts. Commentators sometimes belittle constitutional challenges to laws based on notions of morality by claiming that such laws are not actually enforced (e.g., Bork 1990, 117), but laws that are on the books are available for use by law enforcement officials. Indecent exposure laws are, in fact, enforced against women and can result in jail sentences. In the aftermath of student "riots" at Michigan State University following a loss in the NCAA basketball tournament in 1999, one female student served seventeen days in jail, another was sentenced to fourteen days in jail, and four others were given sentences ranging from ten to fifteen days in jail when they were convicted on charges of indecent exposure after lifting up their shirts in front of crowds of people on a night when mobs were setting fires and damaging property (MacDonald 1999). Why should it be a crime for women to bare their breasts when men's bare chests are an everyday sight in warm weather? What is the harm that society seeks to prevent by imposing criminal punishment for the public exposure of a female breast?

As a matter of logic, the criminalization of female breast exposure is difficult to understand. As one critic of Michigan's statute observed, "The 'crime' she committed [by lifting up her shirt] has no victims [and] violates no right" (McWilliams 1999, 4). Judges could readily take judicial notice of the fact that many men with noticeable body fat in their upper chests—who are permitted to remove their shirts in public—have breasts that are fatter, larger, or rounder than those of many women. This is especially true for men who suffer from a medical condition known as "gynecomastia" (Rothenberg 1991, 95). Because women are permitted to wear bikini tops that reveal nearly everything except their nipples, it almost appears as if the human nipple constitutes the horrible scourge that must be combated if society is to be saved from the harms of indecent exposure. However, men have nipples too, which they reveal quite clearly when shirtless. In addition, women often wear tops of thin or tight-fitting materials that reveal their nipples (albeit thinly covered by fabric) to the eyes of the public. Thus, acceptable sartorial practices in contemporary society clash with the apparent purposes of hiding human nipples from public view.

If the image of the stereotypical female breast is harmful in some way, why do criminal penalties not apply to men who make their breasts visible to the public? In 1952, when Michigan's indecent exposure statute was enacted, the exposure to public view of a woman's breast may have constituted a shocking violation of societal mores. By 1999, however, it was difficult to argue that the same mores existed because female breasts that were uncovered or nearly uncovered were pervasive in advertising and entertainment media. In the September 1999 issue of the women's health and beauty magazine, *Essence*, available for purchase by anyone of any age at any newsstand, there was a two-page advertisement for NIKE sports bras that consisted entirely of a close-up photograph of a naked woman showing everything—breasts, nipples, and even individual hair follicles—from the model's bellybutton to her shoulders (Advertisement 1999, 2–3). Some women go to jail for briefly lifting their shirts to momentarily flash an obscured image of their breasts for public viewing while others gain financial rewards for promoting corporate America's products by baring their breasts in a way that permits complete strangers to stare at their nipples for hours on end.

If equal protection analysis is applied to the unequal treatment of males' and females' breasts under indecent exposure criminal statutes, how can the constitutionality of these statutes be analyzed? The essential question under equal protection analysis is whether criminalization of women's conduct in publicly baring their breasts is substantially related to an important governmental purpose. What can the government assert as its important interest to justify the differential treatment of men's and women's conduct in baring their breasts? While there might be an argument that society's mores require enforcement of a certain degree of morality with respect to modesty about the human body, there would be serious doubts about the adequacy of such a justification in light of the permissibility of near-nakedness (e.g., skimpy bikinis), visible breasts and nipples under thin or stretched fabrics, and naked breasts in widely disseminated national advertisements. How could the protection of society require criminal prosecution for women who lift their shirts in public yet permit breasts and nipples to be visible to the public in other contexts?

An alternative justification, and the one which apparently lurked beneath the prosecution of the Michigan State University students, relies on the notion that the sight of female breasts may trigger undesirable behavior in other people. In the MSU context, two women convicted of indecent exposure were labeled in news reports as "rioters." Even so, they were never charged nor convicted for any of the three rioting offenses under Michigan law (Hudson 1999, 1). The felony of rioting requires proof that the offender engaged in violent conduct and that clearly was not the case when the act was merely lifting up one's shirt (Mich. Compiled Laws section 752.541). The felony of unlawful assembly requires proof of gathering with other people for the purpose of engaging in conduct constituting the crime of riot, conduct which must include proof of violence (Mich. Compiled Laws section 752.543). The felony of inciting to riot requires proof of urging others to commit acts of unlawful force, violence, burning, or destruction of property (Mich. Compiled Laws section 752.542). Does a woman encourage riots by exposing her breasts? In light of the visibility and pervasiveness of naked and nearly naked female breasts in advertising and entertainment media, it seems doubtful that revealing a woman's breast constitutes "urging" others to commit violence and destruction of property, even in the context of exposing one's self to a group of people already engaged in a riot. As one critic of the jail sentences observed in response to the sentencing judge's comment that incarceration of the women was necessary to deter future riots, "In reality, [by exposing her breasts, the offender] probably distracted people who might otherwise have ignited furniture or barfed on [neighbors'] flower[beds]. I think [the offender] was just showing off" (McWilliams 1999, 4).

Clearly, the women convicted of indecent exposure were being held responsible for the riot. One judge who sentenced women to jail for indecent exposure in the riot's aftermath said that the women contributed to the escalation of the riot by exposing their breasts. According to the judge, "The indecent exposures that took place during the course of the riot were a whole different set of circumstances than your normal instance... These were in maintenance of the riot" (Hudson 1999, 1). Moreover, women sentenced for indecent exposure were required to pay restitution of

$2,384 to the City of East Lansing, the same restitution required of people convicted of assembling to riot (Hudson 1991, 1). By sentencing these women to pay the same restitution for riot damage paid by people convicted of actual riot offenses, the courts clearly indicated that the women (and their bare breasts) were being held responsible for the riot.

If a woman baring her breasts was analyzed solely as an issue of free expression rather than as an issue of equal protection, the U.S. Supreme Court's First Amendment decisions might provide a rationale for regulating such conduct. Under the Supreme Court's "fighting words" doctrine in *Chaplinsky v. New Hampshire* (1942), governments are permitted to regulate and prohibit profanity and other statements that tend to incite an immediate breach of the peace. However, there is nothing automatic about the constitutionality of criminalizing profanity. The Supreme Court did not regard the words "Fuck the Draft" on a man's jacket as subject to criminal prosecution under the "fighting words" doctrine (*Cohen v. California* 1971), so it is not certain precisely what words or expressions are subject to regulation under this doctrine. In order to employ this doctrine in criminal cases, states and localities must have narrowly drawn statutes that carefully define the prohibited expressive conduct or statements that tend to incite immediate breaches of the peace. In the case of the MSU students, they were not prosecuted under such a carefully defined statute. They were prosecuted under a general indecent exposure law and the judge merely assumed that their conduct contributed to the riot when he determined their punishments. Thus, the prosecution cannot be readily justified under the "fighting words" doctrine in First Amendment jurisprudence. Indeed, the pervasiveness of imagery and examples of naked and near-naked female breasts in American society refutes any purported assertion that exposure of breasts is analogous to the profane and derisive name-calling that the Supreme Court's decisions address.

If the sight of women's breasts causes riots, then the indecent exposure statute is substantially related to the advancement of the government's purported interest in nipple control as a means of riot prevention. However, the conclusion that women's visible breasts cause riots is highly doubtful in light of the visibility of naked breasts through American society, including national magazines and Home Box Office (HBO) cable television movies. The statute selectively punishes breast exposure in certain contexts while leaving other contexts of breast exposure legal and, in the advertising and entertainment contexts, profitable. Moreover, it seems equally plausible that public disorder can be associated with the exposure of a man's bare chest, as for example when screaming fans surge forward as some male rock singer unbuttons and discards his shirt during a concert. The law, however, singles out women for punishment under this justification for the statute. In reality, the government should carry the burden of doing something more than merely asserting that bare breasts cause riots. The fact that breast exposure occurred as people rioted does not mean that such exposure caused the rioting. If people are going to be deprived of their liberty and endure the life-long stigma of criminal convictions, the government should provide empirical evidence that bare breasts threaten social stability and public peace. Such evidence should be demanded or else the government will not have carried the burden of demonstrating that the statute is substantially related to the government's purported interest in stopping riots.

Beneath the surface of this issue lurks the significant question of whether the women convicted of indecent exposure should be held responsible for the behavior of others. If the sight of a female breast is not a cause of harm, as evidenced by widespread visibility of naked or near-naked breasts, then the attribution of responsibility for rioting to women whose breasts were momentarily bare appears to be a form of vicarious liability. Vicarious liability involves the imposition of criminal liability on one party for the criminal acts of another party. However, vicarious liability is typically imposed only on an individual who has control over the perpetrator and therefore such liability is limited to employer-employee relationships, parent-child relationships, and similar situations. The women convicted of indecent exposure had no control over those who set fires and damaged property. Rioting behavior occurred before the exposure incidents and in geographic locations away from the spots where the convicted women briefly exposed their breasts. The women received sanction and blame as if they had control over the rioters, but there is no basis for regarding them as culpable for the fires and property destruction that occurred.

An alternative justification for an asserted "important governmental interest" that would justify the differential treatment of women might be a paternalistic rationale. Such a justification would claim that women need to be punished for exposing their breasts in order to protect them from being assaulted by men who are excited by the sight of bare breasts. Hypothetically, an advocate of this justification might point to the Woodstock '99 concert in New York in which many people (women and men) removed their shirts, and several women were the victims of sexual assaults. There are three obvious problems with this justification. First, none of the women convicted of indecent exposure at MSU asserted that they had been assaulted in any way. Second, women who did not remove their shirts at Woodstock '99 were sexually assaulted, thus casting doubt on any assertions that bare breasts necessarily are the cause of assaults (Zielbauer 1999, B1). Third, the use of criminal sanctions against women for this policy justification operates to victimize the victims rather than focusing punishment solely on those who were culpable, the actual perpetrators of the violent crimes against women. Again, this asserted justification would appear to require empirical substantiation before it could plausibly be accepted as a sufficiently important justification for the differential treatment of men and women and the punishment of women who briefly expose their breasts.

As indicated by the foregoing discussion, the definition of indecent exposure laws that criminalize the baring of breasts by women and not men should not survive the heightened scrutiny of equal protection analysis. Justifications concerning the prevention of violence, either through societal disorder or directed at individual women, could hypothetically fulfill the requirement of an "important" governmental interest requiring differential treatment by gender, but close examination of these justifications reveals that they lack empirical substantiation and impose either improper vicarious liability or victimize the victims of assaults. In reality, the gender-based definitions of indecent exposure concerning bare breasts reflect an inconsistent and hypocritical conception of morality that holds women to a different standard of behavior than that imposed upon men.

Indeed, one lower court that examined the issue illustrated precisely this point by rejecting an equal protection claim made on behalf of women arrested for being topless at a public beach. In *People v. David* (1989), the judge on the City Court of Rochester, New York, deferred to the legislature's judgment that such applications of indecent exposure laws embody a compelling governmental interest in protecting "public decency." This deferential application of equal protection analysis does not fulfill the judiciary's responsibility to look closely and critically at purported justifications for governmental differentiations by gender. The use of "public decency" as a justification relies on vague definitions and inconsistent applications. As illustrated in the foregoing discussion, nudity and near-nudity are visible, common, and unpunished in other contexts, especially in entertainment and advertising media. Naked or nearly naked breasts are visible throughout society, including on the beach, on the streets, in movies and magazines. However, criminal sanctions are selectively imposed as a reflection of sex role traditionalism that has shaped law and criminal justice. Women who violate their traditional social role and exhibit questionable moral behavior are equated with "bad" women and have historically been subject to punishment (Chesney-Lind 1978), as evidenced by the disproportionate law enforcement attention to female rather than male participants in heterosexual prostitution transactions. Contemporary society's acceptance of near-naked breasts and provocative sexual poses has created a situation in which fine lines are drawn between acceptable breast exposure and unacceptable breast exposure. Revealing virtually everything except the nipple and revealing the nipple under the thin veil of a fabric are acceptable and legal exposures of the female breast. Revealing a bare nipple on a woman, however, is cause for a jail sentence, despite the fact that men also have nipples that they are free to display in public places. The criminalization of bare female nipples constitutes a distinction without a difference when compared to what is permissibly revealed by contemporary clothing and in advertising and entertainment media. It is as if bare female breasts remain a focus of indecent exposure laws as a means, albeit fragmented and inconsistent, for retaining a message about traditional mores concerning women and partial nudity. Thus, indecent exposure laws involving the female breast cannot survive the heightened scrutiny of equal protection analysis for gender discrimination, yet there is little likelihood that a court will collide with established mores by granting women the same equality and freedom to bare their nipples that are enjoyed by men in American society. Decisions by judges are shaped by their personal attitudes, values, and policy preferences (Baum 1997), and thus they are affected by dominant conceptions of morality that regard certain contexts of public exposure of the female breast as improper. Judges also have incentives to avoid controversy in order to prevent damage to the legitimacy and authority of legal institutions. Thus, the path of least resistance would be to view an equal protection challenge to the criminalization of bare female breasts as, in Robert Bork's (1990, 117) terminology, "one more sortie in our cultural war" rather than a constitutional issue that affects the liberty and equality of more than half of the American populace. As a result, the criminal justice system expends resources to sanction nonviolent female offenders who have caused no harm in order to uphold one surviving, inconsistent vestige of a tattered moral concept about modesty and the human body.

The U.S. Supreme Court has applied its equal protection analysis to formal criminal statutes enforcing gender discrimination against men. In *Craig v. Boren* (1976), the Supreme Court established its heightened scrutiny analysis for gender discrimination claims by examining a case pursued by two young men. The men objected to an Oklahoma statute that permitted eighteen-year-old women to purchase beer containing 3.2 percent alcohol but prohibited men from purchasing any beer until they reached the age of twenty-one. Oklahoma sought to justify the mandated gender discrimination by pointing to statistics indicating that young men were more likely than young women to be arrested for drunken driving and public drunkenness. The justices decided that the statistics did not provide a sufficient justification for the discrimination both because the studies were not focused on the purchase of 3.2 percent beer and because the statistics did not provide specific support for the particular three-year age difference for purchasing alcoholic beverages. Thus, the Court used its interpretive authority to strike down a discriminatory statute on equal protection grounds.

By contrast, *Michael M. v. Sonoma County* (1981) presented an equal protection challenge to California's statutory rape law that made it a crime for males to have sexual intercourse with a woman who was under the age of eighteen but did not apply a similar rule to women's sexual contacts with male teenagers. In its decision, the Court accepted California's intention to prevent illicit teenage pregnancies as a sufficiently substantial state interest to justify treating men and women differently for the purposes of defining this sex crime. The Court's opinion placed great emphasis on the biological fact that young women can become pregnant, but young men cannot. Thus, in order to prevent teenage pregnancies, California was entitled to criminalize sexual intercourse and prosecute the man involved, even if it occurred with the consent of both parties, when the woman was of an age that the state legislature deemed too young to make a valid consent and cope with the risk of a consequential pregnancy. The dissenters questioned why California could not pursue the same objectives without discrimination by simply having a gender-neutral statute that applied equally to men and women. The case demonstrates that gender discrimination within the justice system can have detrimental impacts for men as well as women. Because gender-specific statutory rape statutes are based on a presumption that young women need state protection but that young men do not, the Court's decision also serves as a reminder that paternalism continues to affect criminal laws and the Supreme Court's analysis of such laws.

Equal Protection and Discretionary Decisions

As indicated by the foregoing discussion of unequal treatment under formal criminal law, attitudes about women shape the definition of law regarding certain behaviors. Judges are likely to fail to apply equal protection principles to combat this unequal treatment because judicial officers have been socialized in American society and typically share dominant social values. Judges "are drawn from the mainstream of American society... [and] generally come from the affluent political elite whose values and interests favor the maintenance of the general policy preferences of their historical era" (Smith 1997a, 298). Other actors who possess discretionary authority in the criminal justice process, including police officers, prosecutors, and jurors, are also products of their historical era and tend to reflect common social values and prejudices in their decision making (Black 1999). The use of racial profiling as the basis for traffic stops and automobile searches, for example, reflects common stereotypes about the involvement of minority group members in drug crimes. Women have been the objects of stereotypes and prejudice by decision makers in the criminal justice system, especially with respect to punishment for criminal offenses.

Historically, chivalry has been regarded as the most common strategy for punishing women. This concept refers to treating women more leniently than men for comparable crimes (Anderson 1975–76). In the past, this form of favorable differential treatment for women was justified by the claim that women lacked *mens rea* and were incapable of forming the necessary criminal intent required for full culpability and punishment (Sokoloff & Price 1995). In a sense, women were treated as if they were children who were incapable of understanding the difference between right and wrong.

This simple description of chivalry obscures a much more complex phenomenon. Indeed, research shows evidence of chivalry effects in some contexts but not in others (Pollock-Byrne 1990). Chivalry does not operate when women commit crimes that are outside of their accepted gender role. Societal expectations for women may include the notion that when women manifest "masculine" behaviors, associated with physicality and aggressive behavior, such as assault and robbery, they are "abnormal" and deserve harsh punishment (Boritch 1992). In addition, the paternalism and sex role traditionalism connected to the chivalry concept can be manifested through harsher punishments for women than men for morality offenses that label offenders as "bad women" who have failed to fulfill society's expectations for the admirable qualities of femininity and idealized womanhood. For example, the history of juvenile courts includes significant efforts by justice institutions to label and treat girls as offenders because of concerns about their deviations from traditional morality (Chesney-Lind & Shelden 1992). Chivalry may also not benefit poor women and women of color because of the persistence of discrimination and disadvantages by race and social class in the criminal justice system. Chivalry is also complicated by contextual factors, such as whether a woman has dependent children, which may influence decision makers' orientation toward leniency in order to diminish adverse impacts on families (Daly 1999).

The sentencing of offenders related to the MSU riot presented evidence of unequal treatment and the imposition of harsher punishments for women who violated conceptions of morality. Thus, in addition to various fines and restitution orders, women convicted of indecent exposure received jail sentences ranging from ten to seventeen days. By contrast, some male offenders who were convicted of offenses that actually involved rioting behavior received lesser sentences. For example, one conviction for assembling to riot produced a three-day jail sentence. A conviction for obstructing, resisting, or hindering a police officer led to a five-day sentence and another offender convicted of the same charge earned a seven-day sentence (Hudson 1999, 1). Although a recognition of the historic impact of discriminatory paternalism and sex role stereotypes on sentencing leads to the inference that judges applied especially harsh treatment to women convicted of a nonviolent morality offense related to the MSU riot, such discretionary sentencing decisions are virtually immune from scrutiny and remedy by application of an Equal Protection Clause challenge. The Supreme Court has declined to require that judges compare sentences between similarly situated offenders to ensure comparable sentencing. Sentences for similar offenses and offenders vary dramatically from state to state and, sometimes, from courthouse to courthouse within a single state. Moreover, because social science techniques for providing empirical substantiation of unequal treatment claims were put on the shelf after the Court refused to allow judges to examine statistical evidence of systemic racial discrimination in sentencing (*McCleskey v. Kemp* 1987), proof of discrimination would require blatant prejudicial statements by prosecutors or judges. Contemporary sensitivity to overt racism among educated Americans makes it unlikely that these officials would make such open statements, even if they harbored prejudicial attitudes. Discriminatory outcomes are more likely to result from subconscious thought processes in which prosecutors or judges are influenced by gender stereotypes or racial attitudes in attributing intent, blameworthiness, or susceptibility to rehabilitation.

Differential treatment seems evident in the decisions of some prosecutors, judges, and jurors, even in death penalty cases. In some instances, suspicions of chivalry emerge if women are spared from the same punishment as men. For example, when the Supreme Court examined whether felony-murder accomplices could receive the death penalty without actively participating in the killing, a male defendant who had merely driven the getaway car had been sentenced to death while a female defendant who actively participated in the underlying robbery and double murder received a prison sentence (*Enmund v. Florida* 1982). The Supreme Court did not address the lurking issue of gender discrimination because it accepted the case solely for consideration of whether an accomplice could receive the death penalty. In another example, Jesse DeWayne Jacobs assisted his sister, Bobbie Jean Hogan, in abducting the ex-wife of his sister's boyfriend. The abducted woman was shot and killed during the crime. Prosecutors initially claimed that Jacobs did the killing and they succeeded in convincing a jury to sentence him to death. At Hogan's trial, prosecutors changed their theory of the case and claimed that Hogan was the real killer, and they used Jacobs as a witness to testify to that effect (Gwynne 1995). Hogan's jury believed that she was responsible, but they convicted her of involuntary manslaughter rather than murder. Despite the fact that the prosecutor in Jacobs's case later said publicly that he doubted that Jacobs was guilty, Jacobs was executed while his sister was slated to be released from prison in ten years or less (Costanzo 1997, 88). They were co-defendants of apparently unequal culpability, with Hogan ultimately regarded by prosecutors as the actual killer, but they received very different punishments. It is difficult to know whether this case illustrates capriciousness in death penalty cases, heartless cynicism by prosecutors, who changed their theory of the case without caring about who was most culpable, or some other disconcerting defect in the justice process. It is difficult to escape the suspicion, however, that gender considerations may have played a role in determining the crime partners' respective sentences.

Decisions about applying the ultimate punishment to women are influenced by social perceptions of women's roles and decision makers' views about whether the defendant adheres to these roles (Carroll 1997). In some cases, this could encourage decision makers to impose capital punishment. For example, Karla Faye Tucker was sentenced to death in Texas for a 1983 murder in which, after ingesting a wide array of drugs, she used a pickaxe to actively participate in the violent murders of two people in an apartment. Years later, as her execution date approached in 1998, Tucker garnered sympathy and support from around the world because she had become a born-again Christian of apparently exemplary character. Public pressure to spare her from execution included support from Pat Robertson, the conservative president of the Christian Broadcasting Network who is usually a supporter of capital punishment (Pressley 1998). Other offenders on death row discover God as they await their executions, yet they rarely gain international attention and support. News media commentaries made it quite clear that public discomfort with the prospect of Tucker's execution was inextricably linked to her gender ("Gender and the Death Penalty" 1998). When Tucker behaved in a manner far outside expected roles for women by taking drugs and violently employing a pickaxe to commit a double murder, she was sentenced to death. When she reformed herself on death row and became an educated, religious wife of a prison-ministry worker, opposition to her execution garnered significant national media attention and generated a serious (albeit unsuccessful) effort to ask the Texas Board of Pardons and Parole to recommend that her life be spared.

It appears that gender-based stereotypes and attitudes can continue to have an effect on the treatment of men and women in the criminal justice system. Differential treatment by gender in sentencing could conceivably violate the Equal Protection Clause either by discriminating against women in imposing harsh sentences for morality offenses and for behaviors that violate stereotypical sex role expectations or by discriminating against men in giving lesser sentences to women for the same crimes. However, the

Supreme Court's precedents provide scant opportunity for such claims to be pursued because of the nature and clarity of proof required, even when statistical evidence of disparities is available. Moreover, judicial and legislative changes in the habeas corpus process have made it so difficult for many offenders to pursue post conviction remedies that there is a strong likelihood that an offender who had a colorable claim concerning evidence of bias would be denied the opportunity to raise the claim because of procedural barriers to federal habeas corpus review (Smith 1997b).

Advancing Equality Without the Equal Protection Clause

In the definitions of crimes and the application of punishment, the foregoing examples illuminate contexts in which unequal treatment remains unremedied by the application of constitutional law. Opportunities exist for the U.S. Supreme Court and other courts to apply equal protection analysis to ensure that the ideal of equal justice overrides criminal statutes and officials' decisions that appear to be affected by biased attitudes toward women. The absence of judicial action on these issues diminishes the image of justice but does not necessarily imply that other aspects of the criminal justice system cannot move forward toward equality by alternative means.

Throughout American history women have faced various kinds of discrimination within the criminal justice system. This discrimination was not limited to unequal treatment of women who were criminal suspects and convicted offenders. Unequal treatment was also directed at women in their roles as crime victims and aspiring criminal justice officials. Unlike the continuing examples of discriminatory paternalism, such as indecent exposure statutes and sentencing practices, changes have occurred with respect to female crime victims and justice system personnel. These changes have not guaranteed equal treatment but they have demonstrated that political and social forces in society moved in the direction of recognizing and ameliorating some forms of gender discrimination. Following the example of the civil rights movement on behalf of African Americans' aspirations for legal and social equality, advocates for gender equality mobilized a women's movement in the 1960s and 1970s. The mobilization of female advocates of gender equality and their male supporters provided political pressure for new legislative action to advance equal treatment. In addition, litigation resources and strategies, such as those that succeeded in gaining moderate coverage against governmental gender discrimination with the Supreme Court's equal protection jurisprudence (*Craig v. Boren* 1976), helped to advance the beneficial interpretation and implementation of new protective statutes (Cole 1984). Political mobilization increased public awareness about unequal treatment of crime victims and justice system job applicants during a time when societal attitudes about women were changing. Thus, new political pressures helped to push legislatures to enact statutes intended to redress these problems.

The Supreme Court interpreted the Constitution as permitting states to prohibit women from becoming lawyers in *Bradwell v. Illinois* (1873). The Court's action did not foreclose all possibilities of job opportunities for women in the justice system. It merely permitted states and localities to make their own decisions. Although most agencies erected barriers to the employment of women in positions as anything other than the traditional female occupations as nurses and secretaries, a few agencies hired women for other positions. Portland, Oregon's police department was the first to permit a woman to become an officer in 1905, but very few women interested in justice system careers found similar opportunities until the second half of the twentieth century. After the *Bradwell* decision, the potential for constitutional litigation to redress gender discrimination in employment was virtually nonexistent for nearly a century until the Supreme Court decided to apply heightened scrutiny to gender-based equal protection claims in the 1970s.

In the eyes of some observers, the issue of equal employment opportunity within criminal justice institutions may seem distinguishable from the ideal of equal justice for litigants and defendants that is considered a core aspirational element of the justice system's mission. However, the image and legitimacy of the justice system depends, in part, on the operation of its constituent agencies in accordance with the principles that purportedly govern values and decisions of officials within the system. When employment discrimination is pervasive and unredressed, it is apparent that the public can have little confidence in the system's inclination and ability to treat all citizens equally, regardless of their race or gender. Under such circumstances, the decision makers come exclusively from hegemonic demographic groups (i.e., whites and males), and they appear to be disconnected from the diverse society that a democratic system presumes they will represent and understand as they make judgments that determine people's fates. As a result, equal treatment in justice system employment is an important element in the image and reality of the ideal of equal justice.

The legislative action that created the primary vehicle for opening previously closed employment opportunities was the enactment by Congress of Title VII of the Civil Rights Act. The purpose of Title VII was to prohibit various kinds of discrimination in the context of employment. Unlike the Equal Protection Clause, which is focused solely on governmental action, Title VII applies to discrimination by private employers. Title VII makes it "unlawful" for an employer to

> ...fail or refuse to hire or to discharge any individual, or otherwise to discriminate against any individual with respect to his compensation, terms, conditions, or privileges of employment, because of such individual's race, color, religion, sex, or national origin.

Title VII provides the vehicle through which people who believe that they have been victimized by employment discrimination on account of their race, color, religion, sex, or national origin can file legal complaints with the U.S. Equal Employment Opportunity Commission and, in some cases, file lawsuits seeking to remedy the alleged discrimination.

Despite the existence of Title VII, many women's efforts to gain employment in the justice system were met with resistance. Initially, law enforcement agencies and corrections departments often created minimum hiring qualifications that had the effect of excluding women. This effect was not necessarily inadvertent because many male officials in the justice system doubted that women were capable of handling the challenging demands of law enforcement and corrections work, such as arresting unruly suspects, breaking up fights, and controlling violent prisoners. Moreover, women's prospects for employment were hampered by widespread paternalistic attitudes about the proper place of women in subordinate and subservient roles.

The State of Alabama, for example, established a minimum height requirement (5 feet 2 inches) and a minimum weight requirement (120 pounds) for applicants seeking employment in corrections institutions. According to court decisions, these specific requirements had the effect of automatically excluding more than 41 percent of women from consideration for employment while triggering a similar exclusionary impact for less than 1 percent of the state's adult male population. Other agencies had additional requirements such as the ability to lift and carry a specific weight load. These requirements excluded many women from consideration because they lacked the size and physical strength of men. A woman in Alabama who sought employment as a corrections counselor challenged the state's minimum weight requirements by filing an action under Title VII. The U.S. Equal Employment Opportunity Commission examined the case and issued a "right-to-sue" letter that permitted her to pursue her claim through litigation in the federal courts. Because she was otherwise qualified for the job in light of her college degree in correctional psychology, she alleged that the height and weight requirements were not actually necessary for performance of the job's duties and therefore served as an illegal, discriminatory barrier to equal employment under Title VII. The U.S. Supreme Court considered her claim in *Dothard v. Rawlinson* (1977). The Court rejected the physical requirements imposed by the State of Alabama because there was no evidence to demonstrate that these height and weight requirements were essential to job performance. The Court required that employers impose only *bona fide* occupational qualifications that are demonstrably essential to job performance. Thus, a fire department could require that applicants be able to carry a heavy fire hose up a ladder, if such a task is part of the job in question. However, the courts would no longer accept arbitrary requirements, including exclusionary height and weight requirements that bore no demonstrated relationship to job performance.

The Supreme Court's decision helped to prevent criminal justice agencies from using pretextual justifications for rejecting employment applications from qualified women. This action advancing equality was not undertaken as part of the Court's interpretive authority as guardians of the Equal Protection Clause. Instead, it came from the Court's fulfillment of the underlying intentions of a legislative initiative through the justices' authority to interpret statutes. The Court's interpretations of Title VII did not ensure that equal employment existed within the justice system. Decision makers could still employ discretionary judgments to make decisions that were adverse to the interests of qualified women by, for example, rationalizing the hiring and promotion of men through justifications based on subjective criteria. Title VII provided a vehicle for challenging such decisions that was previously not available through the Equal Protection Clause alone. However, the success of such challenges hinged on the availability of legally recognized evidence concerning impermissible gender-based discrimination in employment.

A major problem for women who embarked on careers within the justice system was daily resistance and harassment from male officials opposed to the entry of women into criminal justice-related occupations. The pioneering women who were the first police officers or corrections officers within their agencies frequently heard derogatory comments from their male colleagues and even suffered threats and physical harassment, sometimes of a sexual nature. Instances of sexual harassment in the justice system include physical attacks, demands for sexual favors in exchange for employment opportunities and promotions, and the creation of hostile work environments through unwanted sexual comments and propositions (Grana 2002). Although women eventually earned acceptance in most criminal justice agencies through competent and professional performance of their duties, sexual harassment continues to be a problem when individual male officials harass their female colleagues and subordinates. Title VII provides a vehicle for seeking legal remedies for such actions. Complaints and lawsuits are filed with disappointing regularity concerning sexual harassment issues. In some circumstances, supervisory officials fail to investigate complaints and discipline offending employees. Such inaction facilitates the continuation of discriminatory activity. In 2001, for example, California was ordered to pay $154,000 to a female corrections officer who experienced repeated sexual harassment from a male co-worker despite making complaints to supervisory authorities (Wisely 2002).

Although Title VII forced changes in hiring policies and thereby opened the possibility that women might be eligible for nearly any job in the justice system, disputes still arise about whether women should be permitted in all jobs in correctional settings. Within prisons, corrections officers must view unclothed inmates in residential areas and showers. Moreover, they must conduct intrusive body searches that involve patting down prisoners' bodies and may even require prisoners to disrobe for a visual examination of body cavities. Policies regarding the most intrusive form of searches, actual probing searches of body cavities, frequently require that such searches be conducted by personnel with medical training such as a physician, nurse, or physician's assistant. Prisoners often object to having their bodies frisked or searched by officials of the opposite sex. These objections are usually based on an assertion of privacy rights or rights to religious freedom if such personal contact collides with the precepts of a prisoner's religion. Because states' prison populations are overwhelmingly male, any limitations on cross-gender searches can have significant effects on women's employment opportunities as corrections officials (Bennett 1995). Thus, state regulations often attempt to strike a balance between protecting prisoners' privacy when possible and fulfilling an institution's need for security and obligation to provide equal employment opportunities for women. The policies of Michigan's Department of Corrections state, for example, that

> medical personnel who perform a body cavity search need not be of the same sex as the prisoner being searched. However, all other persons who are present during the search shall be of the same sex as the prisoner, and there shall always be at least one staff member present who is the same sex as the prisoner being searched. (Smith 2000, 130)

Significant movement toward equal employment opportunity within the criminal justice system occurred from the 1970s onward. Because the Supreme Court's pre-1970s interpretation of the Equal Protection Clause provided no opportunity to use constitutional law as the vehicle for prohibiting and remedying gender discrimination, progress in redressing employment discrimination depended on societal change, political mobilization, and legislative action. Similar forces brought changes to the treatment of female crime victims.

Before 1970, many law enforcement agencies regarded domestic violence situations as private "family matters" that did not require intervention from police and prosecutors. As a result, many women were repeatedly victimized by violent spouses and boyfriends without receiving any assistance from government authorities. Political mobilization by women's activists and changing sensitivities about the role of women in society helped to alter justice agencies' prevailing attitudes and policies. Social scientists began to study domestic violence issues, and a widely publicized study concluded that domestic violence could be reduced if perpetrators are arrested and briefly jailed (Sherman 1992). Other studies have cast doubt upon those conclusions, but the original study was very influential in encouraging police departments to create policies that required officers to make arrests whenever they had evidence of interpersonal violence within households. Police were also pressured to change their policies because changing societal attitudes became reflected in decisions by judges and juries that imposed significant financial liability on police departments that failed to protect people whom they knew to be victimized by continuing incidents of domestic violence. In the most famous case, Tracey Thurman won a $2 million judgment against the Torrington, Connecticut, police department after officers were slow to respond to her calls for help and actually observed Thurman's estranged husband holding a bloody knife and kicking her in the head before belatedly pulling the husband away and arresting him. Ms. Thurman suffered severe injuries, including partial paralysis, from being stabbed and beaten by her husband, a man who had previously been arrested and released by police authorities (Kurtz 1988).

Women victimized by sex crimes also frequently experienced insensitive treatment by police officers and traumatic, humiliating questioning when testifying in court. Political mobilization and changing societal attitudes created pressures for statutory reform of laws and procedures concerning the treatment of rape victims. For example, many states changed the definition of the crime of rape by eliminating the traditional requirement that victims prove that they resisted the rapist. The reformed law reflected the reality that many victims are overpowered by their attackers, suffering from shock during the attack, or facing the risk of death if they attempt to fight a stronger and frequently armed attacker. States also eliminated the traditional rule that a rape conviction required corroborating evidence and could not be based solely on the testimony of the victim. It was sometimes difficult to develop corroborating evidence for cases in which the rape occurred in a private place, and the shocked victim delayed before reporting the crime. New "rape shield" statutes also prohibited defense attorneys from placing rape victims "on trial" by asking questions intended to humiliate and intimidate the victim by focusing on the victim's past sexual history rather than on the incident that provided the basis for the charges against the defendant. Prior to the passage of these statutes, some rape victims refused to pursue charges against their attackers because they did not want to be forced to testify in open court about aspects of their personal lives that were not relevant to the crime (Horney & Spohn 1991).

The treatment of domestic violence victims was not conducive to constitutional litigation because it primarily concerned discretionary decisions made by police officers and prosecutors. Moreover, it would have been difficult to prove that justice system officials treated women differently from men. Some men are also victimized by domestic violence and police agencies are not attentive to these victims either. The discretionary practices that ignored the problem of domestic violence had a disproportionately detrimental impact on women because female victims of domestic violence are more numerous than male victims. Even if the U.S. Supreme Court had been receptive to gender-based equal protection claims prior to the 1970s, the absence of formal policies that clearly discriminated against women would have made it difficult to persuade the justices to recognize a constitutional violation. By contrast, the insensitive treatment of rape victims was based on formal statutes and policies. Although these formal governmental rules disproportionately affected women, who are far more frequently victimized by rape than are men, the rules applied equally to women and men, and therefore were not readily challengeable as violating the right to equal protection.

In the examples of domestic violence and rape victims, political pressure and changing societal attitudes led legislatures and agencies to change laws and polices that had previously led to detrimental treatment of women. The limitations of constitutional doctrines and the U.S. Supreme Court's reluctance to inhibit the discretionary authority of justice system officials have guaranteed that rules and practices that produce a disparate impact upon women will seldom receive corrective judicial attention by appellate judges. In these contexts, the advancement of equal justice required legislative action and greater receptivity to women's claims by civil juries. Such changes were the product of political mobilization, public education, and consciousness-raising by advocates of social and legal equality for women.

Conclusion

Over the course of American history, women have made significant progress toward political and legal equality with men. From a constitutional perspective, a particularly notable development was the Supreme Court's enunciation of antidiscrimination doctrines that include women under the coverage of the Equal Protection Clause, albeit with less protection than that granted to victims of racial discrimination. By including gender discrimination under the Equal Protection Clause, the Court created a tool for judges to examine and remedy unequal treatment of women in the criminal justice system. The existence of this tool does not, however, provide assurance that judicial action is sufficiently available and effective to eliminate the vestiges of gender discrimination. At the dawn of the new century, it seems clear that there are lingering issues concerning the equal status of women in the eyes of the law. As indicated by the foregoing examples of indecent exposure prosecutions and capital punishment, there is evidence that prevalent attitudes about women's expected roles and morality continue to shape the treatment of female defendants and offenders in the justice process. Although the Equal Protection Clause provides a plausible basis for redressing the unequal treatment generated by gender-based stereotypes and attitudes, it seems clear that there is little likelihood that constitutional litigation can root out the existing problems. The Supreme Court has not provided doctrinal bases for challenging sentences that appear to be influenced by gender based attitudes. Gender based aspects of formal law provide the strongest foundation for remedial judicial action under equal protection doctrines. However, as the example of indecent exposure law demonstrates, the attainment of equal treatment is not easy or automatic even when formal law is at issue. The continuing prevalence of gender-based attitudes about the applicability of indecent exposure laws to women's, but not to men's, bare breasts makes it likely that many judges share the attitudes that support maintenance of traditional laws, despite obvious changes elsewhere in society that indicate bare breasts are no longer absolutely taboo. Although it is difficult to identify an "important" governmental justification for the current definition of indecent exposure and its differential treatment of women, there are few incentives for claimants to challenge such laws and little reason to expect judges to be responsive to such challenges.

The Equal Protection Clause and judicial decisions interpreting that clause articulate and embody the Constitution's symbolic commitment to equal justice under law. Unfortunately, this examination of examples drawn from the criminal justice system raises questions about the efficacy of law as a means to achieve actual equal treatment of defendants and offenders. The existence of issues concerning gender discrimination in the justice system should serve as a reminder that the new century is less a moment to celebrate the attainment of equality than an opportunity to gain a clearer recognition of the need to grapple with the continuing complex and pervasive problems of unequal treatment.

5

The Poor and Equal Justice

AMERICAN SOCIETY IS highly stratified. Although the people living in the United States are, on average, among the wealthiest in the world, the wealth is not distributed evenly. In contrast to the countries of northern and western Europe, in which governments actively redistribute wealth through social welfare and taxation policies, the United States has millions of poor people. Many people lack jobs or work in occupations with compensation so low that it is difficult for them to pay their basic living expenses. Advertised employment vacancies often require technical skills that were impossible for poor people to obtain in low quality urban and rural school districts. In some metropolitan areas, jobs are available in growing suburbs but public transportation is insufficiently extensive or not designed to take people from the central city to suburbs at the start of the work day. Many Americans lack the basic nutrition, housing, medical care, and educational opportunities that are taken for granted by the majority of citizens who are middle class or above.

Within the criminal justice system, poor people can experience less favorable outcomes for a variety of reasons. Police departments often deploy their resources to apprehend offenders who commit "street crimes" rather than focusing investigative attention on other kinds of crimes. They often concentrate their patrols and surveillance on poor neighborhoods and thereby increase the likelihood that crimes in those neighborhoods will be detected. Historically, laws criminalizing "loitering" and "panhandling" have given police discretionary authority to investigate and arrest poor people. Such laws seldom affect middle-class and affluent people. Police reliance on "profiles" that include descriptive factors such as the type of clothing being worn or the kinds of cars being driven by "suspicious" people typically leads to surveillance and searches directed at poor people rather than affluent people.

While prosecutors may vigorously prosecute poor suspects whose crimes have harmed businesses or affluent people, middle-class people sometimes avoid prosecution by paying compensation or by gaining diversion into substance abuse programs. This differential treatment may stem from effective representation by defense attorneys early in the criminal law process, prosecutorial empathy for "understandable mistakes" made by fellow middle-class citizens, prosecutorial bias against poor people who are perceived as "threatening" to social order, or lobbying from networks of influential people (e.g., elected officials, church leaders, and so forth) who are most likely to be personally acquainted with middle-class and affluent people. Thus, the poor kid who steals a radio from the ground floor of a department store usually has a higher probability of being apprehended and prosecuted than the store manager three floors up who steals larger amounts of money and merchandise on a regular basis.

In addition to the biases embodied in the definition and enforcement of criminal laws, poor people suffer disadvantages. To the extent that modest incomes are associated with educational attainment for many people, many poor people may lack knowledge about the criminal justice system and their rights, at least in their initial encounters with the system. Obviously, some poor people may be very knowledgeable about the criminal law process if they have had many experiences with police and prosecutors. Conversely, affluent people may be unsophisticated and lack knowledge if they have never had personal experience with the system. However, the likelihood of taking classes, encountering books, and reading daily newspapers to gain information about laws, constitutional rights, and police authority may be diminished for people whose lives are absorbed by daily struggles to obtain food, shelter, and the necessities of life for themselves and their families. The Rehnquist Court majority presumes that people know their constitutional rights. For example, *Florida v. Bostick* (1991) was a case concerning a bus passenger whose luggage was searched by the police without a warrant. Justice Sandra O'Connor's majority opinion noted that "an individual may decline an officer's request [to search luggage] without fearing prosecution," yet she does not discuss how people would know that they can refuse such requests because the Supreme Court has said that the police do not need to inform them of their right to refuse. Thus, an individual's knowledge can be an important element in the preservation of rights and limitation of excessive police discretion.

Another element—money—affects whether an individual will be disadvantaged by the operation of criminal law processes, and this lack of financial resources impacts poor people directly and universally. People with money can hire experienced defense attorneys immediately after being arrested. Early intervention by attorneys can improve the quality of the defense's investigation and preparation of the case. Many expensive defense attorneys are known for their ability to gain especially favorable plea agreements. Money can enable a defendant to gain pretrial release, whereas poor defendants who cannot make bail must sit in jail, unable to help with defense preparations. Money permits affluent defendants to hire private investigators, expert witnesses, psychologists, and jury consultants to improve their chances of making the best possible presentation to court. Money enables defendants to pay for DNA tests and other laboratory testing of physical evidence in order to counter the scientific evidence produced for the prosecution by city or state crime labs. Money enables defendants to hire computer consultants and other technical experts who can create simulations and other effective presentations that may help to persuade the judge or jury about the defendant's innocence. Money also enables defendants to carry well-prepared appeals through the various levels of the court system if the trial outcome is disappointing. Poor defendants, by contrast, often have only an overworked and underpaid appointed defense attorney or public defender who tries to arrange a quick plea agreement (Blumberg 1967). These defendants may not have access to investigators, expert witnesses, and other resources that would permit them to challenge the prosecution's evidence. Poor people can be subjected to "assembly-line justice" in which their arrest is followed by a quick guilty plea that is encouraged by both the prosecutor and the defense attorney. Affluent people, on the other hand, can challenge the prosecution's evidence and thereby pressure the government to compromise or abandon its original charges. The resource disparities between the poor defendant, who has little assistance, and the prosecutor, who has the investigative services of the police and evidence preparation expertise of a crime lab, can create unequal and inconsistent outcomes for defendants.

Disparities between the poor and the rest of society are not unique to the criminal law process. Such disparities exist with respect to access to quality education, medical care, and other important, fundamental aspects of American life. Many Americans take these disparities for granted, as if they represent natural or inevitable deservedness (or lack thereof) for people who are rewarded for hard work and initiative. The dominant political ideology of the United States emphasizes individualism, the presumption of equal opportunity and competitive market economics. Viewed through the lens of these ideological elements, poverty is presumed to be the inevitable and deserved outcome for individuals with weak personal characteristics or a lack of initiative. Social scientists from the 1960s onward unmasked these deceptive ideological presumptions as the products of a self-serving inclination to "blame the victims" of racism, unequal distribution of educational resources, and governmental tax policies that favor the rich (McCann 1989). Even if one accepted the ideological premises underlying a Social Darwinian "survival of the fittest" approach of attributing deservedness to social status and wealth, unequal treatment and outcomes pose problems within the criminal law process that differ from the widely accepted existence of inequality in education, medical care, and housing. Unlike other facets of American society in which inequality is accepted, the criminal law process purports to hold out the promise of "equal justice under law" for all people, without consideration of their individual deservedness of fairness and due process. Constitutional rights purport to apply equally to all people. However, in books with such titles as *The Rich Get Richer and the Poor Get Prison* (Reiman 2001) and *Courts and the Poor* (Smith 1991), scholars have documented the pervasiveness of unequal treatment affecting the poor in criminal law processes.

The clash between the reality of unequal treatment and the ideal of equal justice raises an important question: What, if anything, has the U.S.

Supreme Court done to advance the goal of equal justice with respect to poor people? This chapter will discuss the Court's interpretations of the Constitution that affect the reality of differential processes and outcomes for rich and poor. As with other contexts of unequal treatment, the Equal Protection Clause is potentially relevant to the issue of equal justice for the poor. Unlike the situation of racial equality, however, equal protection principles are not the sole or primary basis for seeking equal justice. The Supreme Court's interpretations of other constitutional provisions, such as the Sixth Amendment right to counsel and the Eighth Amendment's protection against excessive bail, provide bases for addressing contexts in which a defendant's lack of resources produces disadvantages.

Equal Protection and the Poor

The Equal Protection Clause, as part of the Fourteenth Amendment, was added to the Constitution following the Civil War. In light of the historical moment of its creation and the primary objective in the minds of its authors, the Supreme Court emphasized that the Clause was intended to address racial discrimination rather than other kinds of discrimination (*The Slaughterhouse Cases* 1873). As noted in Chapter 3, despite its acknowledged purpose to address racial discrimination, the Supreme Court did relatively little to employ the Clause to combat pervasive racial segregation and injustice until the 1950s. Because of the Court's limited interpretation and application of the Equal Protection Clause, it was not used by the justices to address unequal treatment of women, immigrants, and others until the Warren Court era or later. Not surprisingly, there was little effort to apply equal protection principles to the problem of discrimination against the poor.

In 1941, for example, the Supreme Court addressed a California law aimed specifically at poor people and those who assisted them. As famously conveyed by John Steinbeck's novel *The Grapes of Wrath*, the Depression era saw many poor people from Oklahoma's failed "Dust Bowl" farmlands and elsewhere strike out for California in search of steady employment and a chance to escape from poverty. In reacting against the influx of newcomers, California attempted to enforce a criminal law that made it a misdemeanor to bring an indigent person into the state with knowledge of the person's indigent status. The state claimed that the law was necessary to protect the state's social, financial, and moral stability. Whatever the state's justifications, its enforcement fell harshly on poor people seeking to enjoy the benefits of California's rapidly expanding economy. When California prosecuted a man who brought his unemployed brother-in-law to that state from Texas, the case was appealed to the Supreme Court. In *Edwards v. California* (1941), the Supreme Court invalidated the state statute on the grounds that it improperly usurped congressional authority to regulate interstate commerce. According to the Court, the transportation of people constitutes interstate commerce, which is under the legislative control of the national legislature and beyond the reach of state lawmakers. Although the Court's decision sought to end prosecutorial harassment of poor Americans moving to California from other states, it had the ironic consequence of treating poor people as property or commodities under the control of others. While railroads and bus companies transport people for commercial purposes and fit easily under a definition of "commerce," stretching the concept of commerce to cover a man driving his brother-in-law in his personal automobile required the application of the Court's interpretive license. The Court could have used its interpretive authority to address the problem in a manner that treated poor people in a more respectful and humane manner. Several justices wrote concurring opinions to argue that California's law violated the poor people's right to travel or their entitlement to "privileges and immunities of citizenship" under the Fourteenth Amendment. However, the majority of justices did not treat the issue as one affecting the constitutional rights of poor people. Instead, it was treated as an issue concerning federalism and the scope of congressional legislative authority. The Court could have interpreted the Equal Protection Clause to bar criminal laws that single out for prosecution poor people and those who assist them. However, the justices seemed to ignore the apparent equal protection implications of the discrimination against indigent people.

In the 1950s, a minor breakthrough occurred in which a Supreme Court decision recognized the unequal treatment and outcomes affecting poor defendants and used the Equal Protection Clause as a means to combat that unequal treatment. The case concerned an Illinois law that made the opportunity to appeal non-capital criminal convictions contingent on the defendant's ability to pay for a trial transcript (*Griffin v. Illinois* 1956). Defendants who were sufficiently affluent to pay for the transcript could readily present their cases to the state appellate court while poor defendants were denied review if they could not afford to produce the transcript. Justice Hugo Black's opinion (excerpted below) is especially notable for its explicit emphasis on the constitutional requirement of providing equal justice for rich and poor alike. Moreover, he relied specifically on equal protection principles in determining that Illinois is obligated to provide free transcripts for indigent defendants who wish to appeal.

JUSTICE BLACK announced the judgment of the Court and an opinion in which THE CHIEF JUSTICE, JUSTICE DOUGLAS, and JUSTICE CLARK join:

Providing equal justice for poor and rich, weak and powerful alike is an age-old problem. People have never ceased to hope and strive to move closer to that goal. This hope, at least in part, brought about in 1215 the royal concessions of Magna Charta: "To no one will we sell, to no one will we refuse, or delay, right or justice... No free man shall be taken or imprisoned, or disseised, or outlawed, or exiled, or anywise destroyed; nor shall we go upon him nor send him, but by the lawful judgment of his peers or by the law of the land." These pledges were unquestionably steps toward a fairer and more nearly equal application of criminal justice. In this tradition, our own constitutional guaranties of due process and equal protection both call for procedures in criminal trials which allow no invidious discriminations between persons and different groups of persons. Both equal protection and due process emphasize the central aim of our entire judicial system—all people charged with crime must, so far as the law is concerned, "stand on an equality before the bar of justice in every American court."...

Surely no one would contend that either a State or the Federal Government could constitutionally provide that defendants unable to pay court costs in advance should be denied the right to plead not guilty or to defend themselves in court. Such a law would make the constitutional promise of a fair trial a worthless thing. Notice, the right to be heard, and the right to counsel would under such circumstances be meaningless promises to the poor. In criminal trials a State can no more discriminate on account of poverty than on account of religion, race, or color. Plainly the ability to pay costs in advance bears no rational relationship to a defendant's guilt or innocence and could not be used as an excuse to deprive a defendant of a fair trial....

There is no meaningful distinction between a rule which would deny the poor the right to defend themselves in a trial court and one which effectively denies the poor an adequate appellate review accorded to all who have money enough to pay the costs in advance. It is true that a State is not required by the Federal Constitution to provide appellate courts or a right to appellate review at all.... But that is not to say that a State that does grant appellate review can do so in a way that discriminates against some convicted defendants on account of their poverty. Appellate review has now become an integral part of the Illinois trial system for finally adjudicating the guilt or innocence of a defendant. Consequently at all stages of the proceedings the Due Process and Equal Protection Clauses protect persons like petitioners from invidious discriminations....

All of the States now provide some method of appeal from criminal convictions, recognizing the importance of appellate review to correct adjudication of guilt or innocence. Statistics show that a substantial proportion of criminal convictions are reversed by state appellate courts. Thus to deny adequate review to the poor means that many of them lose their life, liberty, or property because of unjust convictions which appellate courts could set aside. Many States have recognized this and provided aid for convicted defendants who have a right to appeal and need a transcript but are unable to pay for it. A few have not. Such a denial is a misfit in a country dedicated to affording equal justice to all and special privileges to none in the administration of its criminal law. There can be no equal justice where the kind of trial a man gets depends on the amount of money he has. Destitute defendants must be afforded as adequate appellate review as defendants who have money enough to buy transcripts. (*Griffin v. Illinois* 1956).

Black's opinion made statements forthrightly reiterating the Supreme Court's motto of "Equal Justice Under Law." According to Black, the United States is a country "dedicated to affording equal justice to all and special privileges to none in the administration of its criminal law." With respect to unequal treatment of the poor, Black emphasized that "[t]here can be no equal justice where the kind of trial a man gets depends on the amount of money he has." Black's statements clashed with the reality of unequal treatment for the poor, racial minorities, and others in courts throughout the United States, especially during the 1950s. However, his opinion took a step toward correcting one important aspect of this unequal treatment by requiring states to provide free transcripts for indigent criminal appellants to enable them to appeal their convictions. In addition, the emphatic, idealistic language of Black's opinion served to employ the Supreme Court's powerful symbolic voice to put states on notice that the high court was beginning to scrutinize their processes to determine whether they hindered or advanced the constitutional objective of equal justice. Although the Supreme Court cannot instantly create social change because of its limited ability to implement and oversee its legal policy directives (Rosenberg 1993), the Court can arguably use its "rights-declaration power" to call attention to problems and push other institutions in the governing system to take action to correct those problems (Tribe 1989).

Although Black's opinion advanced these purposes for the pursuit of equal justice, its precedential power and influence were undercut by its status as a plurality opinion rather than a majority opinion. Only three other justices joined Black's opinion and thus it did not carry the weight of a precedent-setting majority opinion. Justice Felix Frankfurter provided the fifth vote in favor of requiring Illinois to provide free transcripts for indigent appellants, but Frankfurter wrote a separate opinion and declined to join Black's. Moreover, four dissenting justices, a number equal to those supporting Black's opinion, explicitly rejected the use of the Equal Protection Clause as a basis for requiring Illinois to provide free transcripts. Thus, Black's opinion represented only a "minor" breakthrough. Although four justices applied equal protection principles on behalf of poor defendants in the criminal law process, an equal number of justices opposed interpreting the Constitution in this fashion. After the *Griffin* decision, it remained to be seen whether the Court would push forward with additional decisions addressing unequal treatment of the poor or whether a majority of justices would pull back from Black's use of the Equal Protection Clause. Because the Court's composition changes regularly through unpredictable patterns of deaths and retirements among the justices, subsequent appointees would control the balance of power concerning this issue within the evenly divided Court.

A few years after *Griffin*, a Supreme Court opinion again referred to the Equal Protection Clause in examining unequal treatment of the poor. As in *Griffin*, the case concerned criminal defendants' rights in the appellate process. At that time, the Supreme Court was not examining discrimination and disadvantage experienced by poor people in the various sectors of governmental policies and services, such as education, medical care, and taxation. Michael McCann (1989) has argued that the Supreme Court's justices tend to share with other middle-class and affluent Americans the view that the poor are responsible for their own station in life. Thus, the courts did not feel obligated to provide remedies for unequal treatment. According to McCann (1989, 253), the justices' opinions embody a belief that

> state policies that have discriminatory impacts upon the poor are not "suspect" [classifications requiring the application of "strict scrutiny" analysis] because they tend less to inhibit access to social opportunity than to merely recognize the "natural" personal inequalities of ability, character, and motivation...which [the] government, like the market, is not constitutionally obliged to remedy.

In reality, of course, "[w]idespread povery, unemployment, and worker powerlessness" are enduring aspects of our economic system so that people born into poverty have a high probability of remaining poor throughout their entire lives (McCann 1989, 252). The lack of universal access to high-quality basic education, advanced training, and high-paying job opportunities helps to determine people's fates. Despite beliefs about the causes of poverty that inhibit judicial action, the Court took action with respect to criminal law processes. Thus, the justices indicated a recognition that the ideal of equal justice in judicial processes ought to apply to all persons, regardless of their social status or the cause of their social status. The Court's recognition of and action (albeit limited) concerning this issue are laudable. However, in light of the Court's attention to unequal treatment of the poor in criminal law processes, the justices' actions are especially disappointing because they ultimately did so little with respect to the one area of American life in which they acknowledged that wealth discrimination should be unacceptable under the Constitution.

In *Douglas v. California* (1963), the Court considered whether an indigent defendant was entitled to representation on appeal when state law granted the defendant a right to appeal to the state's intermediate appellate court. Under California's procedures, indigent defendants seeking to appeal would have counsel appointed to represent them only if the appellate court determined that counsel would be useful to the case. Some indigent appellants did not receive representation when the appellate court predetermined that their cases were weak. Justice William O. Douglas's majority opinion cited and quoted Black's opinion in *Griffin v. Illinois* (1956) before concluding that this practice was unconstitutional. According to Douglas:

> When an indigent is forced to run this gauntlet of a preliminary showing of merit, the right to appeal does not comport with fair procedure.... The present case, where counsel was denied petitioners on appeal, shows that the discrimination is not between "possibly good and obviously bad cases," but between cases where the rich man can require the court to listen to argument of counsel before deciding on the merits, but a poor man cannot. There is lacking that equality demanded by the Fourteenth Amendment where the rich man, who appeals as of right, enjoys the benefit of counsel's examination into the record, research of the law, and marshaling of arguments on his behalf, while the indigent, already burdened by a preliminary determination that his case is without merit, is forced to shift for himself. The indigent, where the record is unclear or the errors are hidden, has only the right to a meaningless ritual, while the rich man has a meaningful appeal. (*Douglas v. California* 1963, 357–358)

Just prior to and immediately following *Douglas*, the Court issued several decisions reinforcing the idea that there should not be financial barriers to appeals by criminal defendants that prevent indigent offenders from making use of processes available to affluent defendants. In *Lane v. Brown* (1963), the Court prevented a indigent's opportunity to appeal from resting solely on whether his or her public defender decided to request a trial transcript. The indigent defendant can make the request even if the public defender declined to do so. In *Smith v. Bennett* (1961) and *Burns v. Ohio* (1959), the Court mandated that states must waive filing fees for post-conviction processes if indigent defendants cannot pay the fees.

The Court's other decisions regarding legal representation for indigent criminal defendants interpreted and applied the Sixth Amendment right to counsel. The *Douglas* case, however, which concerned appeals, relied on the Fourteenth Amendment and implicitly used the Equal Protection Clause in its language concerning improper discrimination between poor and affluent appellants. In using the Equal Protection Clause, the Supreme Court had not yet fully developed its "suspect classifications" approach in which strict scrutiny was reserved for discrimination by race and moderate scrutiny applied to gender discrimination while other forms of differential treatment were permissible if the government had a rational basis for pursuing a legitimate governmental interest. Indeed, Justice John Harlan's dissenting opinion in *Douglas* criticized the majority for "substitut[ing] resounding phrases for [equal protection] analysis." Because the Court had limited its application of equal protection principles against wealth discrimination to just two cases, *Griffin* in 1956 and *Douglas* in 1963, both of which concerned appellate criminal processes, it was not completely clear that the Court had firmly and finally concluded that the Equal Protection Clause protects the poor from governmental discrimination.

The issue was resolved a decade later in 1973 when the Court decided a case concerning financing for public education (*San Antonio Independent School District v. Rodriguez*). In the education case, two neighboring school districts generated significantly different financial resources for public education in the Texas property tax system that funded schools. The district with the higher tax rate had many poor people and low property values. Thus, this district generated significantly less money per pupil than the affluent district with wealthy residents and high property values, despite the wealthy district's lower tax rate. The formula used by Texas to provide additional state money for school districts compounded the disparity by giving larger sums per pupil to the more affluent district. One of the arguments presented by the parents who challenged the system for funding public schools in Texas was that the property value and tax revenue disparities between districts containing poor people and districts containing affluent people constituted a violation of equal protection by discriminating against the poor. In a narrow five-to-four decision, the Supreme Court rejected the challenge to the Texas education-financing scheme. The majority declared that there is no constitutional right to education guaranteed by the Constitution. Moreover, the majority declined to apply the strict scrutiny test on behalf of the poor to examine the alleged discrimination in the Texas system. Instead, Justice Lewis Powell's majority opinion declared that "A century of Supreme Court adjudication under the

Equal Protection Clause affirmatively supports the application of the traditional standard of review, which requires only the State's system be shown to bear some rational relationship to legitimate state purposes" (*San Antonio Independent School District v. Rodriguez* 1973, 40). The majority concluded that judicial intervention would constitute improper interference into "an area which it has traditionally deferred to state legislatures" (*San Antonio Independent School District v. Rodriguez*). In effect, the Court established that the Equal Protection Clause provides no special protection against state-sponsored discrimination associated with social status and wealth. The majority of justices refused to treat discrimination against the poor as deserving of constitutional prohibition in the same manner as discrimination by race, gender, or national origin. Thus, state laws can discriminate against the poor as long as those laws embody a "rational" approach to pursuing a legitimate governmental purpose. In the decades following the *San Antonio* case, the Court's opinion has been regarded as precluding the possibility that the Equal Protection Clause would be used to closely examine and invalidate state laws and policies that disadvantage the poor.

In the years following 1973, the Court's composition did not change in ways that increased the likelihood of expanded equal protection rights for the poor. Because conservative Republican presidents nominated six of the eight justices appointed to the court from 1973 through the end of the century, the dissenters in *San Antonio* had no chance to gain the additional vote that they needed to overturn the decision and give a more expansive reading to the Equal Protection Clause. Indeed, the four dissenters (Brennan, White, Douglas, Marshall) all left the Court within twenty years after *San Antonio*, and only one of them, White, was replaced by a justice (Ruth Bader Ginsburg) who was as or more liberal in interpreting the Equal Protection Clause.

In the criminal law process, *Griffin* and *Douglas* still stand, but their basis as equal protection precedents has been cast into doubt. In the immediate aftermath of *San Antonio*, the Supreme Court faced the question of whether indigent appellants are entitled to representation in all appeals, including those beyond the first appeal of right addressed in the *Douglas* case. The majority opinion by Justice Rehnquist denied that any such right existed beyond the first appeal. Thus, indigent criminal appellants in North Carolina were not entitled to representation for discretionary appeals to their state supreme court (*Ross v. Moffitt* 1974) The lack of representation for these indigents did not violate the constitutional rights to equal protection, due process, or counsel. In explaining the majority's reasoning, Rehnquist emphasized the weakness of *Griffin* and *Douglas* as equal protection precedents by arguing that they did not clearly rest on the Equal Protection Clause. According to Rehnquist,

> The precise rationale for the *Griffin* and *Douglas* lines of cases has never been explicitly stated, some support being derived from the Equal Protection Clause of the Fourteenth Amendment, and some from the Due Process Clause of that Amendment. Neither Clause by itself provides an entirely satisfactory basis for the result reached, each depending on a different inquiry which emphasizes different factors. (*Ross v. Moffitt* 1974, 608–609)

In examining the equal protection claim concerning indigent appellants' alleged right to representation in North Carolina, Rehnquist cited *San Antonio* as the precedent that justified limiting the application of the Equal Protection Clause in the criminal law process: "Despite the tendency of all rights to 'declare themselves absolute to their logical extreme,' there are obviously limits beyond which the equal protection analysis may not be pressed without doing violence to principles recognized in other decisions of this Court. The Fourteenth Amendment 'does not require absolute equality or precisely equal advantages,' *San Antonio Independent School District v. Rodriguez*, 411 U.S. 1, 24 (1973)…" (*Ross v. Moffitt*, 611–612).

In a subsequent decision indicating that the Sixth Amendment right to counsel applies only in trial courts and not in the appellate process, the Court indicated that the limited entitlement to appellate counsel established in *Douglas* rests primarily on the Fourteenth Amendment right to due process rather than on the right to equal protection (*Martinez v. Court of Appeal of California* 2000). Thus, the importance of *Griffin v. Illinois* and *Douglas v. California* as equal protection precedents has been diminished even further.

By limiting the utility of the Equal Protection Clause as a means to address discrimination and disparities adversely affecting the poor in the criminal law process, the Court forced attorneys and lower courts to look to other provisions of the Constitution as possible sources of relevant rights.

The Right to Counsel and the Poor

The criminal law process in the United States is based on the adversarial model. Unlike the court systems in European countries and elsewhere in which judges take an active role in questioning witnesses and seeking the truth about a defendant's guilt, the adversarial model presumes that the truth about guilt and innocence will emerge from the courtroom clash between prosecutors and defense attorneys. Thus, the availability and effectiveness of defense representation are key elements in the operation of the American system.

For most of American history, the right to counsel in the Sixth Amendment applied only in federal courts. Until the Supreme Court fully incorporated the right to counsel in the 1960s, there was no right to counsel in state criminal cases unless a particular state's legislature or supreme court had created such a right under state statutes or the state constitution. In the federal courts, the right to counsel meant only that the prosecution could not prevent a defendant from obtaining a defense attorney, provided the defendant could afford to hire one. Thus, the Sixth Amendment right to counsel had little meaning for poor defendants in the federal courts until 1938 when the Supreme Court interpreted the provision to require the government to appoint a defense attorney to represent indigent defendants facing serious charges in federal court (*Johnson v. Zerbst* 1938). Throughout the United States, indigent defendants had been forced to represent themselves despite having no capacity to gather evidence while sitting in jail, no knowledge of evidentiary rules and court procedures, and no understanding of the elements of proof in the criminal law process. The complete mismatches between the professional prosecutor and the defendant, who frequently had little formal education, made a mockery of the ideal of the adversary system and did nothing to ensure that innocent people were not wrongly convicted of crimes.

The Supreme Court used the Due Process Clause of the Fourteenth Amendment to make the first expansion of entitlement to counsel for state court defendants. In *Powell v. Alabama* (1932), the Court decided that states must provide defense attorneys for indigent defendants facing the death penalty who are incapable of representing themselves. Three decades later, in *Gideon v. Wainwright* (1963), the Court incorporated the Sixth Amendment right to counsel by requiring states to appoint defense attorneys for indigent defendants facing serious charges in state courts. In taking this step, the Supreme Court was neither leading nor pushing the nation to achieve the ideal of equal justice for the poor. Instead, the Court was merely belatedly following the trend established by more than forty state legislatures and court systems that had already implemented the poor defendants' right to representation in courts within their own borders (Lewis 1964). The Supreme Court's decision in *Gideon* merely forced the remaining half-dozen southern states that required indigent felony defendants to represent themselves in court to catch up with the rest of the country.

In 1972, the Supreme Court expanded the right to counsel to all cases in which the indigent defendant faced the possibility of incarceration, rather than merely limiting the right to serious cases in which the potential sentence was six months or more of imprisonment (*Argersinger v. Hamlin* 1972). However, as noted above, the Court limited the application of a right to appointed counsel on appeal by interpreting the rights to due process and equal protection to limit such entitlements to the first appeal of right and not to subsequent discretionary appeals (*Douglas v. California* 1963; *Ross v. Moffitt* 1974). There is also no right to counsel in post-appeal habeas corpus processes, the traditional legal mechanisms through which people convicted in state courts can ask a federal judge to evaluate whether federal constitutional rights were violated in the course of the investigation, prosecution, and trial of their cases (*Murray v. Giarratano* 1989). In addition, the Court limited the right to trial counsel in cases in which the defendant faced only a fine rather than the possibility of incarceration (*Scott v. Illinois* 1979). Justice Rehnquist's majority opinion asserted that the Court had moved far beyond the Sixth Amendment's original intention of guaranteeing representation in federal cases and that the imposition of a blanket right-to-counsel requirement in all criminal cases, even the most minor ones, would be burdensome, costly, and confusing for the states. He concluded that the deprivation of liberty through incarceration imposes a very different kind of punishment than mere fines for minor offenses, and therefore provision of counsel was justified for defendants facing the possibility of jail or prison but not for other defendants. In limiting the right to trial counsel in this fashion, Rehnquist underestimated the impact of a conviction on poor defendants, even when incarceration is not imposed. Defendants who are not represented by attorneys are, *ipso facto*, at greater risk of being wrongly convicted because of the adversarial process's reliance on professional defense attorneys to investigate and challenge the prosecutor's presentation of evidence. Poor defendants who lack representation as a result of the *Scott* decision find themselves thrust back to an earlier era in American history in which they are virtually defenseless against the substantial investigatory resources and presumed credibility of the police as well as the expertise in law and court procedure possessed by professional prosecutors. Even if a defendant is merely forced to pay a small fine as punishment, an erroneous conviction can have powerful effects on a person's life. A criminal record stigmatizes people and frequently hinders their opportunities for obtaining employment, professional licenses, and credit. Because middle-class and affluent people can afford to hire attorneys to represent them in so-called minor cases for which fines are the mandated punishment, they are not subject to the same risks of stigma and lingering harm from an erroneous criminal conviction. In addition, middle-class and affluent people can afford to hire attorneys to represent them in appeals and habeas corpus processes that provide the corrective mechanisms to undo errors by trial courts, including erroneous convictions. As noted above, indigent defendants are only entitled to representation in their initial appeal from a conviction for an offense that is punishable by incarceration. Thus, the Supreme Court's decision in *Scott* as well as the decision in *Ross v. Moffitt* exacerbate rather than diminish the risk of unequal, disadvantageous outcomes for poor people charged with criminal offenses.

The foregoing cases determined *if* defense attorneys would be appointed. Ostensibly, the Supreme Court's decisions have advanced the ideal of equal justice under the adversarial system in most trial courts by providing indigent defendants with attorneys who will undertake professional advocacy and counteract the advantages long enjoyed by the prosecution. In addition to the flaws in the Court's advancement of equal justice stemming from the application of these rights only to defendants facing incarceration at trial and first appeals of right, there are additional problems that create disadvantages for poor defendants. One problem concerns *when* the defense attorney is provided for the indigent defendant. If the attorney is appointed too late in the process, the defendant may suffer from significant disadvantages and even irreparable harm to the protection of important rights and interests. A second problem concerns the quality of representation. If there are inadequate mechanisms for oversight and weak standards for quality control, then the right to counsel is an illusory promise that falls short of fulfilling the essential elements of the adversarial process.

The Supreme Court addressed the issue of when counsel should be appointed in the famous *Miranda* case in 1966 (*Miranda v. Arizona*). In *Miranda*, the Warren Court required that police officers inform people of their rights before questioning them after they had been taken into custody. Prior to custodial questioning, suspects and arrestees must be informed of their right to appointed counsel if they are indigent and their right to have counsel present during questioning. The decision was based on both the Fifth Amendment privilege against compelled self-incrimination and the Sixth Amendment right to counsel. In *Miranda* and its companion cases, Chief Justice Warren's majority opinion emphasized the vulnerability of indigent suspects subjected to police questioning: "The potentiality for compulsion is forcefully apparent, for example, in *Miranda*, where the indigent Mexican defendant was a seriously disturbed individual with pronounced sexual fantasies, and in *Stewart*, in which the defendant was an indigent Los Angeles Negro who had dropped out of school in the sixth grade" (*Miranda v. Arizona* 1966, 457). Thus, Warren implied that the decision was needed, in part, to protect poor defendants who lack the knowledge and sophistication to preserve their own rights against the psychological ploys and physical coercion employed by police officers during questioning.

The Supreme Court further defined the moments when defendants are entitled to representation in *United States v. Wade* (1967). In *Wade*, a man arrested for robbing a bank was placed in an identification lineup without notice to and outside of the presence of his attorney. Bank employees picked him out of the lineup as the robber. The Court ruled that the man was entitled to have his attorney present at the lineup. The Court's decision relied on a recognition that witness misidentification is a major source of erroneous convictions and that police and prosecutors contribute to erroneous identifications by making suggestive statements and presentations to witnesses. According to Justice Brennan's majority opinion, "A major factor contributing to the high incidence of miscarriage of justice from mistaken identification has been the degree of suggestion inherent in the manner in which the prosecution presents the suspect to witnesses for pretrial identification" (*United States v. Wade* 1967, 228). With a defense attorney present, it would be more difficult for police to influence the identification process by, for example, pointing to one suspect in the lineup and saying, "That's the guy, isn't it?" rather than permitting the witness to make his or her own independent decision.

In *Wade*, the Court attempted to enunciate a principle to guide recognition of the points in the criminal law process in which a person is entitled to be represented by counsel. According to Brennan's opinion, "[O]ur cases have construed the Sixth Amendment guarantee to apply to 'critical' stages of the [criminal law] proceedings" (*United States v. Wade* 1967, 224). In attempting to define the concept of "critical stages," Brennan said that "the accused is guaranteed that he need not stand alone against the State at any stage of the prosecution, formal or informal, in court or out, where counsel's absence might derogate from the accused's right to a fair trial" (*United States v. Wade* 1967, 226). Because so many things can happen at each stage of the criminal law process, Brennan's opinion seemed to imply that indigent defendants (and other defendants) are entitled to be represented counsel throughout the various stages of the process. However, Brennan's conception of "critical stages" did not endure.

The *Wade* decision came at the close of the Warren Court era, and within five years of that decision, four Warren Court justices had retired and been replaced by more conservative jurists appointed by President Richard Nixon. When Nixon campaigned in the 1968 presidential election, he frequently criticized the Warren Court for being "soft" on crime and giving too many constitutional rights to criminals. He promised to appoint "law and order" justices to the Supreme Court who would diminish the scope of criminal defendants' rights and give more authority to police officers (Epstein & Walker 1992). Nixon's four appointees, Warren Burger, William Rehnquist, Harry Blackmun, and Lewis Powell began to turn the Court's criminal justice decisions in a new direction during the 1970s.

By 1972, it was quite clear that the "critical stages" concept had been limited in a manner that would give criminal suspects greater vulnerability than that envisioned by the Warren Court's decision in *Wade*. In *Kirby v. Illinois* (1972), the Court limited the right to counsel at identification procedures to only those contexts in which the arrestee had been charged with a crime. In *Kirby*, the suspect was under arrest and seated at a table at the police station when the witness was brought to the station to identify him. Justice Potter Stewart's plurality opinion concluded that the defendant's full constitutional rights need not be applied until a formal decision to prosecute has been made through the charging of the defendant with a crime. Stewart's opinion indicated that the defendant does not really face the authority of the state and thereby need complete legal protections until the defendant has been charged with a crime:

> The initiation of judicial criminal proceedings is far from a mere formalism. It is the starting point of our whole system of adversary criminal justice. For it is only then that the government has committed itself to prosecute, and only then that the adverse positions of the government and defendant have solidified. It is then that a defendant finds himself faced with the prosecutorial forces of organized society, and immersed in the intricacies of substantive procedural criminal law. (*Kirby v. Illinois* 1972, 689)

Stewart's reasoning seemed to fly in the face of *Miranda*'s concerns about adverse impacts on suspects' rights at the very outset of the criminal law process. Moreover, Stewart's opinion gave no attention to the fact that the same risks of misidentifications and miscarriages of justice that concerned the Court in *Wade* also exist in identification procedures that occur prior to a formal charging decision. The *Kirby* decision did not overturn *Wade* because the defendant in *Wade* had been indicted before the lineup occurred. Instead, the *Kirby* decision strictly limited the "critical stages" concept discussed in *Wade* and, in effect, sent a message to police officers that they could avoid having a defense attorney protect the rights of suspects at lineups and other identification procedures merely by conducting those procedures before filing formal charges. Because of the diminution of the "critical stage" concept, indigent defendants lack a right to representation at important moments, such as bail hearings, which will affect their liberty interests, their ability to assist in the preparation of the defense, and the ultimate odds of successfully defending against the charges (Colbert 1998).

Other decisions also reduced the applicability and effectiveness of the Warren Court's decisions that sought to provide counsel for suspects and defendants in order to protect constitutional rights. For example, in *Moran v. Burbine* (1986), the Court declared that police officers have no obligation to inform a suspect that a specific defense attorney has already informed the police that he or she will represent the suspect during custodial questioning. The suspect must take the initiative to ask for an attorney. Moreover, the Court permitted police officers to lie to the defense attorney by saying that the suspect would not be questioned until the following day when, in fact, the suspect was subsequently questioned during the night. In dissent, Justice Stevens protested that the Court was permitting the police to interfere with communications between attorneys and clients, thereby undermining the core element of the adversarial process. According to Stevens,

> This case turns on a proper appraisal of the role of the lawyer in our society. If a lawyer is seen as a nettlesome obstacle to the pursuit of wrongdoers—as in an

inquisitorial society—then the Court's decision makes a good deal of sense. If a lawyer is seen as an aid to the understanding and protection of constitutional rights—as in an accusatorial society—then today's decision makes no sense at all. (*Moran v. Burbine* 1986, 468)

In another example of the diminution of the right to counsel, the Court decided that police officers can change the content of *Miranda* warnings, even if the new form of the warnings may confuse indigent suspects about the nature of their right to appointed representation during questioning (*Duckworth v. Eagan* 1989). As they delivered the required *Miranda* warnings, the police officers in the case added that a lawyer would be appointed to represent the suspect "if and when you go to court." Chief Justice Rehnquist's majority opinion claimed that the original *Miranda* decision did not require the officers to use any specific words in informing suspects of their rights. Four dissenting justices, however, complained that the warning delivered in the case would mislead a suspect into thinking that she could not get an attorney until she got to court when, in fact, *Miranda* required that she be provided with an attorney upon request prior to any custodial questioning.

In addition to Supreme Court decisions since 1970 that have limited the scope and applicability of the right to counsel for indigent defendants, police practices have also diminished the effectiveness of the Warren Court's original protective intentions in *Miranda*. Police officers have adapted to the *Miranda* requirements by developing techniques and strategies for gaining incriminating statements without defense attorneys impeding suspects' self-incrimination (Leo 1996). These techniques include questioning suspects before they are formally arrested, such as standing on the street or on a doorstep, since *Miranda* only applies to *custodial* interrogations. Officers also lie to suspects during questioning by falsely telling them about evidence they have gathered that demonstrate guilt and then offering to "go easy on them" if they confess immediately. Officers also pretend to befriend suspects during questioning in order to induce them to waive their right to counsel. Imagine if a nervous, bewildered suspect in an assault is told the following by the police: "We understand that people can make you so mad sometimes that you just can't avoid striking out at them. It has happened to all of us. But since you're not really guilty of a real crime, why do you need a lawyer to represent you? Why don't you just tell us what happened? Don't worry. We understand." Although the Court has reiterated that *Miranda* remains the law of the land (*Dickerson v. United States* 2000), police adaptations and Supreme Court decisions diminishing its application have reduced its protective impact for poor defendants. Thus, the question of "when" defense attorneys are appointed to represent indigent defendants has been answered in ways that continue to give police flexibility and to make defendants vulnerable to situations in which their rights will not be fully protected. Some of these situations may increase the risk of erroneous convictions when they reduce the likelihood that defense attorneys will be present during identification procedures and when they permit police to have more opportunities to question suspects outside of the presence of counsel.

Effective Assistance of Counsel

Criminal defendants face serious deprivations of their liberty and, in some cases, even the loss of their lives. If attorneys do not perform in a competent, professional manner, then the right to counsel is merely a symbolic gesture that does little to protect the rights and interests of defendants in the adversarial criminal law process. Thus, it is important to ensure that the attorneys representing defendants meet specified standards for professional performance. This issue is especially crucial for poor defendants served by public defenders and appointed counsel because they cannot fire their attorneys and select new counsel if they are dissatisfied with a lawyer's performance. They did not choose their attorneys and they cannot change attorneys. In effect, they may be captive clients for whomever the judge or county selects to represent them.

The Supreme Court has done little to ensure that attorneys provide effective representation in criminal cases. During the Burger Court era (1969–1986), the Supreme Court indicated its reluctance to actively address the difficult issue of defining minimal performance standards for the effectuation of the Sixth Amendment right to counsel. The Burger-era justices established vague, minimal standards for attorneys' performance that made it nearly impossible for any defendants to demonstrate that their attorneys' actions had been so inadequate as to produce a violation of the constitutional right to counsel. In *Strickland v. Washington* (1984), the Court said that attorneys must perform reasonably under prevailing professional norms but that judicial scrutiny of an attorney's performance must be highly deferential to the attorney. According to Justice O'Connor's majority opinion, "counsel is strongly presumed to have rendered adequate assistance and made all significant decisions in the exercise of reasonable professional judgment" (*Strickland v. Washington* 1984, 690). With respect to attorney performance, the Court spoke of a vague standard involving "reasonable" investigations and advocacy, but simultaneously warned judges not to look too closely nor second-guess attorneys' strategic choices and actions (or inactions). In addition, even if the attorney's performance is somehow outside of the range of reasonableness, the defendant must also show that "there is a reasonable probability that, but for counsel's unprofessional errors, the result of the proceeding would have been different" (*Strickland v. Washington* 1984, 694). Both of these elements, unreasonably poor performance and errors that probably changed the outcome of the case, are extraordinarily difficult for defendants for prove. Moreover, the justices indicated in *United States v. Cronic* (1984) that general complaints about an attorney's poor overall performance will not be sufficient for establishing ineffective assistance of counsel. Instead, the defendant must be able to point to specific errors made by the attorney that were unreasonable and prejudiced the outcome of the case.

Subsequent decisions have reinforced the message that the Supreme Court will rarely second-guess defense attorneys even when their decisions or inaction clearly had an adverse impact on the defendant's case. For example, the Rehnquist Court rejected a claim that an attorney demonstrated ineffective assistance of counsel in a death penalty case by failing to present mitigating evidence during the sentencing hearing prior to imposition of the death penalty (*Burger v. Kemp* 1987). In capital cases, prosecutors present evidence concerning aggravating factors that make the crime or defendant seem worse than other crimes and defendants in order to argue for capital punishment. Defense attorneys are supposed to counteract the prosecutor's presentation with evidence of mitigation, such as information about the defendant's age, IQ, or difficult family circumstances that make the defendant or less crime horrible than those in other cases and therefore deserving of incarceration rather than death. When defense attorneys do not present evidence to oppose the prosecutor's arguments, there may be little reason for judges or juries not to impose a death sentence. In another case, the justices rejected a defendant's ineffective assistance of counsel claim in a case in which he might have received life in prison instead of a death sentence if his attorney had raised an appropriate objection to an improperly presented aggravating factor (*Lockhart v. Fretwell* 1993).

Critics of the Court's vague, deferential standards have ridiculed them as equaling a "mirror test": You put a mirror under the court-appointed attorney's nose, and if the mirror clouds up to demonstrate that the attorney is alive and breathing, that constitutes adequate representation (Bright, Kinnard, & Webster 1990). Because of the weak performance standards, examples arise with troubling regularity in which attorneys' actions were unquestionably detrimental to their clients' interests, yet the courts do not necessarily find the existence of constitutionally deficient, ineffective assistance of counsel. For example, the attorney for a woman facing a death sentence for murdering her abusive husband in Alabama not only failed to obtain hospital records to show the injuries that his client suffered from her husband's abuse, the attorney was also so drunk during the trial that he was found in contempt of court and held in jail overnight until he was sober enough to continue the trial the next day (Lacayo 1992; Bright 1994). Not surprisingly, the defendant was convicted and sentenced to death. A court-appointed attorney for capital defendants in Texas became well known for how quickly he moved his client's cases along through trial—not for his success in representing defendants. He bragged that he spent little time doing legal research or even taking notes (Barrett 1994). Other attorneys in death penalty cases have admitted that they never read their state's capital punishment statute, failed to cite any cases in appellate briefs, and failed to talk to their clients before filing appeals (Gershman 1993). The lax standards created by the Supreme Court have led other judges to the point of declaring that a defendant is not necessarily denied his right to counsel when his defense attorney falls asleep on numerous occasions during a capital murder trial (*Burdine v. Johnson* 2001). If standards are so low that judges must debate whether or not a sleeping attorney provides ineffective assistance to his or her indigent client, then clearly many defendants will be poorly served by their defense lawyers without the Supreme Court providing any meaningful remedy or support through its interpretation of the Sixth Amendment right to counsel.

For poor defendants, the risks of ineffective assistance are exacerbated by the myriad systems in place for appointing and compensating defense counsel for indigents. In counties where attorneys appointed to represent indigent defendants are assigned to cases by elected judges, there are risks that appointments will be based on political patronage rather than experience and expertise. In one Ohio county, for example, the local judges were authorized to bypass experienced and knowledgeable public defenders for death-penalty murder cases and award the cases, with the accompanying $12,500 state-paid fee, to private attorneys who did not necessarily possess significant interest and experience in such legal matters (Torassa 1993). In other locales, low fees may discourage experienced attorneys from accepting cases. Thus, indigent defendants may find their fates determined by inexperienced or unsuccessful attorneys who need to acquire experience or income in any manner that they can (Coyle 1990). The compensation, experience, and commitment of defense counsel can make a major difference in the attainment, or lack thereof, of equal justice. The news media regularly discover examples of poor defendants whose representation by less than stellar attorneys produced miscarriages of justice. For example, Federico Martinez Macias spent nearly 10 years on death row after he was convicted of capital murder in Texas at a trial in which his court-appointed attorney, who was paid only $11.84 per hour, spent only $500 on investigation and expert witnesses, and failed to present testimony from an alibi witness who placed Macias miles from the crime scene at the time of the murder. Macias was convicted based on the testimony of an admitted participant in the robbery-murder who was permitted to plead guilty to lesser charges in exchange for his agreement to identify the "real" killer.

When a prominent Washington, D.C., law firm eventually volunteered to handle the postconviction defense proceedings, Macias gained his freedom after his new lawyers devoted significant resources and expertise to investigating the case thoroughly and presenting new evidence to an appellate court (Cohen 1995).

A key element in the attainment of the ideal of equal justice would be the creation and maintenance of a system to ensure that indigent defendants receive high-quality legal representation. Such a system would require sufficient resources to permit indigent defendants to have experienced attorneys, access to investigators, and compensation for expert witnesses. Under the concept of federalism in the structure of American government, the design of indigent defense systems is left to state and local governments. However, the Supreme Court could affect the operation of those systems by giving greater substantive meaning to the Sixth Amendment right to counsel. As long as the Supreme Court's standards for determining ineffective assistance of counsel remain vague and weak, states and localities retain the freedom to pay minimal compensation to appointed counsel, impose unmanageable workloads on public defenders, and turn a blind eye to ineffective and incompetent lawyering that adversely affects the case outcomes for poor defendants.

Conclusion

"Equal justice under law" remains an unfulfilled slogan for many poor people drawn into contact with the criminal justice system. The ability of defendants to protect their rights and interests in an adversarial criminal law process can depend on the resources and professional assistance available to them. Defendants who can afford to hire a defense attorney immediately after arrest can have professional assistance during identification procedures, bail hearings, early plea negotiations, pretrial discovery, and all of the important steps in the process. In addition, affluent defendants can secure the services of evidence testing laboratories, expert witnesses, private investigators, and jury consultants that enable them to match the expertise and resources that the prosecution will apply against them. By contrast, poor defendants may receive their only assistance from an underpaid appointed attorney, who may lack interest, commitment, knowledge, and experience in criminal law, or from an overworked public defender whose caseload of hundreds of clients precludes careful attention to each individual case (Smolowe 1993; Applebome 1992). Because the American adversary system of justice presumes that the truth will emerge from the clash between equally matched, opposing legal advocates, the disparity in resources and representation necessarily disadvantages poor defendants and presumably increases the likelihood of erroneous convictions.

The Supreme Court has done relatively little to interpret the Equal Protection Clause or Sixth Amendment right to counsel in ways that will advance the ideal of equal justice by ensuring that indigent defendants have access to sufficient resources and the quality of representation necessary to present an effective defense. After initially employing equal protection principles to advance poor defendants' access to appeals (*Griffin v. Illinois* 1956; *Douglas v. California* 1963), the Supreme Court ultimately determined that the Equal Protection Clause does not provide any special protection against governmental discrimination directed at people because of their wealth or social status (*San Antonio Independent School District v. Rodriguez* 1973). In effect, the Court has declared that the government may discriminate against the poor as long as it has a rational reason for doing so. Unlike any differential treatment against people because of their race or gender, unequal treatment of poor people by the government need not be justified by a "compelling" or "important" governmental interest.

The Sixth Amendment has served as the constitutional vehicle for providing resources for indigent defendants. However, the Supreme Court has not led the nation toward ensuring that these resources translate into the promise of equal justice. When the Supreme Court finally declared that all states must provide attorneys for indigent defendants facing serious charges (*Gideon v. Wainwright* 1963), it was merely following a policy that more than forty states had developed and implemented on their own (Lewis 1964). Although the Court expanded the entitlement to representation to all trial-level cases in which defendants face incarceration (*Argersinger v. Hamlin* 1972) and first appeals of right in state courts (*Douglas v. California* 1963), the changing composition of the Supreme Court in the 1970s led to limits on the right to representation. Thus, there is no right to legal representation for poor people in trials of minor offenses that are punishable only by fines (*Scott v. Illinois* 1979), discretionary appeals to courts of last resort (*Ross v. Moffitt* 1974), habeas corpus petitions (*Murray v. Giarratano* 1989), or prisoners' civil rights lawsuits. These contexts in which poor people must fend for themselves in the legal system, usually with few prospects for effectiveness or success, all involve legal proceedings that can have important impacts on the preservation of rights and liberty. In sum, the Court's definition of the contexts in which legal counsel will be appointed has been inadequate for the purpose of advancing the purported goal of equal justice under law.

In addition, the Supreme Court's decisions about the timing of the provision of counsel within the criminal law process have created disadvantages for poor defendants. The Court's original definition of "critical stages" as defining the crucial moments when defense attorneys should be present (*United States v. Wade* 1967) has been diluted to such an extent that attorneys need not be provided for pre-indictment identification procedures or bail hearings, despite the importance of such events for the ultimate fate of the defendant (Colbert 1998). The Court's landmark decision in *Miranda v. Arizona* (1966) mandating appointment of counsel on request prior to custodial questioning has been undercut by other decisions that permit police officers to deceive defense attorneys about when questioning will occur (*Moran v. Burbine* 1986) and to change the nature of the *Miranda* warnings (*Duckworth v. Eagan* 1989). In addition, police have adapted to the *Miranda* requirements by developing techniques to gain incriminating statements without interference by defense attorneys.

Even when defense attorneys are provided for poor defendants at a particular point in the criminal law process, the Supreme Court's weak and vague standards for assessing constitutionally deficient ineffective assistance of counsel ensure that unequal treatment and inconsistent outcomes will be pervasive throughout the legal system. The Court's reluctance to second-guess the decisions, actions, and inaction of defense attorneys means that many defendants are doomed to suffer adverse consequences, including the unnecessary loss of liberty and rights, as a result of attorneys who are disinterested, unprepared, and even asleep in court.

The Supreme Court lacks the authority to address the general societal problems of poverty and income inequality in American society. Within its own bailiwick, however, the Court possesses the authority to interpret and apply the Equal Protection Clause and the Sixth Amendment in ways that will help to ensure that poor people receive greater fairness and equality in the criminal law process. In light of the "Equal Justice Under Law" slogan that literally hovers above the justices' heads at their place of work and permeates the rhetoric of judicial decisions, the Court's actions that prevent the application of equal protection principles and limit the provision of legal resources and representation for the poor are especially disappointing. The Court's tolerance of obvious and pervasive unequal treatment for the poor does not merely reinforce the message that "equal justice" is nothing more than a symbolic slogan; it also conveys the idea that the justices share society's acceptance of unequal treatment for the poor as a natural or inevitable component of the social order.

6

Convicted Offenders
and Equal Justice

WHEN A CRIME has been committed, one definition of the attainment of justice might be the identification, conviction, and punishment of the perpetrator of the illegal act. This definition reflects the underlying purposes of the criminal law, usually stated as protecting public safety through the use of the state's coercive power to punish misconduct. This is not, however, the only conception of justice evident within the legal framework of the American constitutional democracy. With respect to the U.S. Constitution's role in the criminal justice system, the attainment of justice extends beyond the imposition of punishment. The Constitution provides limitations on governmental actions and, simultaneously, provides protections for individuals against actions by government officials that violate the conceptions of liberty and equality embodied in the nation's fundamental legal document. These protections purport to extend even to those who have harmed society.

It would be relatively unremarkable to observe people with status, money, or political connections within a society receiving the benefits of legal protections. These people have access to resources, influence over decision makers, and the ability to create adverse consequences for officials who do not obey the dictates of law in handling criminal cases. However, one hallmark of the constitutional system governing the United States is the claim that the law applies equally to *all* people. The idea that the laws apply equally is, in the abstract, an appealing notion. Indeed, it sounds like an attractive, idealistic slogan when stated publicly or taught as part of the curriculum in schools. A particularly significant test of the validity of this idea comes when it is applied to the nation's most reviled minority: convicted offenders. This politically powerless minority has earned its despised status through actions that harm society. Thus, the rights—or lack thereof—extended to these individuals provide a revealing illustration of the justice system's commitment to its own espoused ideals. To what extent is "Equal Justice Under Law" provided for those who have broken the law?

Convicted Offenders and Constitutional Rights

Many Americans wonder why convicted offenders are entitled to any constitutional protections. Indeed, it is logical to ask why people who have violated the laws of society should not thereby forfeit any entitlement to protection under those laws. Such an analysis relies on a "social contract" approach to understanding constitutional rights. Under a social contract framework, individuals have an implicit social contract with society in which they agree to abide by society's rules in exchange for the benefits of membership in society, including the protections of society's laws. It would be possible to establish a system of rights premised on such reciprocal obligations between individuals and society. However, the U.S. Constitution is not written in terms of reciprocal obligations. Instead, the U.S. Constitution is written in "natural rights" terms that provide legal protections for everyone without explicit exceptions. The Constitution presents rights as legal entitlements possessed by all individuals, no matter what their status in society and no matter what behavior they have undertaken. For example, like other rights in the Constitution, the Fourteenth Amendment right to equal protection of the laws does not include any caveats or conditions about being a law-abiding citizen. Moreover, the Eighth Amendment prohibition in cruel and unusual punishments is clearly intended to provide protections for those individuals who are subjected to governmental sanctions, including sanctions meted out for violating criminal laws. Although judges possess the authority to interpret the Constitution in ways that limit and, in effect, eliminate the practical benefits of these legal protections, the Constitution itself conveys the idea that protections extend to criminal offenders.

It is not surprising to recognize that the Constitution includes protections for lawbreakers as well as law-abiding citizens. The authors of the Constitution and their like-minded civic leaders in the various states had themselves been "lawbreakers" in the eyes of the British government little more than a decade before the creation of the nation's legal charter. Based on their experience in resisting British authorities, the founders were skeptical of governmental power and intent upon protecting fundamental elements of liberty for individuals who fell out of favor with governmental officials. They recognized that individuals who criticized or sought to change governmental policies were often labeled as "criminals" and treated as such by governmental authorities throughout the world. To guard against the mistreatment of individuals and governmental efforts to squelch dissent, the rights within the Constitution are presented broadly, as if they are legal entitlements for every human being. Certainly, constitutional rights have not always been interpreted and applied in such a broad fashion. However, the language of the document, including specific rights for criminal defendants in the Sixth (e.g., confrontation, counsel, trial, and so forth) and Eighth Amendments (e.g., cruel and unusual punishments, excessive bail, excessive fines), demonstrate quite clearly that the framers envisioned legal protections applying to criminal offenders as a matter of course and not being forfeited by virtue of violating some unspecified social contract.

History of the Eighth Amendment

The Eighth Amendment prohibition on cruel and unusual punishments provides the Constitution's clearest textual commitment to legal protections for criminal offenders. Other Amendments also effectively apply to criminal offenders. But most of these rights, such as the Sixth Amendment right to trial by jury, are specifically applied to presumptively innocent defendants whose guilt and status as offenders have not yet been established according to the standards set by law. Although the precise meaning of the ambiguous phrase "cruel and unusual punishments" must inevitably be developed through judicial interpretation, the phrase itself clearly indicates an intention to limit what the government can do in applying "punishments" to individuals.

Before the 1950s, the U.S. Supreme Court had little involvement in cases concerning the rights of criminal offenders. In the nineteenth century, the Supreme Court heard Eighth Amendment cases challenging methods of capital punishment, including public execution by firing squad (*Wilkerson v. Utah* 1879) and the newly invented electric chair (*In Re Kemmler* 1890), but the Court did not favor the offenders' claims. State courts were most relevant for such cases because the Supreme Court did not incorporate the Eighth Amendment for application to state criminal cases until the 1960s (*Robinson v. California* 1962). By contrast, since most states had prohibitions on cruel and unusual punishments in their state constitutions, state courts provided the appropriate forums in which to challenge issues concerning criminal offenders' rights (Berkson 1975). Although a few state courts responded favorably to offenders' legal challenges by, for example, ordering improvements in conditions and practices in jails or prisons (Wallace 1997), courts were generally unresponsive to legal claims seeking the protection of constitutional rights for convicted offenders. Judges deferred to correctional officials because of their presumed expertise in treating offenders (Robbins 1980). Thus, from the creation of corrections institutions in the nineteenth century and continuing through the 1960s, corrections officials generally ran their institutions as they wished with little regard for the possibility that convicted offenders might be entitled to legal protections. As a result, arbitrary decisions, discrimination, and violent actions by corrections officials were common in many institutions.

The U.S. Supreme Court's most important early decision favoring a constitutional rights claim by a criminal offender came in a case concerning the federal government so the issue of incorporation did not impede the Court's authority to interpret and apply the Eighth Amendment. In *Weems v. United States* (1910), the Court decided that the Eighth Amendment prohibited punishments that were disproportionate to the crime. Prior to this decision, the Court had treated the Eighth Amendment as if it only prevented punishments that could be equated with physical torture. In *Weems*, a disbursing officer for the Philippine Branch of the U.S. Bureau of the Coast Guard and Transportation was convicted for falsifying payroll records. The officer received a sentence of fifteen years at hard labor. The

Supreme Court compared the sentence applied to Weems with lesser sentences mandated by statutes for more serious violent offenses and found that his sentence violated the Eighth Amendment by being disproportionate to his offense.

Although the Court had announced that the Eighth Amendment prohibited punishments that were either disproportionate or torturous, the justices had not provided guidance about how lower court judges were to determine which punishments are prohibited. How can one tell when a punishment is disproportionate to the crime? How can one tell when a punishment is the equivalent of torture? Such questions are not easily answered. Thus, the Court sought to provide guidance with its decision in *Trop v. Dulles* (1958).

Albert Trop was a twenty-year-old, native-born American citizen who served in the U.S. military in North Africa during World War II. While stationed in French Morocco in 1944, he was confined to a military stockade for violating disciplinary rules. He escaped but changed his mind less than one day later and surrendered to U.S. Army personnel. A general court-martial convicted Trop of desertion and he received a sentence of three years at hard labor, forfeiture of pay, and a dishonorable discharge. Years later, after serving his sentence and returning to civilian life, Trop applied for a passport. He was denied a passport by the U.S. government because he and seven thousand other men had lost their citizenship under the Nationality Act of 1940, which mandated such forfeiture of citizenship for soldiers convicted of wartime desertion. He brought a claim to the U.S. Supreme Court alleging that loss of citizenship constituted a cruel and unusual punishment in violation of the Eighth Amendment.

The Supreme Court decided that forfeiture of citizenship under these circumstances was unconstitutionally cruel and unusual because "[i]t is a form of punishment more primitive than torture, for it destroys for the individual the political existence that was centuries in development....His very existence is at the sufferance of the country in which he happens to find himself" (*Trop v. Dulles* 1958, 101). The most important aspect of the majority opinion was Chief Justice Warren's articulation of a standard for interpreting and defining the Eighth Amendment. According to Warren, "the words of the Amendment are not precise, and... their scope is not static. The Amendment must draw its meaning from the evolving standards of decency that mark the progress of a maturing society" (Trop v. Dulles 1958, 100). The words "evolving standards of decency" are ambiguous, but they indicate that judicial officers are supposed to evaluate Eighth Amendment cruel and unusual punishment claims according to their assessments of contemporary societal standards. This definition, despite its vagueness, provided the guiding principle for judges making determinations about the constitutionality of criminal punishments.

The application of the Eighth Amendment to the states came in *Robinson v. California* (1962), a case that concerned the constitutionality of criminalizing drug addiction—as opposed to possession, use, or sales of illegal drugs—rather than issues of sentencing or prison policies that are the focus of most noncapital Eighth Amendment cases. Although the primary issue in *Robinson* was not of major importance for the rights of convicted offenders, the Supreme Court's incorporation of the Eighth Amendment in the case opened the door for federal courts throughout the country to hear cruel and unusual punishment claims from offenders in state prisons and local jails.

While *Robinson* officially applied the Eighth Amendment to the actions of state and local officials, other decisions provided the legal vehicles through which claims based on the Bill of Rights and Fourteenth Amendment could be initiated in federal district courts. In 1961, the Court made the federal Civil Rights Statute (42 United States Code section 1983) a powerful vehicle for citizen litigation by permitting civil rights lawsuits in the federal courts when there are claims that state officials have violated individuals' constitutional rights (*Monroe v. Pape* 1961). In effect, the Court resuscitated Reconstruction-era statutes that had lain dormant in the law books because courts during preceding decades had declined to recognize their constitutionality. Shortly thereafter, the Supreme Court explicitly granted convicted offenders in correctional institutions the opportunity to use federal civil rights statutes to file federal legal claims. In *Cooper v. Pate* (1964), the Court declared that prisoners could file federal lawsuits against corrections officials and facilities alleging violations of their constitutional rights. After more than a century and a half, during which time the U.S. Constitution had little applicability to the issue of equal justice and constitutional rights for convicted offenders, the U.S. Supreme Court's decisions in the 1960s made it possible for federal judges to hear and decide cases concerning prisoners' rights.

The Rise and Diminution of Personal Rights

According to James Jacobs (1983, 35), the movement to gain judicial recognition of the existence of constitutional rights for prisoners in the 1960s was part of a larger societal transformation in which various political minorities, including women, ethnic groups, and disabled people, "pressed for admission into the societal mainstream." Although other groups could utilize various political strategies, such as public demonstrations, electoral participation, and legislative lobbying, to achieve their policy goals and gain societal acceptance, incarcerated offenders had few opportunities to seek redress of grievances. Because other branches of government had no reason to be responsive to them, prisoners needed to use the litigation process to seek recognition of constitutional rights. The Supreme Court's decisions of the 1960s opened the door to prisoner civil rights lawsuits in the federal courts by creating the possibility that the U.S. Constitution would apply to all prisoners in both state and federal institutions.

Black Muslim prisoners were important pioneers in the effort to obtain judicial recognition and enforcement of a limited range of constitutional rights (King 1969). Cases filed by Muslim prisoners primarily concerned religious rights and racial discrimination. Thus, their claims asked courts to focus attention on both the Fourteenth Amendment's Equal Protection Clause and the First Amendment's Free Exercise Clause, the constitutional provision concerning the right to practice one's own religion.

Societies often perceive new and unfamiliar religious groups as threatening to the established social order (Beckford 1985). In the United States, the Black Muslims were initially similarly feared, condemned, and harassed. Their assertive rhetoric and hostility toward whites, in particular, led whites to fear their objectives and resulted in suspicion and harassment from government officials. In the early years of the religion's development, there were several instances in which law enforcement officials physically attacked Black Muslims or violated their rights against unreasonable search and seizure and thus generated successful lawsuits for civil damages by the Muslims (Essien-Udom 1962, 288). Black Muslims were typically regarded as members of dangerous gangs or cults when they attracted new recruits inside the walls of prisons. The assertiveness of the African American adherents to the religion threatened the traditional relationships and behavior within prisons. Prior to the 1960s and 1970s, prisons historically emphasized control by officials and compliance (albeit sometimes physically coerced) by prisoners. The Muslims' rhetoric, attitudes, and behavior clashed with this existing social order. As a result, according to James Jacobs (1977, 59–60), Muslim prisoners encountered vehement opposition from correctional officials:

> It is impossible to understand the vehemence and determination with which the prison resisted every Muslim demand, no matter how insignificant, except by understanding that what seemed to be at stake was the very survival of the authoritarian [prison] regime…. The officials countered by purging Muslims from their jobs, blocking their legitimate prison activities, and suppressing them whenever possible. Not surprisingly, many of the leaders ended up in segregation.

Prison officials initially admitted that Black Muslims did not enjoy the same opportunities to practice their religion as those possessed by Christian prisoners, yet judges rejected the Muslims' claims that this discrimination violated their constitutional rights. In an early California case (*In re Ferguson* 1961), although correctional officials acknowledged that they singled out the Muslims for discriminatory treatment by refusing to permit them to have the privileges for worshiping and studying church literature that were granted to all other religious groups, the state supreme court rejected the Muslims' claims concerning rights violations. The court concluded that the Muslims' philosophy and assertive behavior threatened the correctional institution and therefore the institution possessed the authority to deny them the opportunity to worship. A federal judge in New York characterized the Muslims as an organization dedicated to laying secret plans that were likely to lead to unrest among the prisoners (*Pierce v.*

LaVallee 1962). Another federal judge adopted, without examination, a report by the Intelligence Division of the Chicago Police Department, which asserted that the Muslims were dangerous (*Cooper v. Pate* 1963). These decisions reflected attitudes among officials that produced administrative and judicial decisions effectively precluding the Muslims from receiving equal treatment.

Eventually, courts began to recognize the Black Muslims as members of a religion and thereby prohibit corrections officials from discriminating against them. In the 1960s and 1970s, cases brought by Muslims succeeded in gaining recognition for several constitutional rights: opportunity to hold religious services (*Banks v. Havener* 1964); freedom from punishment because of religious faith (*Sewell v. Pegelow* 1961); possess and wear religious medals (*Coleman v. Dist. of Columbia Commissioners* 1964); and a limited right to proselytize (*Fulwood v. Clemmer* 1962). Muslim prisoners won a number of other cases involving First Amendment freedom of religion claims during the 1960s and 1970s (Palmer 1985). With the exception of the important U.S. Supreme Court decision in *Cooper v. Pate* (1964) that created the opportunity for prisoners to file civil rights cases in federal courts, the cases won by the Black Muslims were decided by lower federal courts and state courts. The nation's highest court had little involvement in litigation about the rights of convicted offenders until the 1970s. Instead, lower court judges led the way in applying the Constitution to convicted offenders' claims in order to address the issue of equal justice for prisoners.

The Muslims' legal cases led to decisions that have had a broader impact upon rights for all prisoners. For example, the decision in *Walker v. Blackwell* (1969) helped to limit correctional officials' discretionary power to arbitrarily ban literature as "inflammatory" without demonstrating the existence of an actual threat to institutional security. In a case initiated by a Muslim prisoner that has had especially significant impact, the court decision established limits upon the ability of corrections officials to interfere with correspondence between prisoners and their attorneys (*Sostre v. McGinnis* 1971). In addition, the same case helped to establish the principle that prisoners can recover monetary damages as compensation for the deprivation of constitutional rights. By endorsing the possibility of compensatory damages, the decision in *Sostre* created an incentive for corrections officials to comply with constitutional standards. As one measure of its importance, the decision in *Sostre* has been cited more than 650 times in subsequent cases (Smith 1993a).

The litigation efforts of Black Muslims opened opportunities for members of other religions to have the same access to religious materials, services, and clergy that had been enjoyed by Christian prisoners. The actions of lower court judges in support of the Black Muslims' claims eventually drew the implicit endorsement of the U.S. Supreme Court in a case in which a Buddhist prisoner claimed a denial of constitutional rights because he faced restrictions on his religious practices that prison officials did not apply to other prisoners' religions (*Cruz v. Beto* 1972). The Supreme Court also endorsed the application of the Equal Protection Clause to prohibit racial discrimination in prisons (*Lee v. Washington* 1968). In both of these cases, the justices merely upheld lower court decisions in brief *per curiam* opinions without providing any elaborate statement of the highest court's position on the nature and scope of prisoners' constitutional rights.

Prisoners' right to freely practice their religions under the First Amendment is not unlimited. Courts always balance the permissible extent of prisoners' rights against a correctional institution's need to maintain security and order (Smith 2000). This balancing of interests, which applies to all constitutional rights within corrections, leads to limitations on prisoners' rights. However, the recognition and protection of prisoners' rights, albeit in limited forms, altered the traditional judicial deference to corrections officials that had permitted those officials to use their discretion to grant or deny all rights and privileges to convicted offenders. In particular, judicial decisions required corrections officials to justify the reasons for limiting constitutional rights rather than automatically assuming that corrections officials' decisions were made for appropriate purposes. It is relatively easy for corrections officials to justify limitations on prisoners' Fourth Amendment rights against unreasonable searches and seizures. Corrections officials need to be sure that prisoners do not have weapons, drugs, or other contraband that can threaten security and order within the institution. Consequently, prisoners have little protection under the Fourth

Amendment, except with respect to intrusive and humiliating strip searches and body cavity searches which should require greater justification than cell searches and pat-down body frisks. By contrast, constitutional protections for religious practices and against racial discrimination under, respectively, the Free Exercise Clause and the Equal Protection Clause, do not inevitably collide with institutional safety and security. The Supreme Court originally left open the possibility of permitting temporary racial segregation in the aftermath of a hypothetical prison race riot and of precluding religious practices that threaten safety and security, but the protection of these constitutional rights is supposed to require that prison officials provide clear justifications for imposing limitations.

As the Supreme Court's composition changed during the Burger Court era (1969–1986) and the Rehnquist Court era (beginning in 1986) with the appointment of justices generally less protective of constitutional rights than their Warren Court predecessors, legal protections for prisoners were affected. For example, in 1979, the Court considered the case of *Bell v. Wolfish* in which prisoners confined to a federal jail in New York City brought forth various complaints about conditions and practices in a facility that held many presumptively innocent detainees being held pending trial. One practice challenged by the detainees was the application of body-cavity searches whenever a detainee met with a visitor. In an opinion by Justice William Rehnquist, the Supreme Court majority announced that "Balancing the significant and legitimate security interests of the institution against the privacy interests of the inmates, we conclude that they can [conduct the systematic strip searches and body-cavity inspections]" (*Bell v. Wolfish* 1979, 560). In a body-cavity search, corrections officials do not merely require detainees or prisoners to remove their clothes; they also make a close visual inspection of all body cavities. The justification for such intrusive and humiliating searches is the need to detect and discover hidden contraband that may have been passed from a visitor to a detainee and then secreted inside the detainee's body. When stated as a general matter, the justification for the search is understandable. However, when applied to the context of the case, it becomes less certain that the justification actually demonstrates the necessity of conducting systematic body-cavity inspections of all

detainees who have met with visitors. Doubts about the necessity of the
policy arise because of the application of such searches even in instances in
which there is no reason to suspect that the detainee obtained any
contraband. Instead, the acceptance of the blanket justification appears to
be a form of judicial deference to corrections officials, which symbolically
acknowledges the importance of rights by requiring a justification but
which, in effect, denigrates the effectuation of those rights by not giving
close scrutiny to the context of the justification and the application of the
policy. Justice Thurgood Marshall's dissenting opinion (quoted at length
below) revealed the nature of the Supreme Court's needless and
questionable diminution of detainees' constitutional rights:

> JUSTICE MARSHALL dissenting:
> In my view, the body-cavity searches of MCC inmates represent one of the
> most grievous offenses against personal dignity and common decency. After every
> contact visit with someone from outside the facility, including defense attorneys,
> an inmate must remove all of his or her clothing, bend over, spread the buttocks,
> and display the anal cavity for inspection by a correctional officer. Women
> inmates must assume a suitable posture for vaginal inspection, while men must
> raise their genitals. And, as the [majority] neglects to note, because of time
> pressures [during the search process], this humiliating spectacle is frequently
> conducted in the presence of other inmates.
> The District Court found that the stripping was "unpleasant, embarrassing,
> and humiliating." ...A psychiatrist testified that the practice placed inmates in the
> most degrading position possible.... a conclusion amply corroborated by the
> testimony of the inmates themselves.... There was evidence, moreover, that these
> searches engendered among detainees fears of sexual assault... were the occasion
> for actual threats of physical abuse by guards, and caused some inmates to forgo
> personal visits.
> Not surprisingly, the Government asserts a security justification for such
> inspections. These searches are necessary, it argues, to prevent inmates from
> smuggling contraband into the facility. In crediting this justification despite the
> contrary findings of the two courts below, the Court overlooks the critical facts.
> As respondents point out, inmates are required to wear one-piece jumpsuits with
> zippers in the front. To insert an object into the vaginal or anal cavity, an inmate
> would have to remove the jumpsuit, at least from the upper torso.... Since contact
> visits occur in a glass-enclosed room and are continuously monitored by
> corrections officers,... such a feat would seem extraordinarily difficult. There was
> medical testimony, moreover, that inserting an object into the rectum is painful

and "would require time and opportunity which is not available in the visiting areas,... and that visual inspection would probably not detect an object once inserted.... Additionally, before entering the visiting room, visitors and their packages are searched thoroughly by a metal detector, fluoroscope, and by hand.... Corrections officers may require that visitors leave packages or handbags with guards until the visit is over.... Only by blinding itself to the facts presented on this record can the Court accept the Government's security rationale.

That the Court [majority] can uphold these indiscriminate searches highlights the bankruptcy of its basic analysis. Under the test adopted today, the rights of detainees apparently extend only so far as detention officials decide that cost and security will permit. Such unthinking deference to administrative convenience cannot be justified where the interests at stake are those of presumptively innocent individuals, many of whose only proven offense is the inability to afford bail. (*Bell v. Wolfish*, 441 U.S. 520, 576-579, 1979)

As described in Justice Marshall's opinion, the detainees faced daunting practical obstacles if they wished to hide contraband in their body cavities. Because their interactions with visitors occurred under the observation of corrections officers and while they were wearing full-body jumpsuits, the practical effect of the policy was to subject presumptively innocent detainees to exceptionally invasive inspections, even when corrections officials had no reason to suspect that any wrongdoing had occurred. The Supreme Court effectively revealed an orientation toward judicial deference to corrections officials and nearly nonexistent Fourth Amendment legal protections for prisoners, even under circumstances in which institutional interests did not require such a diminution of rights.

In a similar fashion, the Supreme Court eventually applied its deferential approach to the issue of prisoners' First Amendment rights to free exercise of religion. The case of *O'Lone v. Estate of Shabazz* arose in 1987 during the Rehnquist Court era and concerned an assertion of rights by Muslim prisoners. In *O'Lone*, prisoners at a New Jersey facility who were classified as "gang minimum security" were required to work outside the prison walls in work details. Muslim prisoners requested that they be permitted either to work within the prison on Fridays, use Fridays as a non-work day, or return to the prison at one point during each Friday work day in order to attend Jumu'ah services. Muslim prisoners throughout the federal prison system are permitted to participate in Jumu'ah services each

Friday, and Muslim prisoners in this particular New Jersey prison had previously been permitted to remain inside the prison on Fridays in order to engage in this worship exercise that was central to their religious beliefs. However, prison officials changed the policy and subsequently forbade gang minimum prisoners from returning to the prison in order to participate in the service.

When the new policy was challenged by the Muslim prisoners, the U.S. Supreme Court voted five to four to reject their claim that their rights had been violated. Chief Justice Rehnquist's majority opinion followed a four-part test from a prior case that had rejected prisoners' claimed First Amendment free expression right to write letters to other prisoners (*Turner v. Safley* 1987). The first part of the test requires that the prison regulations colliding with the asserted rights must be logically connected to a legitimate government interest. In this case, the Supreme Court accepted the corrections officials' claim that order and security would be threatened if Muslim prisoners were permitted to return to the prison in order to attend Friday services. The second part of the test asks whether there are alternative means available to permit the prisoners to enjoy the asserted constitutional right. While conceding the "central importance of Jumu'ah" to the prisoners and acknowledging that there was no alternative way provided for them to participate in this key component of their religion's practices, the Court minimized the impact on the prisoners by asserting that they were "not deprived of all forms of religious exercise, but instead are free to observe a number of their religious obligations" (*O'Lone v. Estate of Shabazz* 1987, 351–352). Such reasoning raises important questions about the nature of religious rights. Should judges determine that some aspect of a prisoner's religious practice is not sufficiently important to require accommodation without making a close determination of whether such practices actually threaten order and security? At this prison, the officials' claims about order and security were questionable because they had previously accommodated Muslim prisoners' need to participate in Jumu'ah for the preceding five years without any adverse impact on the institution. There is also a question about whether the justices would actually permit corrections officials to cut out elements of other religions, particularly elements that are most important or familiar to the justices themselves. At the time of the *O'Lone* decision, the Court was comprised of Protestant and Catholic justices, including one justice, Antonin Scalia, whose Catholic religious beliefs appeared to play an especially important role in shaping his life (Kannar 1990). Would the justices actually permit corrections officials to block participation in Mass or Holy Communion for Catholic prisoners by saying, "That's okay. They still get to read the Bible sometimes"?

The other elements of the test applied by the Court ostensibly inquired about the possible impact on the prison of accommodating the asserted right and the availability of ready alternatives for fulfilling the right. The Court's opinion deferred to prison officials in rejecting the possibility of accommodating participation in Jumu'ah or developing alternatives for fulfillment of the right. Once again, the Court's approach effectively demonstrated strong deference to corrections officials and called into question the justices' commitment to safeguarding constitutional rights for convicted offenders. As described in Justice William Brennan's dissenting opinion on behalf of Justices Thurgood Marshall, Harry Blackmun, and John Paul Stevens, the majority opinion's reasoning and application of the *Turner* tests would not withstand scrutiny if the Court were truly committed to carefully effectuating convicted offenders' constitutional rights within the limitations appropriately imposed by the institution's legitimate interests in order and security:

> JUSTICE BRENNAN with whom JUSTICE MARSHALL, JUSTICE BLACKMUN, AND JUSTICE STEVENS join, dissenting:
> The religious ceremony that these respondents seek to attend is not presumptively dangerous, and the prison has completely foreclosed respondents' participation in it. I therefore would require prison officials to demonstrate that the restrictions they have imposed are necessary to further an important government interest, and that these restrictions are no greater than necessary to achieve prison objectives....
> Jumu'ah therefore cannot be regarded as one of several essentially fungible [replaceable with each other] religious practices. The ability to engage in other religious activities cannot obscure the fact that the denial at issue in this case is absolute: respondents are completely foreclosed from participating in the core ceremony that reflects their membership in a particular religious community. If a Catholic prisoner were prevented from attending Mass on Sunday, few would

regard that deprivation as anything but absolute, even if the prisoner were afforded other opportunities to pray, to discuss the Catholic faith with others, and even to avoid eating meat on Friday if that were a preference. Prison officials in this case therefore cannot show that "other avenues remain available for the exercise of the asserted right."

In this case, [prison officials] have not established the reasonableness of their policy, because they have provided only bare assertions that the proposals for accommodation offered by [the prisoners' attorneys] are infeasible....

That Muslim inmates are able to participate in Jumu'ah throughout the entire federal prison system suggests that the practice is, under normal circumstances, compatible with the demands of prison administration. Indeed, the Leesburg State Prison permitted participation in this ceremony for five years, and experienced no threats to security or safety as a result....

As the record now stands, prison officials have declared that a security risk is created by a grouping of Muslim inmates in the least dangerous security classification, but not by a grouping of maximum security inmates who are concentrated in work detail inside the main building, and who are the only Muslims assured of participating in Jumu'ah. Surely, prison officials should be required to provide at least some substantiation for this facially implausible contention.

If the Court's standard of review is to represent anything more than reflexive deference to prison officials, any finding of reasonableness must rest on firmer ground than the record now presents.

Incarceration by its nature denies a prisoner participation in the larger human community. To deny the opportunity to affirm membership in a spiritual community, however, may extinguish an inmate's last source of hope for dignity and redemption. Such a denial requires more justification [by prison officials] than mere assertion that any other course of action is infeasible... *(O'Lone v. Estate of Shabazz,* 482 U.S. 342, 354-359, 1987)

The four-part test developed in the *Turner* decision and applied in the *O'Lone* case provides a basis for the diminution or denial of a variety of rights for convicted offenders, especially when the analysis is applied in a manner that is deferential to the preferences of prison officials. With respect to free exercise of religion, defenders of the Court's approach could accurately note that the Supreme Court also effectively diminished the scope of the First Amendment right generally within a few years after *O'Lone.* Thus, one could argue that any perceived diminution in prisoners' free exercise right was mirrored with a parallel limitation for free exercise rights for all Americans. In *Employment Division of Oregon v. Smith* (1990), the

Supreme Court declared that people must obey general laws, even if those laws hinder the free exercise of religion, so long as those laws are not aimed at stopping a religious practice. The case concerned a Native American drug rehabilitation counselor who lost his job after using peyote in a religious ceremony. His right to engage in a long-standing Native American religious practice did not supercede Oregon's anti-drug law aimed at preventing the use of peyote, even though many other states make exceptions in their drug laws for the use of peyote by Native Americans in traditional religious ceremonies. However, there is a key difference between the *Smith* case and the *O'Lone* case that illustrates the needlessly unequal application of religious rights for convicted offenders. In *Smith*, the law at issue that superceded the right to free exercise was a statute enacted by a state legislature and applied to everyone in the state. The law had to move through democratic legislative processes to which the citizens had an opportunity to respond. Free citizens can lobby, attempt to initiate new legislation, and elect new legislators in response to undesirable legislative actions that collide with freedom of religion. Although these legislation influencing activities may be less likely to succeed when undertaken on behalf of minority religions, such as those practiced by Native Americans, claims about religious freedom sometimes strike a chord of concern among adherents of larger denominations that are better able to contribute effective influence. Indeed, the U.S. Congress enacted the Religious Freedom Restoration Act of 1993 in the aftermath of the *Smith* case in an attempt to require government officials to show a compelling justification for any law that interferes with the free exercise of religion. The law was subsequently invalidated by the Supreme Court as an improperly excessive exercise of congressional authority (*City of Boerne v. Flores* 1997). However, Congress acted again in 2000 to undo the effects of both *Smith* and *O'Lone*. With lobbying from religious groups that were intent on protecting churches' efforts to resist governmental land-use controls, prisoners gained statutory protections when their rights were linked to those of the churches. The "Religious Land Use and Institutionalized Persons Act" was enacted by Congress and signed into law by President Clinton in September 2000. For prisoners, the relevant section of the statute states:

> No government shall impose a substantial burden on the religious exercise of a person residing in or confined to an institution...even if the burden results from a rule of general applicability, unless the government demonstrates that the imposition of the burden on that person (1) is in furtherance of a compelling governmental interest; and (2) is the least restrictive means of furthering that compelling governmental interest.

The statute does not guarantee any particular protections for prisoners, especially because judges can interpret the language loosely and thereby accept a wide range of rationalizations from corrections officials as "compelling." Moreover, the statute may eventually be invalidated by a decision of the Supreme Court or another federal court. The statute's importance is reflected in its symbolic contrast with decisions by the U.S. Supreme Court. The institutional guardians of "Equal Justice Under Law" have done less to set a standard for protecting prisoners' religious rights than have the nation's elected representatives in Congress whose focus, interests, and responsibilities are less frequently directed at incarcerated people's rights. The *O'Lone* decision indicates that convicted offenders' religious freedom rights are subordinate to policies and regulations imposed by corrections officials in the eyes of the Rehnquist Court majority.

Conditions of Confinement

During the 1960s and 1970s, federal judges began to hear claims that conditions inside prisons and jails violated the Eighth Amendment prohibition on cruel and unusual punishments. Federal judges' initial decisions in cases concerning conditions of confinement often focused on prisons in southern states. In particular, judges began by questioning the legality of whippings applied to prisoners in Arkansas prisons (*Talley v. Stephens* 1965; *Jackson v. Bishop* 1968). Such cases raised questions about due process as well as cruelty because such painful punishments were meted out immediately at the discretion of corrections officials and sometimes at the discretion of prisoners who were assigned to use physical threats and force in order to ensure that other prisoners worked diligently in prison jobs. Several states invested little money in correctional institutions and relied on prison thugs rather than correctional officers to maintain order. Southern prisoners worked in harsh, slave-like conditions picking cotton and other crops in order to minimize government expenditures on prisons. Prisoners in other parts of the country often had inadequate nutrition, clothing, and housing, and they were sometimes subjected to rough treatment by corrections officials. Eventually, federal judges began to order prison officials to alter the conditions within their institutions in order to meet humane standards mandated by the Supreme Court's guiding Eighth Amendment principle of contemporary values as enunciated in *Trop v. Dulles* (1958). For example, in 1970 a federal judge in Louisiana found that conditions in the Orleans Parish Prison were so inhumane that they violated the Eighth Amendment's prohibition on cruel and unusual punishments (*Hamilton v. Schiro* 1970):

> [T]he jail was built in 1929 to house 400–450 prisoners, and… at the time, 800–900 prisoners were incarcerated there… The toilets were so badly rusted and corroded that cleanliness was impossible, and in some cells they had to be used as hand basins…. The mattresses were never cleaned and were covered with vomit and urine…. The roof and walls leaked. The jail was infested with rats, mice, and roaches…. The threat of fire and of contamination by contagious diseases was great. (Berkson 1975, 146)

The worst kinds of conditions that drew judicial attention through the litigation process are further illustrated in Judge Frank Johnson's opinion in *Pugh v. Locke* (1976) concerning the Alabama prison system:

JOHNSON, Chief Judge:

The dilapidation of the physical facilities contributes to extremely unsanitary living conditions. Testimony demonstrated that windows are broken and unscreened, creating a serious problem with mosquitoes and flies. Old and filthy cotton mattresses lead to the spread of contagious diseases and body lice. Nearly all inmates' living quarters are inadequately heated and ventilated. The electrical systems are totally inadequate, exposed wiring poses a constant danger to inmates, and insufficient lighting results in eye strain and fatigue.

In general, Alabama's penal institutions are filthy. There was repeated testimony at trial that they are overrun with roaches, flies, mosquitoes, and other vermin. A public health expert testified that he found roaches in all stages of development—a certain indicator of filthy conditions. This gross infestation is due in part to inadequate maintenance and housekeeping procedures, and in part to the physical structure of the buildings themselves. For example, floors in many shower rooms are so porous that it is impossible to keep them clean. Plumbing facilities are in an exceptional state of disrepair. In one area at Draper, housing well over 200 men, there is one functioning toilet. Many toilets will not flush and are overflowing. Some showers cannot be turned off and continually drip or even pour water. Frequently, there is no hot running water for substantial periods of time. Witnesses repeatedly commented on the overpowering odor emanating from these facilities.

One expert witness, a United States public health officer, toured facilities at Draper, Fountain, Holman, and Kilby. He testified at trial that he found these facilities wholly unfit for human habitation according to virtually every criterion used by public health inspectors.

Further effects of the failure to classify are manifold. Violent inmates are not isolated from those who are young, passive, or weak. Consequently, the latter inmates are repeatedly victimized by those who are stronger and more aggressive. Testimony shows that robbery, rape, extortion, theft, and assault are everyday occurrences among the general inmate population. Rather than face this constant danger, some inmates voluntarily subject themselves to the inhuman conditions of prison isolation cells.

The indescribable conditions in the isolation cells required immediate action to protect inmates from any further torture by confinement in these cells. As many as six inmates were packed in four foot by eight foot cells with no beds, no lights, no running water, and a hole in the floor for a toilet which could only be flushed from the outside. The infamous Draper "doghouse" is a separate building, locked from the outside, with no guard stationed inside. Inmates in punitive isolation received only one meal per day, frequently without utensils. They were permitted no exercise or reading material and could shower only every 11 days. Punitive isolation has been used to punish inmates for offenses ranging from swearing at a guard and failing to report to work on time, to murder. *(Pugh v. Locke*, 406 F. Supp. 318, 323-328, M.D. Ala. 1976).

Loud protests emanated from critics who objected to intervention by federal judges into prison administration through litigation by prisoners claiming rights violations (Popeo & Smith 1987). These critics claimed that it was improper for federal judges to interfere with the administration of state institutions. They also claimed that judges were needlessly forcing states and localities to spend large sums of money on corrections facilities and simultaneously undermining the authority of corrections officials who need broad discretion in order to maintain order and security. Despite the controversy surrounding judicial intervention into prisons, the Supreme Court eventually endorsed the authority of federal judges to issue orders requiring improvements in conditions of confinement. The prevalence and severity of problems with prison conditions was such that even conservative Chief Justice William Rehnquist, a frequent critic of judicial decisions protecting defendants' and prisoners' rights, has acknowledged the need to maintain some judicial supervision of standards-enforcing rights. According to Rehnquist,

> There was a time not too long ago when the federal judiciary took a completely "hands-off" approach to the problem of prison administration. In recent years, however, these courts largely have discarded this "hands-off" attitude and waded into this complex arena. The deplorable conditions and Draconian restrictions of some of our Nation's prisons are too well known to require recounting here, and the federal courts have rightly condemned these sordid aspects of our prison systems. (*Bell v. Wolfish* 1979, 562)

In *Hutto v. Finney* (1978), the justices were asked to decide whether these federal judges had exceeded their authority in establishing a minimum diet for prisoners, limiting periods of disciplinary confinement, and limiting the number of prisoners per cell within the prisons of Arkansas. The Arkansas litigation illuminated appalling conditions with prisoner-trusties torturing other prisoners with a homemade electric-shock device, food served to prisoners falling below the minimum caloric level needed for healthy human survival, and groups of prisoners, including those with infectious diseases such as hepatitis, jammed into tiny cells together. The Supreme Court described the inhumane conditions in the isolation cells used to punish Arkansas prisoners and upheld the lower courts' remedial orders. In the majority opinion, Justice Stevens listed the tests to be applied to identify Eighth Amendment violations: "The Eighth Amendment's ban on inflicting cruel and unusual punishments... prohibits penalties that are grossly disproportionate to the offense,... as well as those that transgress today's 'broad and idealistic concepts of dignity, civilized standards, humanity, and decency'" (*Hutto v. Finney* 1978, 685).

The Supreme Court's other major Eighth Amendment decision affecting prisons that recognized the existence of a specific right and thereby implicitly endorsed judicial intervention to protect that right came two years earlier in a case concerning medical treatment (*Estelle v. Gamble* 1976). A prisoner's back was injured when a bale of cotton fell on him as he unloaded a truck while undertaking his prison work assignment. Although he continued to complain about severe pain and lingering medical problems, the prison doctor certified his capability to return to work after giving him painkillers and muscle relaxants for a month. The prisoner refused to return to work because of his pain and he was punished for his refusal. He filed a lawsuit alleging that his constitutional rights had been violated by inadequate medical care. Justice Thurgood Marshall's majority opinion used the *Trop v. Dulles* concept of contemporary standards in declaring that "[t]he infliction of unnecessary suffering is inconsistent with contemporary standards of decency" (*Estelle v. Gamble* 1976, 104). Marshall enunciated an Eighth Amendment-based rule with respect to prisoners' right to medical treatment: "We therefore conclude that deliberate indifference to serious medical needs of prisoners constitutes the 'unnecessary and wanton infliction of pain'… proscribed by the Eighth Amendment" (*Estelle v. Gamble* 1976, 104). In using the phrases "infliction of unnecessary suffering" and "unnecessary and wanton infliction of pain," Marshall enunciated tests that were drawn from the Supreme Court's 1970s capital punishment cases and that represented an effort to clarify, update, and apply the Supreme Court's vague Eighth Amendment test focusing on contemporary standards and values as established in *Trop v. Dulles* (1958).

Justice John Paul Stevens, the lone dissenter in *Estelle*, was concerned that the majority opinion provided too little protection for prisoners' rights. Stevens complained that the subjective standard for determining Eighth Amendment violations depended on the thoughts and motivations in the minds of corrections officials rather than an objective assessment of the treatment provided to prisoners. According to Stevens, "whether a constitutional standard has been violated should turn on the character of the punishment rather than the motivation of the individual who inflicted it" (*Estelle v. Gamble* 1976, 116). By contrast, when Stevens wrote the *Hutto* opinion concerning general prison conditions on behalf of the majority of justices two years later, he focused solely on an objective assessment of whether prison conditions satisfied contemporary standards and values rather than including a subjective assessment of prison officials' thoughts and intentions.

After acknowledging a limited right to medical care (*Estelle v. Gamble* 1976) and endorsing lower court judges' authority to order remedies for unconstitutional conditions of confinement (*Hutto v. Finney* 1978), the Supreme Court's next decisions signaled that the majority of justices wished to define limits for how extensively prisoners' rights would be defined and how actively courts could supervise correctional practices (Call 1995). As previously discussed with respect to body cavity inspections of pretrial detainees, the 1979 case of *Bell v. Wolfish* demonstrated a renewed commitment to show deference to correctional officials when examining constitutional rights claims from incarcerated people. *Bell v. Wolfish* is regarded as heralding a halt to the expansion of judicial activity identifying and protecting prisoners' rights (Robbins 1980). The decision rejecting various claims concerning conditions and practices at the federal jail was technically based on the Fifth Amendment right to due process because pretrial detainees, who have not yet been convicted of a crime, are not considered to be experiencing "punishment" that would place them under the protections of the Eighth Amendment's prohibition on cruel and unusual punishments. However, in determining the application of due process rights to pretrial detainees' legal protections in jails, the Supreme Court relies on the same tests and reasoning that are applied in Eighth Amendment conditions of confinement cases for prisons. Thus, *Bell v. Wolfish* was a precursor to an Eighth Amendment prison case that led the Court to further limit judicial intervention on behalf of prisoners' constitutional rights.

In *Rhodes v. Chapman* (1981), the Supreme Court rejected a claim that prison officials violate the Eighth Amendment when they house two prisoners in a cell specifically designed to house only a single prisoner. Although conditions produced by prison overcrowding can lead to violations of the Eighth Amendment's prohibition on cruel and unusual punishments, the justices found that double-bunking by itself did not automatically trigger the recognition of a rights violation. Justice Lewis Powell's majority opinion reaffirmed the Court's application of contemporary values to define the Eighth Amendment, but warned lower court judges against acting too aggressively to reform prisons. According to Powell, "[C]onditions that cannot be said to be cruel and unusual under contemporary standards are not unconstitutional. To the extent that such conditions are restrictive and even harsh, they are part of the penalty that criminal offenders pay for their offenses against society" (*Rhodes v. Chapman* 1981, 347). As in *Hutto v. Finney* (1978), the Court's prior case concerning prison conditions, Powell applied the objective standard for identifying Eighth Amendment violations by declaring that unconstitutional practices must violate "contemporary standard[s] of decency," involve "wanton and unnecessary infliction of pain," or result in "unquestioned and serious deprivations of basic human needs" (*Rhodes v. Chapman* 1981, 347). His analysis did not focus on the subjective component of corrections officials' thoughts and intentions, which had only been applied in analyzing the limited claim of inadequate medical care rather than general conditions of confinement. Overall, the opinion in *Rhodes v. Chapman* reiterated the Court's theme of the need for judges to show deference to corrections officials. This message was conveyed quite clearly in Powell's statement that "courts cannot assume that state legislatures and prison officials are insensitive to the requirements of the Constitution or to the perplexing sociological problems of how best to achieve the goals of the penal function in the criminal justice system" (*Rhodes v. Chapman* 1981, 352).

The Supreme Court subsequently returned to an emphasis on the subjective standard in another case focusing on a specific Eighth Amendment issue, excessive use of force, rather than general conditions of confinement. In *Whitley v. Albers* (1986), a prisoner was shot by a corrections officer during an inmate disturbance. The prisoner filed suit claiming that the officer's action constituted cruel and unusual punishment. In the case, the inmate was not participating in the disturbance and did not make any threatening actions toward the officer. Instead, the prisoner had been out of his cell altruistically attempting to remove elderly prisoners from the scene of an impending confrontation between corrections officers and an inmate who was holding one corrections officer hostage. When armed corrections officers burst through a prisoner-constructed barricade, the altruistic prisoner was shot as he tried to return to his cell in order to get out of the way. A majority of justices decided that when prison officials need to restore order during a conflict, a prisoner cannot succeed in claiming a rights violation unless the prisoner can show that prison officials acted "maliciously and sadistically for the very purpose of causing harm" (*Whitley v. Albers* 1986, 321). Thus, as in the medical treatment context, the Court established a subjective standard involving an examination of prison officials' motivations and state of mind rather than looking objectively at the action taken and the harm inflicted. The dissenters argued that jurors should be permitted to make an objective determination of the reasonableness of the use of force in order to remedy (and hopefully prevent in the future) any infliction of injuries produced through force that was applied wantonly despite the officers having no preexisting specific intent to injure a particular prisoner.

With respect to litigation challenging prison conditions as a violation of Eighth Amendment rights, the Supreme Court issued its definitive decision that clearly indicated the high degree of deference that judges were expected to evince when considering prisoners' Eighth Amendment claims. *Wilson v. Seiter* (1990) was a unanimous decision with respect to the Court's rejection of the prisoner's claim, but there was a five to four split within the Court concerning the standard of review to be applied in prison conditions cases. Justices Byron White, Harry Blackmun, Thurgood Marshall, and John Paul Stevens disagreed with the direction in which Justice Scalia and the other four members of the majority (Chief Justice William Rehnquist and Justices Sandra Day O'Connor, Anthony Kennedy, and David Souter) steered legal doctrine and public policy concerning convicted offenders' rights. A close division within the Court often creates the possibility that future decisions could swing in the opposite direction with the retirement of one justice or if one member of the majority changes his or her position. In this instance, however, three of the dissenters (White, Blackmun, and Marshall) retired by 1994 so the majority's position does not seem fragile, especially with conservative President George W. Bush poised to appoint the first new justices of the twenty-first century in the event of any additional retirements.

Pearly Wilson was a prisoner at a state prison in Ohio. He filed a civil rights action against Ohio corrections officials alleging that conditions at his prison violated the Eighth Amendment prohibition on cruel and unusual punishment. Wilson's lawsuit made a number of allegations: overcrowding; excessive noise; insufficient locker storage space; inadequate heating and cooling; improper ventilation; unclean and inadequate restrooms; unsanitary dining facilities and food preparation; and housing that mixed all prisoners with those suffering from physical and mental illnesses.

Justice Scalia's majority opinion outlined his interpretation of the history of the Supreme Court's relevant Eighth Amendment decisions. Although lower federal courts began applying the Eighth Amendment to conditions of confinement in prisons during the mid-1960s, Scalia observed that *Estelle v. Gamble* (1976), concerning the alleged deprivation of medical care for prisoners, was the case in which the Supreme Court "first acknowledged that the [cruel and unusual punishment] provision could be applied to deprivations that were not specifically part of the sentence but were suffered during imprisonment" (*Wilson v. Seiter* 1991, 297). He emphasized that *Estelle* required prisoners to show that the deprivation of medical care was due to "deliberate indifference" and not merely to negligence. He described *dicta* in *Estelle* relying on the earlier death penalty case of *Louisiana ex rel. Francis v. Resweber* (1947), concerning a condemned offender who sought to avoid a second scheduled execution after the first execution attempt failed because of a faulty electric chair. The prisoner received severe shocks in the first execution but lost his claim that a second administration of electro-shocks would be cruel and unusual. The justices who rejected Francis's claim emphasized that only the "wanton infliction of pain," which includes evil intentions on the part of corrections officials, rather than accidental equipment malfunctions could serve as the basis for a violation of the Eighth Amendment. Scalia focused on the language used by these justices to emphasize his view that Eighth Amendment violations must be based on intended actions by corrections officials.

Scalia's review of the Supreme Court's Eighth Amendment decisions then omitted the Court's decision in *Hutto v. Finney* (1978). Instead, his opinion implied that the next relevant decision was *Rhodes v. Chapman* (1981), but he indicated that the objective evaluation of prison conditions used in *Rhodes* had been superceded by the test focusing on the subjective state-of-mind of prison officials in *Whitley v. Albers* (1986). He also emphasized that the Court had employed subjective tests in *Estelle*, concerning medical care, and *Louisiana ex rel. Francis* (1947) concerning the death penalty, in order to identify Eighth Amendment violations.

Scalia's review of earlier decisions emphasized the existence of a rule requiring proof about corrections officials' subjective intentions or state-of-mind in order to establish an Eighth Amendment violation. He conveniently ignored language in other decisions indicating that an objective assessment of prison conditions, without regard to corrections officials' intentions, has provided the basis for claims about general conditions. According to Scalia's reasoning, it is not sufficient to show that prison conditions are inhumane. In Scalia's view, the prisoner must also show that corrections officials were deliberately indifferent to the development of those conditions. Under this analysis, if a prison official says, "I knew that the conditions were terrible and I cared deeply about the problem, but I didn't have enough money in the budget to correct the problem," then the official is off the hook for the improper conditions, no matter what suffering the prisoner may have endured.

According to Scalia, "If the pain inflicted is not formally meted out as *punishment* by the statute or the sentencing judge, some mental element must be attributable to the inflicting officer before [the hardship experienced by the prisoner] can qualify [as punishment under the Eighth Amendment]" (*Wilson v. Seiter* 1991, 300). Scalia declined to follow any interpretation of the Eighth Amendment based on evaluations of the human consequences of corrections officials' actions.

Four justices declined to join Scalia's opinion and asserted that the case should be remanded for further consideration by the lower courts. Justice White's concurring opinion criticized Scalia's interpretation of cases because the majority opinion had not examined "those cases involv[ing] a challenge to conditions of confinement. Instead, [Scalia's selected cases] involved challenges to specific acts or omissions directed at individual prisoners" (*Wilson v. Seiter* 1991, 309). In advancing his conclusion that Eighth Amendment violations must be identified based on a subjective assessment of corrections officials' intent, Scalia's review of precedents had included a case on medical care (*Estelle v. Gamble*), the death penalty (*Louisiana ex rel. Francis v. Resweber*), double celling (*Rhodes v. Chapman*), and the shooting of a prisoner (*Whitley v. Albers*). However, none of these cases concerned the issue in *Wilson*: the general conditions within a corrections institution. It seemed remarkable that Scalia omitted discussion of *Hutto v. Finney* (1978), the Arkansas case in which the Supreme Court had addressed most directly the living conditions within a prison. In *Hutto*, the Supreme Court focused only on objective conditions of confinement in that case and did not apply the subjective test of examining corrections officials' intentions. Thus, perhaps it is not surprising that Scalia wanted that precedent to be ignored or forgotten. Justice White also cited other cases to demonstrate that Scalia's erroneous emphasis on officials' subjective intent is not required by prior cases. According to White,

> Not only is the majority's intent requirement a departure from precedent, it likely will prove impossible to apply in many cases. Inhuman prison conditions often are the result of cumulative actions and inactions by numerous officials inside and outside a prison, sometimes over a long period of time. In those circumstances, it is far from clear whose intent should be examined, and the majority offers no real guidance on this issue. In truth, intent is not very meaningful when considering a challenge to an institution, such as a prison system. (*Wilson v. Seiter* 1991, 310)

The concurring opinion warned that "[t]he ultimate result of today's decision, I fear, is that 'serious deprivations of human needs,'... will go unredressed due to an unnecessary and meaningless search for 'deliberate indifference'" (*Wilson v. Seiter* 1991, 311).

Scalia's opinion, in effect, meant that corrections officials no longer needed to defend themselves in Eighth Amendment litigation by claiming that the conditions in their prisons meet the humane standards previously thought to have been required by the Eighth Amendment. After the *Wilson* decision, corrections officials could seek to fend off litigation about inhumane prison conditions by merely claiming that they were helpless to remedy the deficient conditions. Because it is often difficult to provide proof to establish a corrections official's thoughts and intentions, the *Wilson* precedent made it much more difficult for prisoners to pursue legal remedies for inhumane conditions in corrections institutions.

The diminution of Eighth Amendment protections for convicted offenders was not an inadvertent or unanticipated consequence of Scalia's opinion in *Wilson*. In subsequent decisions, Scalia revealed that he was actually seeking to remove all Eighth Amendment protections for inmates in corrections institutions. Scalia joined two dissenting opinions by Justice Clarence Thomas that argued that the original intention of the Eighth Amendment is to protect convicted offenders solely against the pronouncement of cruel and unusual sentences by judges (*Hudson v. McMillian* 1992, *Helling v. McKinney* 1993). According to Thomas and Scalia, the Eighth Amendment does not provide any protections during the course of carrying out the sentence. In Thomas's words:

> Abusive behavior by prison guards is deplorable conduct that properly evokes outrage and contempt. But that does not mean that it is invariably unconstitutional. The Eighth Amendment is not, and should not be turned into, a National Code of Prison Regulation.... [P]rimary responsibility for preventing and punishing [improper conduct by corrections officials] rests not with the Federal Constitution but with the laws and regulations of the various States. (*Hudson v. McMillian* 1992, 28)

The interpretation of the Eighth Amendment advanced by Thomas and Scalia advocates a return to the "hands-off" doctrine that characterized federal judicial review of prisoner cases prior to the 1960s. The "hands-off" doctrine had produced prisons containing horrific conditions in which prisoners were tortured, malnourished, and even murdered (Berkson 1975), yet Thomas and Scalia view judicial deference to correctional officials as the proper application of the Eighth Amendment. Moreover, because Scalia was able to gain the five votes that he needed to support his opinion in *Wilson* without revealing his true viewpoints and intentions, he took a giant step toward diminishing the Eighth Amendment's application to protect prisoners, even though seven other justices disagreed with his subsequently revealed position that the Amendment should not protect prisoners against inhumane institutional conditions and practices.

In a subsequent decision (*Farmer v. Brennan* 1994), the Supreme Court precluded the worst-case scenario raised by dissenters in *Wilson*. After *Farmer*, if prison officials knew about inhumane conditions, they might be liable for failing to implement remedies, even when they sought to claim that a lack of funds prevented them from taking action. The Court held that "a prison official cannot be found liable under the Eighth Amendment for denying an inmate humane conditions of confinement unless the official knows of and disregards an excessive risk to inmate health and safety; the official must both be aware of facts from which the inference could be drawn that a substantial risk of harm exists, and he must also draw the inference" (*Farmer v. Brennan* 1994, 1979). In setting this standard, the Court reiterated that mere negligence by corrections officials would not be sufficient to violate the Eighth Amendment. However, the Court also emphasized that prisoners need not prove the much higher standard of malicious acts that intentionally seek to harm the prisoner. Although the Court adopted a middle-ground standard for the subjective intent requirement of *Wilson*, the Court's definition of this "deliberate indifference" standard still poses substantial difficulties for prisoners seeking to prove unconstitutional conditions of confinement. However, because of the continued existence of the subjective intent requirement from *Wilson* as well as *Farmer*'s definition of that requirement, corrections officials are still invited to seek to avoid liability by claiming ignorance about inhumane conditions.

In concurring opinions in *Farmer*, Justices Stevens and Blackmun continued to criticize the existence of *Wilson*'s subjective intent requirement. These justices preferred a rule that would require officials to seek out and remedy inhumane conditions without the option of tolerating such conditions out of ignorance or claimed ignorance. However, because Scalia was able to gather five votes in favor of imposing the "deliberate indifference" test in *Wilson*, the subjective intent test continues to exist as the basis for a significant impediment to prisoners' Eighth Amendment claims and a substantial diminution of convicted offenders' rights.

Congress compounded the challenges facing prisoners who wish to file Eighth Amendment claims concerning their conditions of confinement by enacting the Prison Litigation Reform Act (PLRA) in 1996 (Solano 1997). The PLRA sought to deter frequent litigation by prisoners by, for example, making it more difficult for indigent prisoners to have filing fees waived. The Act also limited the authority of federal judges concerning such matters as ordering and overseeing continuing remedies, especially with respect to prison overcrowding. Of particular interest with respect to the judicial system's purported dedication to "equal justice under law," is one provision of the PLRA which limits prisoners' opportunities to file lawsuits, even when clear violations of their constitutional rights may be occurring. The relevant provision (28 U.S.C. 1915g) says:

> In no event shall a prisoner bring a civil action or appeal a judgment in a civil action or proceeding under this section if the prisoner has, on 3 or more prior occasions, while incarcerated or detained in any facility, brought an action or appeal in a court of the United States that was dismissed on the grounds that it is frivolous, malicious, or fails to state a claim upon which relief may be granted, unless the prisoner is under imminent danger of serious physical injury.

This provision of the Act seems to presume that any indigent prisoner who has previously had three cases dismissed must have been abusing opportunities to litigate by filing groundless lawsuits solely for the purpose of harassing corrections officials. In reality, because prisoners have no right to assistance of counsel in preparing civil rights lawsuits, it is very easy for prisoners to misstate genuine grievances as constitutional claims or fail to clearly identify the constitutional basis for alleged rights violations. The term "frivolous" is applied by courts to a variety of claims that are not eligible for consideration under the technical requirements of federal law, even though they may embody a good faith presentation of genuine harms suffered by a prisoner (Fradella 1998). For example, a prisoner who suffered severe discomfort from allergic skin reactions to the laundry soap and certain foods used in a correctional institution sought to alleviate his genuine physical pain by requesting special accommodations (e.g., the use of a different soap, a special diet, additional medical attention, and so forth) as well as financial compensation for his suffering. However, the federal court dismissed the case for failing to state a claim because the prisoner could not show deliberate indifference to his medical care (*Estelle v. Gamble* rule) in light of the fact that corrections officials provided some pain medications, even if those medications were allegedly not effective in remedying the problem (Smith 2000, 67). In addition, because some prisoners in the United States serve sentences that last for decades, a prisoner could have had three cases dismissed, yet those cases could have been spaced over a period of fifteen or more years. Thus, three dismissals do not indicate that the prisoner files illegitimate claims or that the prisoner repeatedly uses the litigation process for harassment purposes.

Despite the fact that there are legitimate, understandable, and predictable reasons that a prisoner may have three or more civil rights actions dismissed by the federal court, the PLRA bars additional civil rights filings by the prisoner unless the prisoner is in "imminent danger of serious physical injury." Consequently, after the third dismissal, an indigent prisoner could not receive the necessary waiver of filing fees to permit new litigation even if prison officials were openly denying the prisoner the opportunity to read the Bible or were subjecting the prisoner to intrusive body-cavity searches purely for the purpose of harassing and humiliating the prisoner. Such actions would violate, respectively, the First Amendment right to free exercise of religion and the Fourth Amendment right against unreasonable searches. However, because the officials' actions would not create "imminent danger of serious physical injury," the prisoner would not be able to seek federal court protection to prohibit further rights violations.

Prisoners and free citizens are similarly situated in the sense that neither has a right to counsel for filing federal civil rights lawsuits intended to gain judicial protection of constitutional rights. Free citizens, however, have no statutory barriers to filing lawsuits whenever they believe that their rights have been violated. Prisoners have been singled out for a limitation that will effectively deny some of them protection of constitutional rights that they are clearly entitled to possess. Ideally, the U.S. Supreme Court would intervene to ensure that no statutes prevent people from enjoying the protection of constitutional rights to which they are entitled. By 2002, however, the nation's highest court had not yet declared any aspect of the PLRA to be unconstitutional. Indeed, no observers anticipated that the Court would do so in light of the efforts by the majority of justices to limit the scope and enforcement of prisoners' rights through their own judicial decisions (e.g., *Wilson v. Seiter*).

It is not surprising that elected officials, such as members of Congress, would use their authority to limit litigation and the effectuation of constitutional rights for a political minority (i.e., prisoners) that is despised and feared by the public. These legislators reflect the popular values and emotions in society by seeking to curtail prisoners' rights. In the constitutional governing system of the United States, the federal judiciary, with its life-tenured judges and authority to interpret the Constitution in order to undo improper actions by other government officials, is positioned to prevent actions by legislators that impinge on the constitutional rights of those who are disfavored by the dominant political interests. In the case of prisoners, however, the Supreme Court, widely regarded as the chief guardian of the Constitution and purported defender of constitutional rights, did not act to block excessive actions by legislators during the final decades of the twentieth century. In fact, the legislators merely followed in the Supreme Court's footsteps by making decisions that limit the constitutional rights of convicted offenders.

Access to Justice

A key factor in determining whether convicted offenders enjoy the protections contained in the U.S. Constitution is their ability to initiate litigation in order to enable judges to intervene with remedial orders. If prisoners cannot gain access to the courts and make effective use of judicial processes, then constitutional rights are mere slogans that have no practical impact for prisoners who need to seek judicial attention to ensure the implementation of those rights. The Supreme Court has recognized a right of access to the courts (*Ex parte Hull* 1941). The justices appear to presume that right of access is an inherent element of the right to due process, but the justices' opinions have not explicitly explained the constitutional source of the right. The right of access to the courts does not, however, ensure that prisoners can actually litigate with sufficient effectiveness to guarantee that their rights will be protected by the courts. In criminal trials, indigent defendants have a right to be represented by counsel, and, therefore, the government must provide a public defender or appointed defense counsel. However, the Sixth Amendment only applies to criminal trials and an initial appeal. It does not apply to other postconviction legal processes, including civil rights lawsuits filed by prisoners to vindicate their rights after incarceration (*Ross v. Moffitt* 1974; *Murray v. Giarratano* 1989). Thus, prisoners must either hire their own attorneys, which very few can afford to do, or represent themselves in court. Because legal processes are complicated and technical, it is extremely difficult for prisoners to gain enough self-education about law to litigate effectively. The litigation process is especially difficult for the many prisoners who have low IQs, literacy problems, mental illnesses, or do not speak English as their native language (Smith 1987). One judge sarcastically described the extreme difficulties most prisoners face in attempting to represent themselves in court:

> In this court's view, access to the fullest law library anywhere is a useless and meaningless gesture in terms of the great mass of prisoners.... To expect untrained laymen to work with entirely unfamiliar books, whose content they cannot understand, may be worthy of Lewis Carroll['s *Alice in Wonderland*], but hardly satisfies the substance of constitutional duty. Access to full law libraries makes about as much sense as furnishing medical services through books like: "Brain Surgery Self-Taught," or "How to Remove Your Own Appendix," along with scalpels, drills, hemostats, sponges, and sutures. (*Falzerano v. Collier* 1982, 803)

In order to permit prisoners to prepare their own cases, the Supreme Court ruled in *Bounds v. Smith* (1977) that corrections officials must supply prisoners with access to a law library or assistance from people trained in law. Most prisons opted to provide libraries rather than assistance. As a result, many prisoners struggled fruitlessly with complex legal materials as they sought to find a means to file lawsuits alleging violations of their rights. Federal courts have attempted to make it easier for these *pro se* litigators to file cases by providing standard forms that guide the prisoners through the steps needed to file a claim. However, prisoners still need the capability to distinguish constitutional rights claims from other kinds of legal and non-legal complaints in order to avoid immediate dismissal. More than 95 percent of prisoners' section 1983 cases are dismissed in their initial stages (Hanson & Daley 1995a). Some of these cases may contain potentially valid claims concerning constitutional rights violations, but these claims can easily be misunderstood, overlooked, and lost if they are not presented clearly and effectively. Moreover, there are questions about whether federal court decision making processes give prisoners' petitions evaluations that are careful and thorough enough to detect valid claims presented in garbled English by uneducated prisoners. This problem may be especially acute because prisoners' cases are typically delegated by judges to inexperienced law clerks who regard them as routine, undesirable cases rather than as interesting, important legal filings (Smith 1988).

Some federal judges attempted to address the deficiencies produced by reliance on law libraries through judicial orders mandating special assistance for offenders manifesting special difficulties in their attempts to use the prison libraries. For example, some judges were concerned that prisoners who had problems with literacy, developmental disabilities, or fluency in English could never effectively use a law library on their own in order to seek protection of constitutional rights. Therefore, they need assistance from paralegals or lawyers provided by the prison. In 1996, however, the U.S. Supreme Court sharply curtailed the ability of lower court judges to tailor judicial orders to address such problems. Justice Scalia's majority opinion in *Lewis v. Casey* ostensibly acknowledged that certain prisoners cannot make effective use of law libraries and therefore may be entitled to special assistance. However, Scalia imposed a requirement that such prisoners demonstrate to a court an "injury-in-fact" in order to obtain a judicially ordered remedy. Although it may be superficially attractive to expect that a clear disability will be demonstrated to a court before a judge can order additional legal resources or special assistance for a prisoner, in practice the requirement creates a classic "Catch-22" situation. After *Lewis v. Casey*, how will an illiterate or mentally ill prisoner demonstrate that he or she has been harmed by inadequate legal resources? If a prisoner can use legal materials well enough to file a section 1983 lawsuit claiming that the prison library is inadequate, why wouldn't the court say, "The library must not be so bad for your purposes if you were able to file a lawsuit asking us to examine the prison's legal resources." If a prisoner is really unable to use the law library, how will he or she be able to file the necessary section 1983 action to prove the existence of a disability and ask the court to examine the library's adequacy? Prisoners who could actually demonstrate an injury-in-fact from inadequate legal assistance are unlikely to be able to do so because no judicially ordered assistance can be provided until *after* the prisoners make effective demonstrations of their disabilities in court. It remains to be seen how effectively prisoners who can demonstrate that they are harmed by inadequate legal resources will be able to bring such problems to a court's attention.

The Supreme Court's decision in *Lewis v. Casey* is regarded as a warning to federal judges. Because the Supreme Court majority insists that individual prisoners must demonstrate how they were harmed by the legal resources offered, district judges cannot easily make a broad examination of flaws in law libraries and legal assistance programs. Even if flaws are identified, judges cannot order remedies unless prisoners can prove that they were harmed by those flaws. Scalia's *Lewis v. Casey* opinion even indicates that corrections officials rather than judges should take the lead in deciding how to solve problems that are discovered. Judges are supposed to let corrections officials run things as much as possible.

An alternative means for prisoners to use the judicial process to seek protection of their constitutional rights is to permit knowledgeable prisoners to assist those who have less understanding of law and the litigation process. In one of its first cases concerning prisoners' constitutional rights (*Johnson v. Avery* 1969), the U.S. Supreme Court said that prison officials cannot prevent prisoners from helping each other with their cases unless the prison provides an alternative source of legal resources. In most prisons, the prison law library itself provides the alternative source of legal resources despite the deficiencies in relying on the presence of library materials as the means to ensure access to the courts for all prisoners. A prisoner subsequently asserted that he had a First Amendment free speech right to provide legal advice and assistance to another prisoner. However, in 2001, the Supreme Court applied the *Turner* test to reject that claim and permit corrections officials to punish a prisoner for providing legal assistance to another prisoner (*Shaw v. Murphy* 2001).

Prisoners' access to the courts is the key constitutional entitlement upon which the effectuation of all other constitutional rights necessarily rests. If prisoners do not have access to the courts and cannot effectively present cases in the litigation process, they have little hope of preventing corrections officials from violating all of their constitutional rights. They also have little hope of using post-appeal processes for raising questions about alleged rights violations by police and prosecutors that contributed to their criminal convictions. Convicted offenders use the habeas corpus process to challenge the legitimacy of their convictions and punishments when constitutional rights violations allegedly occurred during either the investigation of their cases by police or the processing of their cases by prosecutors and judges. If prisoners believe their federal constitutional rights were violated in the course of the state prosecutions that produced their convictions, they may petition federal judges to review the actions of state criminal justice officials. There is no right to counsel in the habeas corpus process so prisoners must rely on prison law libraries to prepare their own cases and, as with civil rights lawsuits about alleged rights violations in prisons, it is very difficult for prisoners to present their habeas corpus petitions effectively. More than 98 percent of habeas corpus petitions in the federal courts are dismissed, most often for violating a procedural rule about how such cases are to be filed (Hanson & Daley 1995b).

The importance of habeas corpus is underscored by the fact that it is one of the few individual rights protected in the original Constitution. Two years before the framers of the Constitution placed individual rights and liberties in the Constitution's Bill of Rights, they had stated in Article I, Section 9 that "[t]he Privilege of the Writ of Habeas Corpus shall not be suspended, unless when in Cases of Rebellion or Invasion the public Safety may require it." Although Congress cannot suspend habeas corpus except in extraordinary national emergencies, Congress can enact statutes to determine the procedures for habeas corpus petitions. Congress used its authority to define habeas corpus procedures through the Habeas Corpus Act of 1867 and through subsequent legislative enactments (28 U.S.C. sec. 2254). While some critics would like to bar state prisoners' cases from the federal courts, Congress has clearly endorsed the role of federal courts in reviewing state convictions through the vehicle of habeas corpus. As Larry Yackle (1994, 702) observed, "recent [congressional] enactments, particularly the establishment of the federal rules for habeas practice in 1977, close the books on the question whether current law makes the federal forum available to state prisoners."

Chief Justice William Rehnquist appointed retired Justice Lewis Powell to head a committee to recommend reforms to streamline the processing of death penalty cases. The Committee was instructed to place a particular emphasis on habeas corpus procedures. When Rehnquist submitted the Powell Committee proposals to Congress without gaining the approval of the Judicial Conference, the body of federal judges that communicates with Congress about policies affecting the courts, a majority of judges on the Judicial Conference sent a letter to Congress dissociating the Conference from Rehnquist's proposals for habeas corpus reform (Greenhouse 1989). This episode revealed Rehnquist's desire to limit convicted offenders' access to habeas corpus and helped to explain the Supreme Court's decisions creating limitations that made it more difficult for offenders to raise claims concerning alleged rights violations.

Despite the fact that habeas procedures are presumptively under the control of Congress because they are defined by statutes, the Supreme Court acted on its own in a series of decisions to change habeas corpus procedures in ways that would limit state prisoners' access to review of their cases by federal judges. In *Teague v. Lane* (1989), for example, the Court announced that prisoners could not base habeas claims on new rules announced after their trials. In effect, the federal courts can acknowledge that a prisoner's constitutional rights were violated during the investigation and prosecution processes but decline to order a new trial by asserting that the existence of the particular right at issue was not clearly recognized by judges at the time that the violation occurred. The problem with this superficially plausible position is that the Supreme Court justices themselves often disagree about whether a particular right was recognizable at the time that a violation occurred. For example, in *Butler v. McKellar* (1989), a defendant jailed on unrelated charges and represented by counsel on those charges was questioned by police about a murder case without having his attorney present. The incriminating statements that the defendant made during that interrogation were used to convict him of the murder. He subsequently claimed that his statements should be excluded from evidence because the police violated his rights by questioning him without his attorney present. In *Arizona v. Roberson* (1988), the Court ruled that a defendant in jail on one charge and represented by counsel cannot be questioned outside of the presence of his or her attorney concerning a separate charge. Butler's rights were clearly violated under the rule in *Roberson*, but five justices said that the rule did not apply to Butler because *Roberson* was not decided until after Butler's interrogation took place. By contrast, four dissenting justices traced a series of cases leading up to the *Roberson* decision and concluded that judges should have recognized that such questioning was not permitted under the Court's prior interpretations of the Constitution. Thus, the Court-created rules for habeas corpus permitted Butler to remain on death row despite the fact that his questioning violated the Constitution. Sadly, the Court's decision left Butler with no avenue to challenge his conviction despite the rights violation *and* significant questions about his guilt. The prosecutor and jury were never told by Butler's original inexperienced defense attorney that Butler had the mental functioning of a nine-year-old with an IQ of 61 and he had never even completed third grade. Thus, the accuracy of any statements he made to the police while being questioned in jail without an attorney present is questionable. Moreover, an FBI agent determined that hairs found on the victim's clothing were definitely not from Butler (Marcus, 1990). Butler's conviction and death sentence rested heavily on admissions of doubtful validity obtained in violation of his rights. Even so, the Supreme Court majority closed the door on any opportunity to gain a new trial through the habeas corpus process.

In other cases restricting the availability of habeas corpus, the Court limited the ability of prisoners to submit multiple habeas petitions, even after they obtained new information about rights violations that may have occurred. As a result of *McCleskey v. Zant* (1991), Warren McCleskey was executed, despite the fact that prosecutors had sought to hide from his attorney information about a deal between a key witness and the police. The witness claimed that McCleskey, his jail cellmate, confessed to him that he was guilty of the murder. However, the jury and the defense were never told that the witness was planted in McCleskey's cell and told that several criminal charges against him would be dropped if he would testify that McCleskey had admitted to the crime. There is no way to know if this self-interested criminal offender was telling the truth in claiming that McCleskey admitted guilt. Two jurors later declared that they would not have voted to impose the death penalty if they had known that the witness may not have been reliable because of his personal motive to implicate McCleskey in order to reduce his own potential criminal punishment ("Warren McCleskey" 1991). The use of a police informer to question a defendant about charges for which he is represented by counsel violates the defendant's rights under *Massiah v. United States* (1964), yet McCleskey could not challenge this right's violation because the Supreme Court decided in his case that convicted offenders must raise all of their claims in their initial petition. They cannot file a second petition raising additional issues except in extraordinary circumstances. As discussed in Chapter 3, McCleskey had used his first petition to use statistical evidence about the existence of racial discrimination in Georgia's death penalty sentencing. The majority of justices, however, refused to accept this form of evidence as proof of an equal protection violation (*McCleskey v. Kemp* 1987). The Court expected McCleskey to discover and raise the *Massiah* claim in the first petition despite the fact that the police and prosecutor had hidden the information about the cellmate's status as a police informer at the time that the first petition was filed.

An additional procedural limitation was imposed by the Supreme Court in *Coleman v. Thompson* (1991). Any violations of state procedural rules, such as filing an appeal late, will cause offenders to waive and forfeit any habeas corpus claims about rights violations. This is a burdensome rule because convicted offenders can lose their constitutional rights through errors and incompetence by their attorneys, many of whom may be unenthusiastic and undercompensated appointed counsel. In *Coleman*, attorneys misunderstood a confusing date stamp on a judicial order and filed an appeal a few days late. This violation of procedural rules invalidated Coleman's appeal in state court but the attorneys still knew that they had an opportunity to contest any rights violations through the habeas process in federal courts. The Supreme Court, however, foreclosed this opportunity by imposing the rule about any error in state processes precluding federal court review, too. Such rules emphasize efficient case processing over careful consideration of proper legal procedures and the protection of constitutional rights. Moreover, such rules place into the hands of state judges, who are frequently elected officials closely tied to the local political environment, the final authority over determining the existence of any constitutional rights violations, whether federal or state. By precluding federal habeas corpus review, the Supreme Court's decision increased the likelihood that constitutional errors will remain undetected and uncorrected. Thus, convictions will stand despite rights violations, and there is a greater risk that innocent people will be convicted of crimes and have no opportunity to have their cases reexamined. In the case of the rape-murder for which Coleman was convicted and sentenced to die, a subsequent investigation by an attorney-turned-writer who was unconnected to the case revealed serious deficiencies in the police investigation and defense representation at trial as well as important evidence that pointed to the guilt of a man other than Coleman (Tucker 1997). However, because the Supreme Court's decision enforcing the habeas corpus procedural rule effectively blocked any opportunity to have these issues examined in court, Coleman was executed for a crime that he very likely did not commit.

The Supreme Court has used other mechanisms to limit opportunities for the vindication of constitutional rights. For example, prior to 1991, Justice Byron White had been the Circuit Justice responsible for emergency petitions from the Fifth Circuit, which is comprised of Texas, Louisiana, and Mississippi and is the source of a disproportionate number of death penalty cases. White routinely granted extensions for the filing deadlines facing prisoners who did not have the assistance of counsel in preparing their post-conviction claims. However, Chief Justice Rehnquist decided that White should be replaced by Justice Antonin Scalia who immediately announced that all prisoners must adhere to strict time limits for filing petitions, whether or not they have attorneys to assist them (Greenhouse 1991). This policy increases the likelihood that some prisoners will forfeit their claims because they lack the knowledge, intellect, and literacy skills necessary to research, prepare, and present legal claims effectively.

In 1996, Congress took action to support and advance the Supreme Court's efforts to limit convicted offenders' access to habeas corpus. The Antiterrorism and Effective Death Penalty Act imposed new deadlines and limits on successive habeas petitions ("New Antiterrorism Law" 1996). The law also imposed more difficult standards of proof for offenders seeking to gain federal judicial recognition of certain alleged constitutional rights violations (Reuben 1996). The statutory impediments to effective use of the habeas corpus process are especially burdensome because offenders do not have a right to assistance of counsel in preparing their petitions. As a result, the statute increases the likelihood that violations of constitutional rights in criminal cases will go unremedied.

When Congress enacts legislation that effectively hinders the protection of constitutional rights, the U.S. Supreme Court can use its power of judicial review to examine and invalidate such statutes as contrary to the Constitution. In the case of the Antiterrorism and Effective Death Penalty Act, the Supreme Court not only endorsed the validity of the statute and the limitations that it imposed, the justices also rushed with uncharacteristic haste to give the limitations on habeas corpus their stamp of approval. Normally, the Court hears its final cases for each annual term during April and then devotes itself to writing opinions so that decisions can be announced for all of the term's cases by the end of June. The new statute was signed into law on April 24th so observers presumed that any consideration of the statute's constitutional validity would have to wait until the Court's next term began in October. However, the Court accepted a case challenging the Act on May 3rd and set oral arguments for June 3rd. It is extraordinarily rare for justices to hear an oral argument in June rather than carrying the case over until the next regular term in the fall. Previously, the Court had taken such action in hearing the Watergate case concerning whether President Nixon would be required to give the independent prosecutor tapes of conversations recorded in the White House (*U.S. v. Nixon* 1974). That case concerned a looming constitutional crisis and thus required immediate attention from the high court. A case concerning habeas corpus reforms did not seem to be as urgent. Despite protests from four of the justices that adequate examination and deliberation would be impossible when giving attorneys just one month to prepare a case which the justices would then have only a few weeks to decide, the Court proceeded to hear and decide the case very quickly. By endorsing the limitations on habeas corpus so quickly (*Felker v. Turpin* 1996), as if deciding an urgent case of national importance, the Supreme Court reinforced the appearance that it placed a high priority on limiting opportunities for convicted offenders to receive consideration and vindication of claims concerning constitutional rights (Smith 1997b).

Conclusion

A central element in the conception of justice underlying the constitutional governing system of the United States is the protection of constitutional rights. The authors of the Constitution and the Bill of Rights were wary of the manner in which excessive governmental power might be applied to misuse criminal justice processes in order to improperly search, arrest, imprison, and mistreat those individuals whose conduct is regarded as violating criminal statutes. The Bill of Rights provides legal protections in the criminal justice process for all citizens, including the most deservedly despised individuals who have harmed others while violating criminal statutes.

In interpreting and applying the constitutional provisions relevant to convicted offenders, the U.S. Supreme Court in the final decades of the twentieth century diminished the scope of constitutional rights and created impediments to the examination and vindication of those rights. It is clear that convicted offenders cannot enjoy all constitutional rights in the same manner as other citizens because of the need to maintain security and order in correctional settings. Thus, the Supreme Court must necessarily strike a balance between protection of rights and maintenance of correctional objectives. In striking the balance, however, the Court makes choices about priorities and about whose determinations will control the scope of legal protections. Rather than closely scrutinize correctional policies and practices to ensure that convicted offenders obtain the fullest measure of rights consistent with security, order, and other correctional objectives, the Court has adopted a deferential approach that subordinates even less threatening rights, such as free exercise of religion, to discretionary preferences of correctional administrators (e.g., *O'Lone v. Estate of Shabazz* 1987). Moreover, the Court has enhanced impediments to the vindication of all rights by preventing lower court judges from actively seeking reasonable mechanisms to ensure the adequacy of legal resources and assistance needed by *pro se* litigators in correctional settings (*Lewis v. Casey* 1996). As a result, the limited rights that exist as a formal matter of law are not necessarily implemented to protect the legitimate interests of convicted offenders.

The Supreme Court also imposed and endorsed impediments to the vindication of constitutional rights violated in the process of investigating and prosecuting criminal cases. The Court's restrictions on habeas corpus processes impose difficult burdens on convicted offenders who have no right to counsel for habeas proceedings and therefore must usually attempt to prepare and present their own cases. As a result, constitutional rights violations go uncorrected if they are not quickly discovered and proven by convicted offenders or if procedural errors preclude their consideration by the courts. In the most troubling cases, the impediments to consideration and vindication of constitutional rights can lead to the incarceration or execution of individuals who have been erroneously convicted of crimes for which they were not guilty. Such outcomes occur with appalling regularity in the American criminal process, and the public is reminded of this fact repeatedly as hardly a month goes by without news reports of innocent prisoners being released, sometimes after serving many years in prison (e.g., Cooper 2001; Maguire 2001; "Wrongly Held Man" 2001). When the

Supreme Court's actions facilitate these errors by limiting the Constitution's potential to provide legal protections, the high court bears responsibility for contributing to case outcomes that are the very antithesis of any definition of justice.

7

Judicial Behavior
and the Ideal of Equal Justice

IF THE CRIMINAL law process of the United States is compared with those
of many other countries, there is much to be appreciated about the
American system. Criminal suspects, defendants, and convicted offenders
are entitled to legal protections that help to guard against abusive actions by
police and other government officials. These legal protections, in the form
of constitutional rights, limit police authority to conduct searches, provide
attorneys for indigent defendants, permit the use of trials to determine guilt,
and otherwise supply a variety of procedural entitlements designed to create
fair proceedings. Legal protections are not always implemented as intended
by the judicial decisions that define the rights contained within the
Constitution, but there are mechanisms available to create the possibility of
enforcing these protections. Defendants may make motions in trial courts
to exclude evidence that was obtained in violation of their rights.
Sometimes they succeed in gaining judicial orders to bar the presentation of
improperly obtained incriminating evidence. After conviction, defendants
may file appeals or *habeas corpus* petitions to request that other courts review
the actions by police, prosecutors, and trial judges to ensure that all
constitutional rights were respected and protected. In some circumstances,
people can file civil lawsuits against the police or corrections officials
seeking monetary compensation for harms caused by the violation of
specific constitutional rights. Such lawsuits may be successful when
presenting claims about the excessive use of force, improper arrests, and
illegal searches. Lawsuits may be filed by innocent, free citizens as well as by

incarcerated convicted offenders. The existence of constitutional rights and mechanisms to enforce those rights stands in stark contrast to the relative absence of such protections in many countries where the ruling elite controls governmental institutions and processes, including legal processes in court, and uses those processes to advance regime maintenance rather than fair outcomes. Unfortunately, the existence of rights within the American system often obscures recognition of the ways in which these rights either fail to fulfill the words of the Constitution or receive inconsistent application in the justice system.

Unfulfilled Rights

Although it is true that American criminal law processes compare favorably by some measures to those of many other countries, the use of such comparisons can inappropriately mask the deficiencies of the American system. Comparisons of the United States with nondemocratic governing systems, in particular, give Americans an appreciation for what they have without illuminating those aspects of the criminal law process that fail to deliver the quality of justice promised by the Constitution and by the judiciary that portrays itself as the guardian of the nation's foundational document. Some of the legal system's deficiencies may be considered illusory promises or even illusory rights if people believe in the existence and effectiveness of legal protections that are applied inconsistently or inefficaciously. For example, the right to trial by jury, usually referred to as "a jury of one's peers," is trumpeted as a hallmark of the American justice system. Even so, few Americans realize that the Sixth Amendment right to trial by jury has been interpreted to apply only to "serious" charges that might each produce a sentence of more than six months of imprisonment. In reality, a defendant could be sentenced to twenty years in prison without having a right to trial by jury if he or she was charged with forty separate "petty" offenses (e.g., such as stealing forty letters from the U.S. mail) that each drew sixth-month sentences that were to be served consecutively (*Lewis v. United States* 1996). The right to trial by jury is real, but its limited applicability makes public perceptions of its universality misguided. Similarly, the Sixth Amendment right to counsel is illusory in the sense that its actual implementation guarantees indigent defendants little more than the opportunity to have a defense attorney stand next to them in the courtroom while they plead guilty. The Supreme Court's decisions that make it extremely difficult to prove unconstitutionally ineffective counsel reflect a reluctance to second-guess the actions (and inactions) of defense attorneys (*Lockhart v. Fretwell* 1993). The lax standards created by the Supreme Court have led some judges to the point of declaring that a defendant is not necessarily denied his right to counsel when his defense attorney falls asleep on numerous occasions during a capital murder trial (*Burdine v. Johnson* 2001). If some judges believe that a defense attorney can sleep during the presentation of evidence in a death penalty trial without violating his client's Sixth Amendment rights, then what extreme malfeasance would these judges require to identify an attorney's performance that falls below constitutional standards? The purported right to counsel is obviously illusory with respect to defendants whose attorneys provide poor or nonexistent representation.

Constitutional rights, such as the examples of the right to a jury trial and the right to counsel, are illusory when people mistakenly believe that these rights exist in a form that provides much broader legal protections than those actually guaranteed in practice. By contrast, the legal system's purported promise of "equal justice under law" is not an *illusory* goal of the system. In reality, it is a *chimerical* goal; one that is a fantasy that much of society recognizes has little connection with reality. Responses to public opinion polls provide evidence that many Americans believe that the criminal law process falls short of its purported aspiration for fair and equal justice. For example, in a national survey conducted by the Gallup Poll in September 2000, only 16 percent of respondents believed that the criminal justice system is "very fair." Approximately half of the respondents implicitly recognized deficiencies in criminal law processes when they called the system "somewhat fair" and nearly 30 percent said it was either "somewhat unfair" or "very unfair" (Gallup Poll 2000). In another national poll, nearly 40 percent of respondents said that, in general, "blacks are accused and convicted of criminal acts more than whites simply because they are black" (Locke 1999, 204). The public's awareness of and skepticism about fairness and equal treatment in the criminal law process are not surprising in light of the regular news media attention to such persistent problems as racial profiling, excessive use of force by police, and erroneous convictions, especially in death penalty cases. In light of the public's expressed concerns about the fairness of the criminal law process, perhaps the most surprising aspect of this issue is the relative lack of such expressions of skepticism and concern among the justices of the Supreme Court whose decisions help to determine the extent to which the Constitution advances "equal justice under law." The Rehnquist Court majority's lack of skepticism and disinclination to use their authority to enhance fairness and equal treatment reflect the political events that determined which individuals would be selected for service on the high court as well as historical developments that shaped the justices' experiences and values.

Supreme Court Justices'
Orientation Toward the Expansion of Rights

The justices of the Warren Court era (1953–1969) incorporated most criminal justice related rights in the Bill of Rights for application to state and local officials. In addition, their interpretations expanded the definitions of numerous rights and thereby established a variety of nationwide legal protections, such as *Miranda* warnings and the exclusionary rule, that previously existed only in some of the nation's jurisdictions, if at all. Many politicians and law enforcement officials complained that the Warren Court went too far in expanding rights affecting criminal justice. As a result, "law and order" became a political issue in many electoral campaigns with candidates pledging to work toward installing new judges who would diminish the scope of rights for suspect, defendants, and convicted offenders. The "law and order" campaign themes espoused by Republican presidential candidate Barry Goldwater in 1964 attracted public attention and forced subsequent candidates to respond to the issue of crime (Gest 2001). As a presidential candidate in 1968, Richard Nixon publicly complained that "some of our courts in their decisions have gone too far in weakening the peace forces as against the criminal forces in this country"

(Epstein & Walker 1992, 335). Thus, he and the Republican presidents that followed him for the next quarter of a century attempted to nominate new justices to the Supreme Court who would interpret the Constitution in ways that reduced the scope of rights and thereby diminished limitations imposed on police, prosecutors, and corrections officials. The values and policy preferences of most justices appointed since 1969 reflect an orientation toward limiting criminal justice rights. With the exception of President Clinton's appointees, Justices Ginsburg and Breyer, and President Ford's appointee, Justice Stevens, justices were selected for the high court because they were perceived to share the Republican presidents' preference for relaxing requirements for criminal justice officials, even if it meant either enhancing or failing to confront less than equal treatment of suspects, defendants, and convicted offenders in the criminal justice process.

The happenstance of political events that placed Republican presidents in the White House at most of the moments when justices retired or resigned contributed to an ideological orientation within the Court that has impeded efforts to interpret the Constitution in ways that would advance the purported goal of "equal justice under law." The individuals selected to serve as Supreme Court justices have favored goals other than equal treatment in their interpretation of the Constitution. In speculating about why the majority of justices are generally unreceptive to claims concerning the rights of suspects, defendants, and convicted offenders, some observers have pointed to the prior professional experiences of these justices as a potentially important element in shaping their viewpoints and values. For example, none of the justices on the Rehnquist Court at the turn of the twenty-first century had ever represented a defendant in a criminal case (Fortunato 1999). Service as a criminal defense attorney arguably provides an opportunity to recognize the complexity of criminal cases, the human consequences of prosecution for defendants and their families, and the importance of legal protections for those who must square off against the state in court proceedings. By contrast, several of the justices had experience representing the government in the enforcement of various laws against individuals. Chief Justice William Rehnquist and Justice Antonin Scalia had both served as assistant attorneys general in the U.S. Justice

Department. Justice David Souter had been Attorney General of New Hampshire and Justice Clarence Thomas served as an assistant attorney general in Missouri. The possible causal link between prior professional experience and judicial decision making is debated in the social science literature, particularly because one cannot know whether prosecutorial experience builds a particular worldview or set of values (Tate 1981). It may simply be that people who possess those viewpoints and values choose to become prosecutors rather than their experience in the job of prosecutor influencing the development of these values. However, because attitudes and values are believed to be shaped by experiences in life, especially teachings by parents and early experiences, the possibility exists that early professional experience is a component of that value-shaping process.

The Protection of Rights and Generational Socialization

One of the most striking aspects of comparing contemporary Supreme Court justices with their predecessors in the Warren Court era is the differences in their life experiences and personal knowledge about the need for individual rights and rules for law enforcement officials in the criminal law process. The Warren Court justices grew up in an era in which they gained personal knowledge of unprofessional and abusive conduct by law enforcement officials. By contrast, the Rehnquist Court justices came to adulthood after professionalization processes impacted criminal justice occupations, and officials' abusive actions had already been constrained by Supreme Court decisions. Differences in experience and knowledge could readily affect the justices' relative skepticism about officials' motives and conduct as well as a corresponding recognition of the need for strong individual rights in order to create legal guidelines for officials' permissible authority and behavior (Smith 1990).

Historically, the police worked for the prevailing political establishment within each community. According to Samuel Walker (1984, 84), they "enforced the narrow prejudices of their constituencies, harassing 'undesirables' or discouraging any kind of 'unwelcome' behavior." Harassment and brutality were directed at racial minorities, religious minorities, immigrants, and the poor as well as at political opponents.

Moreover, there were generally few qualifications necessary for becoming a law enforcement officer. Frequently, nearly any adult white male could become a police officer through loyalty to the controlling political interests. The risks of abusive behavior from the politically motivated and untrained law enforcement officers were exacerbated by the absence of constitutional protections for criminal suspects. For most of American history, police officers were relatively free to employ coercive and even violent methods against criminal defendants because the Supreme Court did not apply many of the provisions of the Bill of Rights to limit actions by state and local criminal justice officials until the 1960s.

Early in the twentieth century a movement began to professionalize police departments. Advocates of reform sought to make police officers act as neutral civil servants and remove law enforcement from the control of partisan political machines. The professionalization movement was motivated by the same forces generating other Progressive Era reforms in government and politics, such as civil service and juvenile courts (Walker 1977).

The police reform movement arose, in part, from public concern about brutal treatment of criminal suspects by law enforcement officers. The Wickersham Commission in 1931 released a report documenting police violence and brutal methods used to extract confessions from suspects. According to Walker, this report both generated and reflected changing public expectations about police behavior:

> The significance of the third degree controversy was twofold. On the one hand it reflected the heightened public concern about the police. At the same time, however, it represented a dramatic shift in public expectations about the quality of law enforcement. Brutality and uncivil conduct had long been part of the American police tradition. However, by the early 1930s the public was not only increasingly intolerant of the more flagrant abuses of power but also began to expect the police to conform to constitutional standards of due process (Walker 1977, 133).

Warren Court decisions on defendants' rights also pushed the police to professionalize. These decisions defined rules for proper police procedures by identifying which police practices caused rights violations. For example, in the famous *Miranda* decision in 1966 requiring police to inform suspects of their rights, Chief Justice Warren devoted much of his opinion to a critique of abusive police practices. The decision provided relatively clear rules about what police must say to arrestees and clearly limited the potential for abusive interrogation practices. As a result of these changes, historians documented reductions in police lawlessness and corruption in urban police departments in the 1960s and thereafter (Fogelson 1977).

The forces of professionalism and court decisions defining rights eventually had similar effects on policies and practices in prisons. In corrections, the introduction of judicial mandates and opportunities for convicted offenders to seek enforcement of those mandates in court coincided with an influx of college-educated administrators in prisons. These twin developments helped to transform correctional institutions from fiefdoms under the absolute and arbitrary control of officials to bureaucratic governmental organizations guided by legal norms (Jacobs 1977).

Because police made significant strides toward professionalization as a result of the reform movement and the Warren-era decisions, perceptions of the risks of police abuse have apparently diminished in the minds of recent Court appointees. Warren and other justices during the 1960s could not only remember the publicity from the Wickersham report and other exposes of the 1930s, they also had personal experience with the problems of police misconduct. Chief Justice Warren, who served on the Court from 1953 to 1969, had observed and even participated in coercive interrogations during his tenure as a prosecuting attorney in California during the 1930s (White 1982). Justice William O. Douglas, who served on the Court from 1939 to 1975, had several unpleasant encounters with local law enforcement officials during his impoverished youth in the early twentieth century. He hopped aboard freight trains to travel from town to town in search of work picking crops. In his autobiography's discussion of his youth in Yakima, Washington, Douglas (1974, 78) declared:

The police, in my view, represented the ultimate personality of the Establishment that owned and ran the Yakima Valley. They were harsh and relentless and bore down heavily on the nonconformist. They caused a close sifting of loyalties in a young man who felt the roughness of their hand. I knew their victims too intimately to align myself with the police.

Other members of the Warren Court also had personal experience with abusive behavior by criminal justice officials. Justice Thurgood Marshall, who served from 1967 to 1991, experienced racism firsthand as an African American youth in Baltimore in the early twentieth century. In addition, he traveled throughout the South as an attorney for the NAACP during the 1930s and 1940s documenting discriminatory and abusive police actions and litigating cases against various state and local governments. Indeed, he was nearly lynched by a mob of law enforcement officers in Tennessee when his car was stopped on a dark highway (Rowan 1993). As a youngster, Justice William Brennan, who served from 1956 to 1990, saw his father beaten bloody by the police for attempting to help organize a labor union (Eisler 1993). While serving as a prosecutor and police court judge in Alabama during the World War I era, Justice Hugo Black, who served on the Supreme Court from the 1930s through 1971, undoubtedly knew about abusive practices applied during the preprofessional era in a time and place in which criminal justice officials used their legal authority to oppress and harass African Americans. In other words, because they had firsthand knowledge of unrestrained, abusive practices in the criminal law process, several members of the Court during the Warren era had a concrete reference point for awareness of the risks of harmful, inhumane behavior by criminal justice officials.

By contrast, the members of the Rehnquist Court's conservative majority (i.e., Rehnquist, O'Connor, Scalia, Kennedy, and Thomas) were children during the 1930s and 1940s, and did not reach adulthood until after many abusive practices had been altered by the professionalism movement. Some of them did not reach adulthood until after the Warren Court had mandated additional restrictions on officials' authority through constitutional decisions that defined rights for suspects, defendants, and convicted offenders. In addition to their policy orientation toward relaxing rules for criminal justice officials, these justices do not possess the same skepticism about the potential for abuse of authority that was possessed by their predecessors who had personal knowledge of such activities. In effect, the professionalization of criminal justice officials and reduction in blatant abusive practices has dimmed the Supreme Court's institutional memory about the reasons that *Mapp v. Ohio* (1961), *Miranda v. Arizona* (1966), and other Warren-era decisions sought to draw relatively clear lines for the acceptable behavior of criminal justice officials.

As discussed in the preceding chapters of this book, the Rehnquist Court's decisions interpreting the Constitution have tended to place a higher value on providing criminal justice officials with flexible, discretionary authority than on seeking to effectuate the goal of equal justice. For example, when the Court turned a blind eye to the statistical evidence of racial discrimination in the imposition of the death penalty, Justice Lewis Powell's majority opinion emphasized the importance of maintaining criminal justice officials' discretionary decision making authority (*McCleskey v. Kemp* 1987). Similarly, the Court's diminution of rights for convicted offenders is based on the justices' reluctance to interfere with decision making by corrections officials (*O'Lone v. Shabazz* 1987).

An argument asserting that the justices should be more sensitive to the risks of abusive and discriminatory actions by criminal justice officials should not be equated with a condemnation of police, prosecutors, and judges as immoral, unethical, cruel, or corrupt. As Yale Kamisar (1989, B9) noted, one can raise concerns about police misbehavior without a jaded view of law enforcement officers themselves: "[The risks are] not because the police are more dishonest than the rest of us... [but] rather because they are no less human than the rest of us—no less inclined to further their own interests if given the leeway to do so." H. Richard Uviller (1988) reached similar conclusions about the risks of police misbehavior after his study of police in New York City.

Because they lack the firsthand knowledge and personal experiences of their Warren era predecessors, the justices comprising the Rehnquist Court majority have few influences to constrain their values and policy preferences that favor justice system officials' autonomy and discretion at the expense of equal treatment for suspects, defendants, and convicted offenders. Moreover, in examining their interpretations of the Equal Protection Clause, there is additional evidence that several justices are motivated by political values rather than recognition of and sensitivity to unequal treatment.

The Rehnquist Court Majority's Priorities and Values

A central theme for the majority of Rehnquist Court justices is restraining the activity and influence of the federal government and, especially, the federal courts. This theme emerges under two different but related labels. In some cases, the justices emphasize the need for "judicial restraint." In other cases, the justices emphasize the importance of their vision of "federalism" which involves permitting states to handle their own affairs as much as possible without interference by Congress, the president, or the federal courts. By judicial restraint, they typically mean the importance (in their eyes) of federal judges permitting other branches of government and the states handle their own affairs without interference. In equal protection related cases, the Rehnquist Court majority permitted school districts to end busing plans, even if the result would be a return to racially segregated schools (*Board of Education of Oklahoma City v. Dowell*, 1991). They also permitted the withdrawal of judicial supervision over school districts that had not yet achieved desegregation in all areas of operation (*Freeman v. Pitts*, 1992) and reined in federal judges whose remedial orders aggressively sought to ensure the success of school desegregation plans by attracting the enrollment of additional white students (*Missouri v. Jenkins*, 1995). In the area of public education, Professor Gary Orfield of Harvard University has labeled the Rehnquist Court's cases as "resegregation" decisions "authorizing school districts to return to segregated and unequal public schools" (Orfield & Eaton 1996, 1).

The majority's emphasis on judicial restraint in the context of federalism is evident in other decisions. For example, justices' opinions have argued that federal judges should defer to determinations by state judges when examining prisoners' habeas corpus petitions (*Wright v. West*,

1992). The Rehnquist Court majority altered the definition of "cruel and unusual punishment" applied to Eighth Amendment cases challenging conditions of confinement in correctional institutions by creating a standard that makes it extraordinarily difficult to justify judicial intervention. The subjective test established in *Wilson v. Seiter* (1991) asks whether prison officials were "deliberately indifferent" to deficient conditions rather than whether the conditions caused unnecessary pain and suffering. As a result, prison officials are able to make many of their own decisions about their institutions without fear of intervention by federal judges, even if improper conditions exist, so long as they assert that they were concerned about the conditions within their institution. By generally adopting a deferential posture toward decisions by corrections officials (e.g., *O'Lone v. Shabazz*, 1987), the Rehnquist Court majority has limited the scope of prisoners' rights and restrained federal judges from making decisions that will affect policies and practices in prisons and jails.

Chief Justice Rehnquist, Justice Scalia, Justice O'Connor, and Justice Kennedy regularly write opinions that emphasize the limited role of judges in shaping law and public policy. They all appear to agree with Justice Clarence Thomas's statement that

> it is important certainly that judges not confuse their role as judges in interpreting the Constitution with [Congress's] role..., the important role making policies and determining statutory and legislative policies that we should have in this country in a variety of areas. I think it is very important that judges realize that their role is a limited one. (*Nomination*, 1991, 341)

With respect to federalism in general, since 1937 the Supreme Court had recognized the power of Congress to legislate broadly with respect to matters related to interstate commerce. Article I, section 8 of the Constitution grants to Congress the power to regulate "interstate commerce." Prior to 1937, the Court had often interpreted that phrase narrowly and thereby permitted states to regulate many commercial activities within their own borders, even if those activities, such as manufacturing and mining, produced goods sold throughout the nation and had a significant impact on the national economy. After President Franklin

Roosevelt began to appoint new justices to the Court in the 1930s, the Court defined congressional power so broadly that a farmer growing a small plot of wheat for consumption on his own farm was determined to be subject to federal regulations (*Wickard v. Filburn* 1942). Congress subsequently used this broad interpretation of its authority to regulate interstate commerce as the basis for wide-ranging legislation concerning minimum wages, working conditions, employment discrimination, and even criminal matters. After a sixty-year period in which the federal government applied this broad authority, the Rehnquist Court suddenly shifted gears and limited federal authority in favor of states having power over their own affairs. In 1995, Rehnquist, O'Connor, Kennedy, Scalia, and Thomas stunned constitutional law professors by suddenly limiting the power of Congress to regulate under the Commerce Clause. This five-member majority invalidated the Gun-Free School Zones Act that had made it a federal crime to possess a firearm in or near a school (*United States v. Lopez* 1995). By declaring the law to be unconstitutional, the justices emphasized that states should handle their own affairs without interference from the federal government. Similarly, in *Printz v. United States* (1997), the five-member majority decided that Congress could not mandate that local sheriffs conduct background checks on gun purchasers. In *United States v. Morrison* (2000), the Court said that Congress exceeded its authority in the Violence Against Women Act of 1994 by authorizing civil lawsuits in federal courts by victims of gender motivated violence. These decisions reflected a preference for permitting state and local control of policies and keeping all of the federal governmental branches, including courts, from interfering with states' development and implementation of their own laws.

The Rehnquist Court majority also revealed its priorities and values in decisions concerning equal protection issues. As discussed in Chapter 3, the dawn of the Rehnquist Court era saw the majority of justices reject an equal protection claim based on strong statistical evidence that African American defendants and victims were treated differently from their white counterparts in Georgia murder cases that led to death sentences (*McCleskey v. Kemp* 1987). In subsequent years, the Court addressed a number of other equal protection claims. Since the retirements of Warren-era holdovers,

Justice William Brennan (1990) and Thurgood Marshall (1991), the Supreme Court has supported individual claimants by identifying violations of the Equal Protection Clause in only a few cases. The Court found in favor of a white-owned company that challenged federal government affirmative action policies that steered a fraction of highway contracts to "disadvantaged business enterprises" owned by members of minority groups (*Adarand Constructors, Inc. v. Pena* 1995). The Court effectively expanded an earlier decision favoring a white-owned business that challenged similar policies by state and local governments (*City of Richmond v. Croson* 1989). The Court found a denial of equal protection in the exclusion of women from the Virginia Military Academy (*United States v. Virginia* 1996). The Court also invalidated a Colorado law that prohibited state and local governments from enacting or enforcing laws prohibiting discrimination against gays and lesbians (*Romer v. Evans* 1996). The only decisions favoring individuals that affected the criminal law process concerned the prohibitions on discrimination based on race and gender in applying peremptory challenges in jury selection (*J.E.B. ex rel Alabama v. T.B.* 1994; *Georgia v. McCollum* 1992; *Edmonson v. Leesville Concrete* 1991). However, as discussed in Chapter 3, these decisions provided illusory protections because the Court subsequently permitted trial judges to accept pretextual excuses for exclusions apparently based on race and gender, even if those excuses were silly or irrational (*Purkett v. Elem* 1995).

In *United States v. Armstrong* (1996), by contrast, the justices blocked an investigation into possible racial discrimination by prosecutors. A defense attorney presented evidence that one U.S. attorney was prosecuting only members of minority groups for cocaine offenses, yet the Supreme Court would not permit the attorney to gather additional information from the prosecutor's files that might clearly establish the existence of racial discrimination in prosecution policies. In dissent, Justice Stevens noted, "While 65% of the persons who have used crack cocaine are white, in 1993 they represented only 4% of the federal offenders convicted of trafficking in crack. Eighty-eight percent of such defendants were black" (*United States v. Armstrong* 1996, 479–480). Although evidence has been presented to the Supreme Court concerning racial discrimination in capital punishment

(*McCleskey v. Kemp* 1987) and in cocaine prosecutions and sentencing (*United States v. Armstrong* 1996), a majority of justices have stopped the Court from taking action against these manifestations of unequal justice, despite the fact that all of the justices agree that the Equal Protection Clause should protect against racial discrimination. By contrast, the justices disagree with each other about the extent to which the clause should protect against governmental discrimination by gender, sexual preference, social class, and other characteristics. As other issues of discrimination, such as racial profiling by police in traffic stops, gain more attention from the news media and public, the Supreme Court has increased the autonomous authority of the police to undertake discretionary stops (*Whren v. United States* 1996) and to take motorists into custody for minor offenses, such as failure to wear a seatbelt (*Atwater v. City of Lago Vista* 2001). Such decisions serve to expand opportunities for discrimination rather than to assess accurately the realities of police behavior in order to develop legal rules that will diminish the risks of unequal treatment.

The decisions also apparently reflect the priorities and values of the majority of justices who frequently trumpet the importance of judicial restraint and the need to prevent the federal government from intruding into the affairs of state and local governments. As indicated by the foregoing discussion, the Rehnquist Court majority seldom identifies any violations of the Equal Protection Clause but increasingly emphasizes the importance of federalism and judicial restraint. The perception that these justices do not place a high priority on the eradication of discrimination has been further enhanced by their decisions that limit the scope of federal civil rights statutes that permit victims of unequal treatment to seek remedies in the federal courts (*United States v. Morrison* 2000; *Alexander v. Sandoval* 2001; *Board of Trustees of the University of Alabama v. Garrett* 2001). Such decisions may provide an additional indication of the justices' priorities by limiting the reach of federal laws against discrimination. As a result, statutory legal tools to combat unequal treatment are eliminated in the Court's effort to limit federal authority and judicial involvement in antidiscrimination efforts.

Apparent Inconsistencies and Justices' Priorities

If these justices consistently adhered to their preferences for judicial restraint and federalism, it would be easy to conclude that they simply believe that those two priorities receive greater consideration in their hierarchy of values than do equal protection and the advancement of equal justice under law. Such a conclusion could serve as the basis for disagreeing with and criticizing the Court for failing to use its authority to advance the system's purported goal of equal treatment in the criminal law process and other aspects of the legal system. Despite such disagreements, these justices could honestly claim that their view of the American constitutional governing system obligates them to advance the democracy enhancing qualities and functions purportedly served by judicial restraint and federalism as premier values and objectives. Moreover, they could assert that their advancement of democracy will ultimately advance equal treatment because it permits the voters to push state and local elected officials toward the fulfillment of societal objectives. A major flaw in this line argument would arise, however, if these justices were not, in fact, consistent advocates of judicial restraint and federalism. If they selectively utilized equal protection principles and judicial intervention to advance alternative objectives, then it would be clear that equal treatment is not merely an extant value that happens to reside below federalism and judicial restraint on the justices' hierarchy of values. Instead, such selective use of equal protection principles and judicial intervention would provide evidence that "equal justice under law" is actually a *disfavored* objective that the justices reject for reasons other than their purported fidelity to federalism and judicial restraint. In this context, a "disfavored" objective need not imply that the justices actively oppose the advancement of equal treatment within the legal system. It may also mean that the justices are so insensitive to the problems of unequal treatment that these issues remain unrecognized and misunderstood as the justices utilize their authority to advance their priorities and values.

Bush v. Gore (2000), the Supreme Court's monumental decision that put an end to the controversial presidential election of 2000, shed light on the Rehnquist Court majority's concern (or lack thereof) for "equal justice under law" by revealing the justices' willingness to use the Equal Protection Clause and judicial intervention in a context in which issues of federalism and judicial restraint loomed large. Moving against the trend of its federalism decisions that favored state autonomy and authority, a five-member majority (Rehnquist, O'Connor, Kennedy, Scalia, Thomas) effectively decided the outcome of the presidential election by terminating the Florida Supreme Court's order for a recount under state law. The majority said the state court's recount order violated the equal protection rights of certain voters. By preserving the existing vote tallies that gave Bush a slim margin of victory, the justices effectively ignored myriad voting irregularities that kept many voters, especially Al Gore's supporters, from having their ballots properly counted as expressing their preferences. Subsequent statistical analyses by social scientists demonstrated that the confusing and illegal "butterfly ballot" in Palm Beach County by itself led Bush to prevail after the terminated recount because so many Gore voters accidentally punched their ballots for Reform Party candidate Patrick Buchanan when Buchanan's punch spot ("chad") on the ballot was placed to the right of Gore's name (Wand et al. 2001). The "butterfly ballot" with candidates' names spread across two pages clearly violated the state statute mandating that candidates be listed in a single column with the spot for indicating the vote to be placed "at the right of the name of the candidate for whom you desire to vote" (Fla. Stat. 101.151(3)(a)). The U.S. Supreme Court's action in the name of equal protection did nothing to ensure equal treatment for these voters or for voters in other counties who were erroneously removed from the voting rolls, denied access to Spanish-language ballots, and myriad other problems that denied them the opportunity to express their preferences at the polls. Indeed, the electoral problems perpetuated by the Court's abrupt termination of the recount had a disproportionate impact on the original intended beneficiaries of the Equal Protection Clause. According to the preliminary investigation of voting problems conducted by the U.S. Civil Rights Commission, African American voters suffered disproportionate adverse effects from erroneous exclusions from voting rolls, antiquated and error-prone punch card ballot systems, and inadequately staffed and equipped polling places ("Rights

Commission's Report" 2001). African Americans comprised only 11 percent of all Florida voters, but they cast 54 percent of the ballots that were rejected by elections officials ("Rights Commission's Report" 2001).

The Court's selectively-applied and limited interpretation of the Equal Protection Clause created the illusion of protecting equal treatment for voters. The illusory nature of the majority's purported concern for unequal treatment of voters became clear to readers of the Court's opinion who noticed one sentence subtly buried in the text that indicated the Court's application of equal protection principles to elections was *for this case only*. In the Equal Protection Clause's 132-year history preceding *Bush v. Gore*, the Court had never before identified an equal protection based constitutional right to have ballots counted according to a common standard. Then, having created this new constitutional right, the majority announced that this right applied only to this particular case. The right was not intended to apply to other cases. In effect, it only applied to protect Bush's Florida supporters in the 2000 presidential election. The majority clearly indicated that it did not intend to address unequal treatment in other elections, other states, or Florida counties in which Gore supporters were treated unequally when it said: "Our consideration is limited to the present circumstances, for the problems of equal protection in election processes generally present many complexities" (*Bush v. Gore* 2000, 109). Linda Greenhouse (2000, 1), the *New York Times*' Pulitzer Prize-winning analyst of Supreme Court decisions observed that "Among the most baffling aspects of the opinion was its simultaneous creation of a new equal protection right not have ballots counted according to different standards and its disclaimer that this new constitutional principle would never apply in another case."

Unfortunately, the Court's decision in *Bush v. Gore* had the appearance and effect of ensuring that the candidate who shared a political party affiliation with the five members of the majority would become president. Concerns about federalism and judicial restraint, which are so frequently trumpeted as premier values by Rehnquist, Scalia, Thomas, O'Connor, and Kennedy, seemed to have disappeared when it appeared that Governor Bush's lead in the Florida voting might vanish if the all of the ballots were counted to determine the intent of the voters. Furthermore, these five justices have been the least inclined of all Rehnquist Court justices to apply equal protection principles in circumstances of racial discrimination. None of these justices would identify an equal protection violation when presented with statistical evidence of systemic racial discrimination in death penalty sentencing (*McCleskey v. Kemp* 1987). Even Clarence Thomas, the Court's lone African American who was not yet a justice at the time of the *McCleskey* case, has sharply criticized the use of social science evidence in Supreme Court cases (Smith & Baugh 2000, 60–62). Despite their unwillingness to recognize strong evidence of racial discrimination, these justices were quick to rely on the Equal Protection Clause to preserve the electoral interests of Bush voters in Florida while simultaneously ignoring the numerous equally (if not more) compelling forms of unequal treatment that adversely affected voters who generally supported Vice President Gore.

A closer look at the justices' personal connections and possible motivations reveals troubling elements. National news organizations reported witnesses' descriptions of Justice O'Connor's distraught outburst at a party on election night when it appeared that Vice President Gore would win the election. Her husband reportedly explained to bystanders that the justice planned to retire if Bush won the election so that she could be replaced by a Republican appointee. However, she would be disappointed to be forced to remain on the Court at least four more years if Gore became president (Thomas & Isikoff 2000). As the litigation unfolded, Justice Thomas's wife was responsible for gathering resumes at the Heritage Foundation in order to advise Governor Bush on whom to appoint to government jobs in the executive branch (Krugman 2000). Although Thomas's defenders claimed that Mrs. Thomas was employed by the Heritage Foundation and not by the Bush campaign, there was no denying the fact that her work was on behalf of the Bush campaign. In light of his spouse's paid employment on Bush's behalf, there is a serious question about whether Thomas should have recused himself and declined to participate in a decision in which his family had an apparent conflict of interest. Similar problems regarding the appearance of potential bias or conflict of interest existed concerning Justice Scalia, who had sons working at each of the two law firms representing the Bush campaign in the post-election litigation. According to Title 28, section 455 of the U.S. Code, judicial officers must recuse themselves when they have a spouse who has an interest that could be substantially affected by the outcome of a proceeding or in circumstances in which their impartiality might reasonably be questioned (Romano 2001). Instead of withdrawing themselves from consideration of this case, these justices, along with Rehnquist and Kennedy, produced a questionable decision creating a new "for-this-case-only" constitutional right that involved repudiating or ignoring their usual themes of enhancing federalism and advocating judicial restraint.

The Court's decision in *Bush v. Gore* made it clear that the justices' disinclination to apply the Equal Protection Clause to advance the ideal of equal justice in the criminal justice system is a choice based on personal values and policy preferences. The justices are willing to interpret and apply equal protection rights in situations that fit with their priorities. Unfortunately, a number of justices give scant attention to recognizing and remedying aspects of unequal treatment that affect criminal defendants and convicted offenders.

The Prospects for Equal Justice Under Law

Unequal treatment of suspects, defendants, and convicted offenders in the criminal law process stems from several sources. Foremost among these causes is the application of discretionary authority by criminal justice officials. Police officers make choices about which individuals to stop, search, and arrest. Prosecutors make choices about which charges to pursue or whether to drop all charges in a case. Judges often have discretion in ruling on evidentiary disputes and other matters, including sentences. Corrections officials employ discretion in making work assignments, conducting searches, imposing discipline, and respecting constitutional rights. The U.S. Supreme Court and other courts cannot issue decisions that guarantee equal treatment for people in the system. Law, including judicially created law through court decisions, is not self-effectuating. Moreover, judges do not have the capacity to oversee the implementation of their decisions. Despite these limitations on judicial power, justices of the Supreme Court are not impotent when considering the problems of unequal treatment. Through their authority to interpret the Equal Protection Clause, the Sixth Amendment right to counsel, and other constitutional provisions, the justices can establish new rules and norms that push criminal justice officials toward the objective of "equal justice under law." The Supreme Court's decisions provide a basis for appeals and civil rights lawsuits by individuals whose rights were violated by criminal justice officials. The Court's decisions also shape college criminal justice curricula and training programs for police officers.

The Rehnquist Court has not adequately utilized its decision-making authority to advance the goal of equal justice. A majority of justices turned a blind eye to statistical evidence of racial discrimination in the death penalty and in prosecution policies. The Court's decisions on police authority to stop people and conduct searches have generally preserved or expanded broad discretionary authority that facilitates racial profiling in traffic stops and other aspects of the continuing problem of unequal treatment by race. In the one area in which the Court acted to limit discrimination, the use of race and gender in peremptory challenges for jury selection, the Court's decisions turned out to be largely symbolic. In the aftermath of *Purkett v. Elem* (1995), it became clear that attorneys can continue to employ categorical discrimination in jury selection as long as they do not admit what they are doing and the trial judge is willing to accept pretextual excuses.

Problems abound in other aspects of the criminal law process. Criminal laws remain on the books that treat women differently from men. However, the Supreme Court has done little to eradicate such laws by analyzing them in light of equal protection principles. Poor people suffer significant disadvantages in the bail process and in having their fates determined by the decisions of appointed defense attorneys who sometimes lack commitment and skill. Despite these problems, the Supreme Court has avoided creating strong standards for attorney performance that would serve to "level the playing field" in the adversarial processes of criminal justice and thereby reduce the risks of erroneous convictions, rights violations, and unequal treatment. Through the decisions of the U.S. Supreme Court, convicted offenders have seen their legal protections shrink and become increasingly illusory. Corrections officials may be able to avoid ensuring that prison conditions meet standards for human habitability merely by claiming that they were not deliberately indifferent to the poor conditions within their institutions (*Wilson v. Seiter* 1991). Prisoners' legitimate desires to conduct standard religious services can be outweighed by corrections officials' claims that the timing of such services will disrupt prison routines. The Court's deferential posture in examining corrections officials' assertions has needlessly widened the gap between the free exercise of religious rights of free persons and those of incarcerated offenders for whom religion may be a central focus of their self-rehabilitation efforts.

Further progress toward the espoused ideal of "equal justice under law" is possible if a majority of justices on the Supreme Court make that ideal a central focus of their priorities and values. Time and again, dissenting justices in such cases as *McCleskey v. Kemp* (1987), concerning racial discrimination in capital punishment, and *O'Lone v. Shabazz* (1987), concerning the free exercise of religion in prisons, have demonstrated that the Constitution provides a basis for establishing legal principles that will advance the goal of equal treatment. Unfortunately, however, the historical quirks of fate that have shaped the timing of changes in the U.S. Supreme Court's composition have favored the appointment of justices who are relatively unconcerned about and insensitive to the continuing problems of unequal treatment within the criminal law process. These justices are not unaware that the Constitution provides them with the authority to advance equal treatment. Indeed, they are willing to interpret and apply the Equal Protection Clause on occasion. The central problem lies not with their unwillingness to use their interpretive authority but instead with their inclination to use that authority selectively to advance narrow interests. The Rehnquist Court majority has interpreted and applied the Equal Protection Clause to protect the interests of whites and males against affirmative action programs in government contracting (*City of Richmond v. Croson* 1989; *Adarand Constructors v. Pena* 1995). They have used the Equal Protection Clause to create a new one-time-only right to have votes counted in a uniform manner in order to ensure that George Bush would win the presidential election of 2000 (*Bush v. Gore* 2000). By contrast, they have not used the Equal Protection Clause, Due Process Clause, or other constitutional provisions to adequately address unequal treatment of African Americans by police officers, criminal statutes that treat women differently from men, or criminal law processes, such as bail and the right to counsel, that significantly disadvantage poor defendants.

In the affirmative action and presidential election examples in which the majority of justices employed the Equal Protection Clause, their use of the Clause conflicted with their usual advocacy of judicial deference to state and local officials. Moreover, these selective uses of equal protection principles amid numerous glaring and unremedied problems of unequal treatment in the criminal law process, in electoral processes, and elsewhere in society demonstrate clearly the Rehnquist Court majority's insensitivity to the harsh realities of discrimination and their strong commitment to a specific policy agenda. After examining the decisions of the Rehnquist Court, Professor Stephen Gottlieb focused on the conservative justices in concluding that the Court majority's values and decision making do not protect the rights of people who lack power and status in society. According to Gottlieb (2000, 197):

> What unites a portion of the conservative group [of justices] on the Court has been a focus not on the consequences of law but on the purity of official motives.... What unites the core of the conservative group on the Court has been skepticism about law and government and a hostility toward the underdogs who seek their protection.

In light of the gap between the promise of "equal justice" and the reality of unequal treatment in the criminal law process, it is difficult to be optimistic about the prospects for meaningful change through judicial avenues. The Rehnquist Court majority's selective application of equal protection principles that ensured the election of George W. Bush effectively positioned the new president to use his appointment power to select justices who, like the five-member majority in the 1990s, share his antipathy for critical analysis of the sources of inequality and error in the criminal justice system. As governor of Texas, Bush blocked efforts to ensure that capital defendants had adequate defense representation, and he reflexively defended his record as the state chief executive who presided over the largest number of executions while serving as governor. Unless and until a majority of judicial decision makers make equal treatment in the legal system a priority in their hierarchy of interpretive values, change (if it occurs) will be incremental and limited. Any changes that occur will depend on public reactions and political pressure generated by news media descriptions of continuing problems rather than judicial action. At the dawn of the twenty-first century, such media attention and pressure led to scattered legislative and executive efforts to analyze and remedy problems associated with racial profiling by police and inadequate defense representation for capital defendants, such as the death penalty moratorium declared by the governor of Illinois. U.S. Supreme Court decisions advancing equal treatment could have broader impact by creating rules with national applicability, by raising the visibility of existing problems, and by warning criminal justice officials throughout the country that a higher authority stood ready to examine instances of discrimination and unfairness. Unfortunately, both the goal of "Equal Justice Under Law," so prominently displayed on the Supreme Court building, and the means to advance that goal through the Equal Protection Clause and other provisions of the Constitution will remain, respectively, illusory and misused. As long as the majority of decision makers on the highest court emphasize their own narrow policy preferences when they selectively address those circumstances that they define as impermissible unequal treatment, the judiciary's statue of the blindfolded goddess of justice will not embody its intended ideals. Instead of symbolizing neutral decision making and fair outcomes, it will actually stand for an unwillingness to recognize the reality of discrimination and disadvantage in the legal system.

Bibliography

Abraham, Henry J. *The Judicial Process.* 6th ed. New York: Oxford University Press, 1993.

Acker, James. "A Different Agenda: The Supreme Court, Empirical Research Evidence, and Capital Punishment Decisions, 1986–1989." *Law and Society Review* 27 (1993): 65–72.

Ackerman, Bruce A. *We the People: Transformations.* Cambridge, Mass.: Belknap Press, 1998.

Advertisement. "NIKE Inner Actives." *Essence*, September 1999, 2–3.

"ACLU Moves to Have Maryland State Police Held in Contempt." American Civil Liberties Union Press Release. www.aclu.org. November 14, 1996.

Allen, Ronald J. "Foreword." *The Judicial Role in Criminal Proceedings.* Edited by Sean Doran and John Jackson. Oxford: Hart Publishing, 2000.

Anderson, Etta. "The 'Chivalrous' Treatment of the Female Offender in the Arms of the Criminal Justice System: A Review of the Literature." *Social Problems* 23 (1975–76): 350–369.

Applebome, Peter. "Indigent Defendants, Overworked Lawyers." *New York Times*, May 17, 1992, E18.

Baer, Judith A. "The Fruitless Search for Original Intent." *Judging the Constitution: Critical Essays on Judicial Lawmaking.* Edited by Michael W. McCann and Gerald L. Houseman. Glenview, Ill.: Scott, Foresman, 1989, 49–71.

Baldus, David C., George Woodworth, and Charles A. Pulaski. *Equal Justice and the Death Penalty: A Legal and Empirical Analysis.* Boston: Northeastern University Press, 1990.

Barak, Gregg, Jeanne M. Flavin, and Paul S. Leighton. *Class, Race, Gender, and Crime.* Los Angeles: Roxbury Publishing, 2001.

Barker, Lucius, and Jesse J. McCorry, Jr. *Black Americans and the Political System.* Cambridge, Mass.: Winthrop Publishers, 1976.

Barrett, Paul M. "Lawyer's Fast Work on Death Cases Raises Doubts About System." *Wall Street Journal.* September 7, 1994, 1.

Baum, Lawrence. *The Supreme Court.* 4th ed. Washington, D.C.: Congressional Quarterly Press, 1992.

———. *The Puzzle of Judicial Behavior.* Ann Arbor: University of Michigan Press, 1997.

Beckford, J. A. *Cult Controversies: The Societal Response to New Religious Movements.* London: Tavistock, 1985.

Begley, Sharon, and Debra Rosenberg. "The Latest Trouble with Racial Profiling." *Newsweek*, January 14, 2002, 8.

Bell, Derrick. *Faces at the Bottom of the Well.* New York: Basic Books, 1992.

Bennett, Katherine. "Constitutional Issues in Cross-Gender Searches and Visual Observation of Nude Inmates by Opposite-Sex Officers: A Battle Between and Within Sexes." *Prison Journal* 75 (1995): 90-112.

Berkson, Larry C. *The Concept of Cruel and Unusual Punishment.* Lexington, Mass.: Lexington Books, 1975.

Black, Donald. "Dispute Settlement by the Police." In *The Social Organization of Law.* 2nd ed., Edited by M. P. Baumgartner. San Diego, Calif.: Academic Press, 1999.

Blumberg, Abraham. *Criminal Justice.* Chicago: Quadrangle Books, 1967.

Bohm, Robert M. "Capital Punishment in Two Judicial Circuits in Georgia: A Description of the Key Actors and the Decision-Making Process." *Law and Human Behavior* 18 (1994): 319–326.

Boritch, Helen. "Gender and Criminal Court Outcomes: An Historical Analysis." *Criminology* 30 (1992): 293–309.

Bork, Robert H. *The Tempting of America: The Political Seduction of the Law.* New York: Free Press, 1990.

Bowers, William J. "The Pervasiveness of Arbitrariness and Discrimination under Post-*Furman* Capital Statutes." *Journal of Criminal Law and Criminology* 74 (1983): 1067–1100.

Bray, Karen M. "Reaching the Final Chapter in the Story of Peremptory Challenges." *U.C.L.A. Law Review* 40 (1992): 517–555.

Brennan, William. "The Constitution of the United States: Contemporary Ratification." *Judges on Judging.* Edited by David M. O'Brien. Chatham, N.J.: Chatham House, 1997, 200–210.

Bright, Stephen B. "Counsel for the Poor: The Death Sentence Not for the Worst Crime but for the Worst Lawyer." *Yale Law Journal* 103 (1994): 1835–1883.

Bright, Stephen B., Stephen O. Kinnard, and David A. Webster. "Keeping *Gideon* from Being Blown Away." *Criminal Justice* (Winter 1990): 11–13, 46–48.

Brooks, Roy. *Rethinking the American Race Problem.* Berkeley, Calif.: University of California Press, 1990.

Butterfield, Fox. "States Easing Stringent Laws on Prison Time." *New York Times* (on-line edition). September 2, 2001.

Call, Jack E. "The Supreme Court and Prisoners' Rights." *Federal Probation* 59 (March 1995): 36–46.

Carpenter, Dave. "Russians Work to Avoid Being Drafted into the Harsh Army." *Seattle Times* (on-line edition). May 14, 1997.

Carroll, Jenny E. "Images of Women and Capital Sentencing Among Female Offenders." *Texas Law Review* 75 (1997): 1413–1452.

Chesney-Lind, Meda. "Chivalry Reexamined: Women and the Criminal Justice System." In *Women, Crime, and the Criminal Justice System.* Edited by Lee Bowker. Lexington, Mass.: Lexington Books, 1978.

Chesney-Lind, Meda, and Randall G. Shelden. *Girls, Delinquency and Juvenile Justice.* Pacific Grove, Calif.: Brooks/Cole Publishing, 1992.

Claiborne, William. "Illinois Governor to Block Executions During Death-Penalty Probe." *Seattle Times.* www.seattletimes.com. January 31, 2000.

Clary, Mike. "Boy Gets Life in Prison for Death of Playmate." *Seattle Times* (online edition). March 3, 2001.

Cohen, Adam. "The Difference a Million Makes." *Time.* March 29, 1995, 43.

Colbert, Douglas. "Thirty-five Years after *Gideon*: The Illusory Right to Counsel at Bail Proceedings." *University of Illinois Law Review* (1998):1–51.

Cole, David. "Strategies of Difference: Litigating for Women's Rights in a Man's World." *Law and Inequality* 2 (1984): 33–59.

———. *No Justice: Race and Class in the American Criminal Justice System.* New York: New Press, 1999.

Cole, George F., and Christopher E. Smith. *The American System of Criminal Justice.* 9th ed. Belmont, Calif.: Wadsworth Publishing, 2001.

Cooper, Aaron. "Oklahoma Inmate Freed 15 Years after Conviction." Associated Press Wire Service. May 8, 2001.

Costanzo, Mark. *Just Revenge: Costs and Consequences of the Death Penalty.* New York: St. Martin's Press, 1997.

"Court Ends Federal Jurisdiction over Female Prisons." Associated Press Wire Service. December 14, 1999.

Cox, Archibald. *The Court and the Constitution.* Boston: Houghton Mifflin, 1987.

Coyle, Marcia. "Counsel's Guiding Hand Is Often Handicapped by the System It Serves." *National Law Journal.* June 11, 1990, 36.

Daly, Kathleen. "Structure and Practice of Familial Based Justice in a Criminal Court." In *The Social Organization of Law.* 2nd ed. Edited by M. P. Baumgartner. San Diego, Calif.: Academic Press, 1999.

DeYoung, Karen, and Eric Pianin. "China Trade, Cuban Embargo: More Legislators Question the Distinction." *Seattle Times* (on-line edition). May 24, 2000.

Dorin, Dennis D. "Far Right of the Mainstream: Racism, Rights, and Remedies from the Perspective of Justice Antonin Scalia's McCleskey Memorandum." *Mercer Law Review* 45 (1994): 1035–1088.

Douglas, William O. *Go East, Young Man.* New York: Random House, 1974.

Edmonds, Thomas N., and James A. Fink. *Michigan Criminal Law and Procedure.* Lansing, Mich.: Michigan Sheriffs' Association Educational Services, 1998.

Eisler, Kim Isaac. *A Justice for All: William J. Brennan and the Decisions that Transformed America.* New York: Simon & Schuster, 1993.

Epstein, Lee, and Joseph Kobylka. *The Supreme Court and Legal Change.* Chapel Hill: University of North Carolina Press, 1992.

Epstein, Lee, and Thomas G. Walker. *Constitutional Law for a Changing America: Rights, Liberties, and Justice.* Washington, D.C.: Congressional Quarterly Press, 1992.

Essien-Udom, E. U. *Black Nationalism: A Search for Identity in America.* Chicago: University of Chicago Press, 1962.

Eversley, Melanie. "Bar Group Joins Archer to Fight Racial Profiling." *Detroit Free Press,* August 11, 1999, p. 1A.

Finkelman, Paul. "The Color of Crime." *Tulane Law Review* 67 (1993): 2063–2112.

Finucane, Martin. "Sister's Legal Battle Frees Man Convicted of Murder." Associated Press Wire Service (online report). March 15, 2001.

Flesher, John. "Free Speech, Decency Clash in Cursing Trial." *Lansing State Journal,* June 11, 1999, 1B.

Fogelson, Robert. *Big-City Police.* Cambridge, Mass.: Harvard University Press, 1977.

Foner, Eric. *Reconstruction, 1863–1877: America's Unfinished Revolution.* New York: HarperCollins, 1988.

Fortunato, Stephen J. "The Supreme Court's Experience Gap." *Judicature* 82 (1999): 251.

Fradella, Henry F. "A Typology of the Frivolous: Varying Meanings of Frivolity in Section 1983 Prisoner Civil Rights Litigation." *The Prison Journal* 78 (1998): 465–492.

Friedman, Lawrence. *Crime and Punishment in American History.* New York: Basic Books, 1993.

"From Mao Apologist to Prisoner." *Seattle Times* (on-line edition). February 24, 2001.

Gallup Poll. "Social Science: Crime." www.gallup.com. August 29–September 5, 2000.

"Gender and the Death Penalty." *Washington Post,* January 14, 1998, A18.

General Accounting Office. *U.S. Customs Service: Better Targeting of Airline Passengers for Personal Searches Could Produce Better Results.* Washington, D.C.: Government Printing Office, 2000.

Gershman, Bennett. "Themes of Injustice: Wrongful Conviction, Racial Prejudice, and Lawyer Incompetence." *Criminal Law Bulletin* 29 (1993): 502–515.

Gest, Ted. *Crime and Politics: Big Government's Erratic Campaign for Law and Order.* New York: Oxford University Press, 2001.

Gey, Steven G. "Justice Scalia's Death Penalty." *Florida State University Law Review* 20 (1992): 67–132.

Gibson, James L. "From Simplicity to Complexity: The Development of Theory in the Study of Judicial Behavior." *Political Behavior* 5 (1983): 7–49.

Goldstein, Leslie Friedman. *The Constitutional Rights of Women.* Rev. ed. Madison, Wis.: University of Wisconsin Press, 1988.

Gottlieb, Stephen. *Morality Imposed: The Rehnquist Court and Liberty in America.* New York: New York University Press, 2000.

Grana, Sheryl J. *Women and (In)Justice: The Criminal and Civil Effects of the Common Law on Women's Lives.* Boston: Allyn and Bacon, 2002.

Greenhouse, Linda. "Judges Challenge Rehnquist's Role on Death Penalty: An Extraordinary Move." *New York Times,* October 6, 1989, A1.

———. "Scalia Tightens Policy on Death Penalty Appeals." *New York Times,* February 22, 1991, B16.

———. "News Analysis: Another Kind of Bitter Split When Jurisprudence Is Pulled into Politics." *New York Times* December 14, 2000, 1.

Gwynne, S. C. "Guilty, Innocent, Guilty." *Time,* January 16, 1995, 38.

Hanson, Roger A., and Henry W. K. Daley. *Challenging the Conditions of Confinement of Prisons and Jails.* Washington, D.C.: Bureau of Justice Statistics, 1995a.

————. *Federal Habeas Corpus Review: Challenging State Court Convictions.* Washington, D.C.: Bureau of Justice Statistics, 1995b.

Harris, David A. *Driving While Black: Racial Profiling on Our Nation's Highways.* www.aclu.org/profiling/report/index.html, June 1999.

Hensley, Thomas, and Christopher E. Smith. "Membership Change and Voting Change: An Analysis of the Rehnquist Court's 1986–1991 Terms." *Political Research Quarterly* 48 (1995): 837–856.

Hensley, Thomas R., Christopher E. Smith, and Joyce A. Baugh. *The Changing Supreme Court: Constitutional Rights and Liberties.* St. Paul, Minn.: West/Wadsworth, 1997.

Herbert, Bob. "In America." *New York Times.* December 7, 2001 (www.nytimes.com).

Higginbotham, A. Leon. *In the Matter of Color: The Colonial Period.* New York: Oxford University Press, 1978.

Horney, Julie, and Cassia Spohn. "Rape Law Reform and Instrumental Change in Six Urban Jurisdictions." *Law and Society Review* 25 (1991): 118–153.

Hudson, Mike. "Riot Cases Continue to Tie Up Local Courts." *MSU State News,* August 31, 1999, 1.

Human Rights Watch. *All Too Familiar: Sexual Abuse of Women in U.S. State Prisons.* New York: Human Rights Watch, 1996.

Irwin, John. *The Jail: Managing the Underclass in American Society.* Berkeley, Calif.: University of California Press, 1992.

Jacobs, James. *Stateville.* Chicago: University of Chicago Press, 1977.

————. *New Perspectives on Prisons and Imprisonment.* Ithaca, N.Y.: Cornell University Press, 1983.

Johnson, Sheri Lynn. "Black Innocence and the White Jury." *Michigan Law Review* 83 (1985): 1611–1708.

————. "Unconscious Racism and the Criminal Law." *Cornell Law Review* 73 (1988): 1016–1037.

Jones, James M. *Prejudice and Racism.* Reading, Mass.: Addison-Wesley, 1972.

Kamisar, Yale. "Court Chomped at *Miranda* Rights." *Cleveland Plain Dealer,* July 18, 1989, B9.

Kannar, George. "The Constitutional Catechism of Antonin Scalia." *Yale Law Journal* 99: 1297–1357.

Karmen, Andrew. *Crime Victims: An Introduction to Victimology.* 2nd ed. Pacific Grove, Calif.: Brooks/Cole,1990.

King, D. P. "Religious Freedom in the Correctional Institution." *Journal of Criminal Law, Criminology, and Police Science* 60 (1969): 299–305.

Kluger, Richard. *Simple Justice: The History of Brown v. Board of Education and Black America's Struggle for Equality.* New York: Knopf, 1975.

Kolchin, Peter. *American Slavery.* New York: Hill & Wang, 1993.

Krugman, Paul. "Reckonings." *New York Times* December 13, 2001 (www.nytimes.com).

Kurtz, Howard. "Battered Women, Reluctant Police." *Washington Post*, February 28, 1988, A1.

Lacayo, Richard. "You Don't Always Get Perry Mason." *Time*. June 1, 1992, 38.

Ladd, Everett Carll. *The American Polity* 2nd ed. New York: W.W. Norton, 1987.

Leo, Richard. "*Miranda*'s Revenge: Police Interrogation as a Confidence Game." *Law and Society Review* 30 (1996): 259–288.

Lewis, Anthony. *Gideon's Trumpet*. New York: Random House, 1964.

Locke, Shmuel. *Crime, Public Opinion, and Civil Liberties: The Tolerant Public*. Westport, Conn.: Praeger Publishers, 1999.

MacDonald, Christine. "City Wants Rioters to Pay—Literally," *Lansing State Journal*, May 27, 1999, 1A.

Macedo, Stephen. *The New Right v. the Constitution*. Washington, D.C.: Cato Institute, 1987.

Maguire, Kathleen, and Ann L. Pastore, eds. *Sourcebook of Criminal Justice Statistics*. Washington, D.C.: Bureau of Justice Statistics, 1997.

Maguire, Kenneth. "Wrongly Jailed Man Gets Apology." Associated Press Wire Service. May 3, 2001.

Maltese, John Anthony. *The Selling of Supreme Court Nominees*. Baltimore: Johns Hopkins University Press, 1995.

Marcus, Ruth. "Waiting Forever on Death Row." *Washington Post National Weekly Edition*, June 18, 1990, 12.

McCann, Michael W. "Equal Protection for Social Inequality: Race and Class in Constitutional Ideology." in *Judging the Constitution: Critical Essays on Judicial Lawmaking*. Edited by Michael W. McCann and Gerald L. Houseman. Glenview, Ill.: Scott, Foresman, 1989.

McWilliams, Tom. "Judgment Shows How We Are Responsible for Others' Actions." *MSU State News*, June 14, 1999, 4.

Mezey, Susan Gluck. *In Pursuit of Equality: Women, Public Policy, and the Federal Courts*. New York: St. Martin's Press, 1992.

Michigan Complied Laws, 2002.

Miller, Eleanor M. *Street Women*. Philadelpha: Temple University Press, 1986.

Milner, Neal A. *The Court and Local Law Enforcement: The Impact of Miranda*. Beverly Hills, Calif.: Sage, 1971.

Mintz, John, and Peter Slevin. "Human Factor Was at Core of Vote Fiasco." *Washington Post*, May 31, 2001 (www.washingtonpost.com).

Morash, Merry, Robin N. Haarr, and Lila Rucker. "A Comparison of Programming for Women and Men in U.S. Prison in the 1980s." *Crime and Delinquency* 40 (1994): 197–221.

Morrow, Lance. "A Trial for Our Times." *Time*, October 9, 1995, 28.

Mydans, Seth. "23 Dead After 2nd Day of Los Angeles Riots: Fines and Looting Persist Despite Curfew." *New York Times*, April 30, 1992, A1.

Myrdal, Gunnar. *An American Dilemma: The Negro Problem and Modern Democracy*. New York: Harper & Brothers, 1944.

Nakell, Barry, and Kenneth A. Hardy. *The Arbitrariness of the Death Penalty.* Philadelphia: Temple University Press, 1987.

"New Antiterrorism Law Contains Habeas Reform and Victim Restitution." *The Third Branch* 28 (May 1996): 4.

Nomination of Judge Clarence Thomas to Be Associate Justice of the Supreme Court of the United States: Hearings before the Senate Committee on the Judiciary, 102nd Cong. Washington, D.C.: U.S. Government Printing Office, 1991.

Nowell, Paul. "Lawyer Says He Sabotaged Inmate." Associate Press Wire Service (on-line edition). November 2, 2000.

Olsen, Frances. "Statutory Rape: A Feminist Critique of Rights Analysis." In *Legal Theory: Readings in Law and Gender.* Edited by Katharine T. Bartlett and Rosanne Kennedy. Boulder, Colo.: Westview Press, 1991.

Orfield, Gary, and Susan Eaton. *Dismantling Desegregation: The Quiet Reversal of Brown v. Board of Education.* New York: New Press, 1996.

Palmer, John W. *Constitutional Rights of Prisoners.* Cincinnati, Oh.: Anderson Publishing, 1985.

Peltason, Jack. *Fifty-eight Lonely Men: Southern Federal Judges and School Desegregation.* New York: Harcourt, Brace, 1961.

Pettigrew, Thomas F. *Racial Discrimination in the United States.* New York: Harper & Row, 1975.

———. "New Patterns of Racism: The Different Worlds of 1984 and 1964." *Rutgers Law Review* 37 (1985): 673–695.

Pierre, Robert E. "Botched Name Purge Denied Some the Right to Vote." *Washington Post* May 30, 2001 (www.washingtonpost.com).

Pollock-Byrne, Joycelyn M. *Women, Prison, and Crime.* Pacific Grove, Calif.: Brooks/Cole Publishing, 1990.

Popeo, Daniel J., and George C. Smith. "Court Supervision of Prisons Is Unnecessary." In *Criminal Justice Sources.* Vol. 2. St. Paul, Minn.: Greenhaven Press, 1987.

Pressley, Sue Anne. "Pro-Death Penalty But Chivalrous Texans Debate Fate of Karla Faye Tucker." *Washington Post,* January 25, 1998, A3.

Provine, Doris Marie. "Courts in the Political Process in France." In *Courts, Law, and Politics in Comparative Perspective.* Edited by Herbert Jacob, Erhard Blankenburg, Herbert M. Kritzer, Doris Marie Provine, and Joseph Sanders. New Haven, Conn.: Yale University Press, 1996.

Reasons, Charles E., Darlene J. Conley, and Julius Debro, eds. 2002. *Race, Class, Gender, and Justice in the United States.* Boston: Allyn and Bacon.

Rehnquist, William H. *The Supreme Court: How It Was, How It Is.* New York: William Morrow, 1987.

Reiman, Jeffrey. *The Rich Get Richer and the Poor Get Prison.* 6th ed. Boston: Allyn & Bacon, 2001.

Reuben, Richard C. "New Habeas Restrictions Challenged." *American Bar Association Journal* 82 (July 1996): 22, 25.

"Rights Commission's Report on Florida Election." *Washington Post.* June 5, 2001 (www.washingtonpost.com).

Robbins, Ira. "The Cry of Wolfish in the Federal Courts: The Future of Federal Judicial Intervention in Prison Administration." *Journal of Criminal Law and Criminology* 71 (1980): 211–225.

Romano, Carlin. "The Supreme Court Fumbled Democracy." *The Chronicle of Higher Education.* January 5, 2001 (http://chronicle.com).

Rosenberg, Gerald. *The Hollow Hope: Can Courts Produce Social Change?* Chicago: University of Chicago Press, 1993.

Rothenberg, Robert E. *The New Illustrated Medical Encyclopedia and Guide to Family Health.* New York: Lexicon Publications, 1991.

Rowan, Carl. *Dream Makers, Dream Breakers.* Boston: Little, Brown, 1993.

Schultz, David A., and Christopher E. Smith. *The Jurisprudential Vision of Justice Antonin Scalia.* Lanham, Md.: Rowman & Littlefield, 1996.

Schwartz, Bernard. *A History of the Supreme Court.* New York: Oxford University Press, 1993.

———. *Decision: How the Supreme Court Decides Cases.* New York: Oxford University Press, 1996.

Sharp, David. "Bush Rejects Death-Penalty Doubts." *Seattle Times* (www.seattletimes.com). June 12, 2000.

Sherman, Lawrence. *Policing Domestic Violence: Experiments and Dilemmas.* New York: Free Press, 1992.

Smith, Christopher E. "Examining the Boundaries of Bounds: Prison Law Libraries and Access to the Courts." *Howard Law Journal* 30 (1987): 27–44.

———. "United States Magistrates and the Processing of Prisoner Litigation." *Federal Probation* 52 (December 1988): 13–18.

———. "Police Professionalism and the Rights of Criminal Defendants." *Criminal Law Bulletin* 29 (1990): 155–166.

———. *Courts and the Poor.* Chicago: Nelson-Hall, 1991.

———. "Supreme Court Surprise: Justice Anthony Kennedy's Move Toward Moderation." *Oklahoma Law Review* 45 (1992): 459–476.

———. "Black Muslims and the Development of Prisoners' Rights." *Journal of Black Studies* 24 (1993a): 131–146.

———. *Justice Antonin Scalia and the Supreme Court's Conservative Moment.* Westport, Conn.: Praeger Publishers, 1993b.

———. "Imagery, Politics, and Jury Reform." *Akron Law Review* 28 (1994): 77–95.

———. *Courts, Politics, and the Judicial Process.* 2nd. Chicago: Nelson-Hall, 1997a.

———. *The Rehnquist Court and Criminal Punishment.* New York: Garland, 1997b.

———. *Law and Contemporary Corrections.* Belmont, Calif.: Wadsworth Publishing, 2000.

Smith, Christopher E., and Joyce A. Baugh. *The Real Clarence Thomas: Confirmation Veracity Meets Performance Reality.* New York: Peter Lang, 2000.

Smith, Christopher E. and John Hurst. "The Forms of Judicial Policymaking: Civil Liability and Criminal Justice Policy." *Justice System Journal* 19 (1997): 341–354.

Smith, Roger. "Custodial Rape of Female Prisoners Widespread in U.S." *Prison Legal News* 12 (June 2001): 6–7.

Smith, Rogers. *Civic Ideals: Conflicting Visions of Citizenship in U.S. History.* New Haven: Yale University Press, 1997.

Smolowe, Jill. "The Trials of a Public Defender." *Time.* March 29, 1993, 48.

Sokoloff, Natalie J., and Barbara Raffel Price. "The Criminal Law and Women." In *The Criminal Justice System and Women: Offenders, Victims, and Workers.* 2nd ed. Edited by Barbara Raffel Price and Natalie J. Sokoloff. New York: McGraw Hill.

Solano, Ricardo, Jr. "Is Congress Handcuffing Our Courts?" *Seton Hall Law Review* 28 (1997): 282–311.

Sorenson, Jonathan R., and Donald H. Wallace. "Capital Punishment in Missouri: Examining the Issue of Racial Disparity." *Behavioral Science and Law* 13 (1995): 61–72.

Spohn, Cassia, and Jeffrey Spears. "The Effect of Offender and Victim Characteristics on Sexual Assault Case Processing Decisions." *Justice Quarterly* 13 (1996): 649–679.

Staples, Robert. *Introduction to Black Sociology.* New York: McGraw-Hill, 1976.

Steele, Shelby. *The Content of Our Character: A New Vision of Race in America.* New York: St. Martin's Press, 1990.

Stumpf, Harry P. *American Judicial Politics.* San Diego, Calif.: Harcourt, Brace, Jovanovich, 1988.

Tate, C. Neal. "Personal Attribute Models of the Voting Behavior of U.S. Supreme Court Justices: Liberalism in Civil Liberties and Economics Decisions, 1946–1978." *American Political Science Review* 75 (1981): 355–367.

Thomas, Evan, and Michael Isikoff. "The Truth behind the Pillars." *Newsweek.* December 25, 2000 (republished at www.msnbc.com).

Tonry, Michael. *Malign Neglect: Race, Crime, and Punishment in America.* New York: Oxford University Press, 1995.

Torassa, Ulysses. "Public Defenders Do Little Public Defending." *Cleveland Plain Dealer* June 27, 1993, 3B.

Tribe, Laurence. "The Curvature of Constitutional Space: What Lawyers Can Learn from Modern Physics." *Harvard Law Review* 103 (1989): 1–39.

Tucker, John. *May God Have Mercy.* New York: W.W. Norton, 1997.

Tyack, David B. *The One Best System: A History of American Urban Education.* Cambridge, Mass.: Harvard University Press, 1974.

Urofsky, Melvin I. *A March of Liberty: A Constitutional History of the United States.* New York: Alfred A. Knopf, 1988.

"U.S. Marshal's Conviction for Raping Prisoners Affirmed." *Prison Legal News* 13 (January 2002): 30.

Uviller, H. Richard. *Tempered Zeal.* Chicago: Contemporary Books, 1988.

Van Horn, Carl E., Donald C. Baumer, and William T. Gormley, Jr. *Politics and Public Policy.* Washington, D.C.: Congressional Quarterly Press, 1992.

Vela, Susan. "Lawsuit Charges Bias in Curfew Arrests." *Cincinnati Enquirer,* April 21, 2001 (www.enquirer.com).

Walker, Samuel. *A Critical History of Police Reform.* Lexington, Mass.: Lexington Books, 1977.

———. "'Broken Windows' and Fractured History: The Use and Misuse of History in Recent Police Patrol Analysis." *Justice Quarterly* 1 (1984): 75–90.

——— *Taming the Systems: The Control of Discretion in Criminal Justice, 1950–1990.* New York: Oxford University Press, 1993.

Walker, Samuel, Cassia Spohn, and Miriam DeLone. *The Color of Justice: Race, Ethnicity, and Crime in America.* 2nd ed. Belmont, Calif.: Wadsworth Publishing, 2000.

Wallace, Donald H. "Prisoners' Rights: Historical Views." In *Correctional Contexts: Contemporary and Classical Readings.* Edited by James W. Marquardt and Jonathan R. Sorenson. Los Angeles: Roxbury, 1997.

Wand, Jonathan N., Kenneth Shotts, Jasjeet S. Sekhon, Walter R. Mebane, Jr., Michael C. Herron, and Henry E. Brady. "The Butterfly Did It: The Aberrant Vote for Buchanan in Palm Beach County, Florida." *American Political Science Review* 95 (2001): 793–810.

"Warren McCleskey Is Dead." *New York Times*, September 29, 1991, E16.

West, Cornel. *Race Matters.* Boston: Beacon Press, 1993.

White, G. Edward. *Earl Warren: A Public Life.* New York: Oxford University Press, 1982.

White, Mitzi. "The Nonverbal Behaviors in Jury Selection." *Criminal Law Bulletin* 31 (1995): 414–445.

White, Welsh. *The Death Penalty in the Nineties.* Ann Arbor, Mich.: University of Michigan Press, 1991.

Wiecek, William. *Liberty Under Law: The Supreme Court in American Life.* Baltimore, Md.: Johns Hopkins University Press, 1988.

Wilbanks, William. *The Myth of a Racist Criminal Justice System.* Monterey, Calif.: Brooks/Cole.

Wilkinson, J. Harvie. *From Brown to Bakke: The Supreme Court and School Integration, 1954–1978.* New York: Oxford University Press, 1979.

Wisely, W. "California Pays for Guard's Sexual Misconduct." *Prison Legal News* 13 (January 2002): 17–18.

"Wrongly Held Man Gets $3.2 M." Associated Press Wire Service. April 13, 2001.

Yackle, Larry W. "The Habeas Hagioscope." *Southern California Law Review* 66 (1993): 2331–2431.

———. "Form and Function in the Administration of Justice: The Bill of Rights and Federal Habeas Corpus." *University Michigan Journal of Law Reform* 24 (1994): 685–732.

Yalof, David Alistair. *Pursuit of Justices: Presidential Politics and the Selection of Supreme Court Nominees.* Chicago: University of Chicago Press, 1999.

Zielbauer, Paul. "Inquiry Pressed into Reported Rapes at Woodstock." *New York Times*, July 30, 1999, B1.

Cases Cited

Douglas v. California, 372 U.S. 353 (1963)

Duckworth v. Eagan, 492 U.S. 195 (1989)

Duncan v. Louisiana, 391 U.S. 145 (1968)

Edmonson v. Leesville Concrete, 500 U.S. 614 (1991)

Edwards v. California, 314 U.S. 160 (1941)

Elem v. Purkett, 25 F.3d 679 (8th Cir. 1994)

Employment Division of Oregon v. Smith, 494 U.S. 872 (1990)

Enmund v. Florida, 458 U.S. 782 (1982)

Estelle v. Gamble, 429 U.S. 97 (1976)

Ex parte Hull, 312 U.S. 546 (1941)

Falzerano v. Collier, 535 F. Supp. 800 (D.N.J. 1982)

Farmer v. Brennan, 511 U.S. 825 (1994)

Felker v. Turpin, 518 U.S. 651 (1996)

Ferguson v. City of Charleston, 532 U.S. 67 (2001)

Foley v. Connelie, 435 U.S. 291 (1978)

Florida v. Bostick, 501 U.S. 429 (1991)

Freeman v. Pitts, 503 U.S. 467 (1992)

Frontiero v. Richardson, 411 U.S. 677 (1973)

Fulwood v. Clemmer, 206 F. Supp. 370 (D.D.C. 1962)

Furman v. Georgia, 408 U.S. 238 (1972)

Georgia v. McCollum, 505 U.S. 42 (1992)

Gideon v. Wainwright, 372 U.S. 335 (1963)

Glover v. Johnson, 478 F. Supp. 1075 (E.D. Mich. 1978)

Goesart v. Cleary, 335 U.S. 464 (1948)

Graham v. Collins, 506 U.S. 461 (1993)

Gregg v. Georgia, 428 U.S. 153 (1976)

Griffin v. Illinois, 351 U.S. 12 (1956)

Hamilton v. Schiro, 338 F. Supp. 1016 (E.D. La. 1970)

Helling v. McKinney, 509 U.S. 25 (1993)

Holland v. Illinois, 493 U.S. 474 (1990)

Hoyt v. Florida, 368 U.S. 57 (1961)

Hudson v. McMillian, 503 U.S. 1 (1992)

Hurtado v. California, 110 U.S. 516 (1884)

Hutto v. Finney, 437 U.S. 678 (1978)

Illinois v. Wardlow, 528 U.S. 119 (2000)

In re Ferguson, 361 P.2d 417 (Cal. 1961)

In re Kemmler, 136 U.S. 436 (1890)

In re Griffiths, 413 U.S. 717 (1973)

Jackson v. Bishop, 404 F.2d 371 (8th Cir. 1968)

J.E.B. v. Alabama *ex rel.* T.B., 511 U.S. 127 (1994)

Johnson v. Avery, 393 U.S. 483 (1969)

Johnson v. Transportation Agency, 480 U.S. 616 (1987)

Johnson v. Zerbst, 304 U.S. 458 (1938)

Kelley v. Johnson, 425 U.S. 238 (1976)

Kirby v. Illinois, 406 U.S. 682 (1972)

Lane v. Brown, 72 U.S. 477 (1963)

Lee v. Washington, 390 U.S. 333 (1968)

Lewis v. Casey, 518 U.S. 343 (1996)

Lewis v. United States, 518 U.S. 322 (1996)

Lockhart v. Fretwell, 506 U.S. 364 (1993)

Louisiana ex rel. Francis v. Resweber, 329 U.S. 459 (1947)

Madsen v. Women's Health Center, 512 U.S. 753 (1994)

Mapp v. Ohio, 367 U.S. 643 (1961)

Massiah v. United States, 377 U.S. 201 (1964)

Martinez v. Court of Appeal of California, 528 U.S. 152 (2000)

McCleskey v. Kemp, 481 U.S. 279 (1987)

McCleskey v. Zant, 499 U.S. 467 (1991)

Michael M. v. Superior Court of Sonoma County, 450 U.S. 464 (1981)

Miranda v. Arizona, 384 U.S. 436 (1966)

Mississippi University for Women v. Hogan, 458 U.S. 718 (1982)

Missouri *ex rel.* Gaines v. Canada, 305 U.S. 337 (1938)

Missouri v. Jenkins, 515 U.S. 70 (1995)

Monroe v. Pape, 365 U.S. 167 (1961)

Moran v. Burbine, 475 U.S. 412 (1986)

Murray v. Giarratano, 492 U.S. 1 (1989)

New York v. Quarles, 467 U.S. 649 (1984)

O'Lone v. Estate of Shabazz, 482 U.S. 342 (1987)

Payne v. Tennessee, 501 U.S. 808 (1991)

People v. David, 549 N.Y.S.2d 564 (1989)

Pierce v. LaVallee, 212 F.Supp. 865 (N.D. N.Y. 1962)

Planned Parenthood v. Casey, 505 U.S. 833 (1992)

Plessy v. Ferguson, 163 U.S. 537 (1896)

Powell v. Alabama, 287 U.S. 45 (1932)

Powers v. Ohio, 499 U.S. 400 (1991)

Printz v. United States, 521 U.S. 898 (1997)

Pugh v. Locke, 406 F.Supp. 318 (M.D. Ala. 1976)

Purkett v. Elem, 514 U.S. 765 (1995)

Reed v. Reed, 404 U.S. 71 (1971)

Regents of the University of California v. Bakke, 438 U.S. 265 (1978)

Rhodes v. Chapman, 452 U.S. 337 (1981)

Robinson v. California, 370 U.S. 660 (1962)

Romer v. Evans, 517 U.S. 620 (1996)

Ross v. Moffitt, 417 U.S. 600 (1974)

Rostker v. Goldberg, 453 U.S. 57 (1996)

San Antonio Independent School District v. Rodriguez, 411 U.S. 1 (1973)

Scott v. Illinois, 440 U.S. 367 (1979)

Sewell v. Pegelow, 291 F.2d 196 (4th Cir. 1961)

Shaw v. Murphy, 532 U.S. 223 (2001)

Sipuel v. Board of Regents of the University of Oklahoma, 332 U.S. 631 (1948)

Slaughterhouse Cases, 83 U.S. 36 (1872)

Smith v. Bennett, 365 U.S. 708 (1961)

Sostre v. McGinnis, 334 F.2d 906 (2d Cir. 1964)

South Carolina v. Gathers, 490 U.S. 805 (1989)

State of Minnesota v. Russell, 477 N.W.2d 886 (1991)

Strauder v. West Virginia, 100 U.S. 303 (1880)

Strickland v. Washington, 466 U.S. 668 (1984)

Swain v. Alabama, 380 U.S. 202 (1965)

Talley v. Stephens, 247 F. Supp. 683 (E.D. Ark. 1965)

Taylor v. Louisiana, 419 U.S. 522 (1975)

Teague v. Lane, 489 U.S. 288 (1989)

Terry v. Ohio, 392 U.S. 1 (1968)

Tison v. Arizona, 481 U.S. 137 (1987)

Trop v. Dulles, 356 U.S. 86 (1958)

Turner v. Safley, 482 U.S. 78 (1987)

United States v. Armstrong, 517 U.S. 456 (1996)

United States v. Cronic, 466 U.S. 684 (1984)

United States v. DeGross, 960 F.2d 1433 (9th Cir. 1992)

United States v. Lopez, 514 U.S. 549 (1995)

United States v. Morrison, 529 U.S. 598 (2000)

United States v. Nixon, 418 U.S. 683 (1974)

United States v. Paradise, 480 U.S. 149 (1987)

United States v. Virginia, 518 U.S. 515 (1996)

United States v. Wade, 388 U.S. 218 (1967)

Walker v. Blackwell, 411 F.2d 23 (5th Cir. 1969)

Walton v. Arizona, 497 U.S. 639 (1990)

Wards Cove Packing Co. v. Atonio, 490 U.S. 642 (1989)

Weems v. United States, 217 U.S. 349 (1910)

Whren v. United States, 517 U.S. 806 (1996)

Whitley v. Albers, 475 U.S. 312 (1986)

Wickard v. Filburn, 317 U.S. 111 (1942)

Wilkerson v. Utah, 99 U.S. 130 (1879)

Wilson v. Seiter, 501 U.S. 294 (1991)

Woodson v. North Carolina, 428 U.S. 280 (1976)

Wright v. West, 505 U.S. 277 (1992)

Index

GENERAL EDITORS
David A. Schultz & Christina DeJong

Studies in Crime and Punishment is a multidisciplinary series that publishes scholarly and teaching materials from a wide range of methodological perspectives and explores sentencing and criminology issues from a single nation or comparative perspective. Subject areas to be addressed in this series include, but will not be limited to: criminology, sentencing and incarceration, policing, law and the courts, juvenile crime, alternative sentencing methods, and criminological research methods.

For additional information about this series or for the submission of manuscripts, please contact:

> David A. Schultz
> Peter Lang Publishing
> Acquisitions Department
> 275 Seventh Avenue, 28th floor
> New York, New York 10001

To order other books in this series, please contact our Customer Service Department:

> (800) 770-LANG (within the U.S.)
> (212) 647-7706 (outside the U.S.)
> (212) 647-7707 FAX

Or browse online by series:
> www.peterlangusa.com